The

New

American

Studies

Critical American Studies Series

George Lipsitz, University of California–San Diego, Series Editor

The
New
American

John

Studies

Carlos

Rowe

Critical American Studies Series

University of Minnesota Press

Minneapolis / London

Published by the University of Minnesota Press
111 Third Avenue South, Suite 290
Minneapolis, MN 55401-2520
http://www.upress.umn.edu

Library of Congress Cataloging-in-Publication Data

Rowe, John Carlos.
    The new American studies / John Carlos Rowe.
        p.   cm. —   (Critical American studies series)
    Includes bibliographical references and index.
    ISBN 0-8166-3577-3 (hc.) — ISBN 0-8166-3578-1 (pbk.)
    1. American literature—History and criticism—Theory, etc.   2. American literature—History and criticism.   3. Popular culture—United States.   4. United States—Civilization.   I. Title.   II. Series.
    PS25 .R69 2002
    810.9—dc21

                                                                2002001361

Printed in the United States of America on acid-free paper

The University of Minnesota is an equal-opportunity educator and employer.

12 11 10 09 08 07 06 05 04 03 02   10 9 8 7 6 5 4 3 2 1

For Kristin

Contents

Preface

The following chapters were written between 1987 and 2000 for different occasions and not originally designed for this book. I have organized them into two major sections and revised them to address each other in ways appropriate to a sustained reflection on the future directions of American Studies as a field. Wherever possible, I have revised these essays to be readable today and to contextualize as much as possible historical events and popular works that may have lost their currency. In completing these revisions, I was interested to find that the most dated materials were not those drawn from popular and mass culture or the local news, but certain methodological and academic discourses and their rhetorical conventions. Critics of cultural studies often call attention to the ephemerality of the mass and popular cultural materials this approach treats. But what strikes me is that the ephemerality of any particular object of study is less an inherent quality of that object than of the hermeneutic practices that are used to interpret it in a particular historical moment. Rather than worry about the distinction between transitory and classic cultural artifacts and phenomena, then, we should pay more attention to the methods and theories we employ to contextualize and interpret our historical examples.

I have divided the book into theoretical approaches and textual examples in response to American Studies' healthy skepticism regarding abstract theories and its insistence upon historical evidence and close textual analyses to support theses. By the same token, I think that the new American Studies is characterized by theoretical interests that give greater coherence to the discipline and help its teachers develop coherent curricula to suit many different institutional and pedagogical situations. The theoretical essays in the first part of this book argue generally that traditional American Studies has often been resistant to critical theory, especially of the philosophical cast taken by much Continental structuralism and poststructuralism. Often the exceptionalist bias of traditional American Studies has prompted its scholars to reject theories and models developed outside the United States, even when such approaches have had considerable relevance for the field. In still other cases, a certain overdetermination of material culture and socioeconomic forces has led intellectuals in the field to distrust theories lacking historical specificity and concreteness.

The textual examples in the second part of the book are not intended to work out in a rigorous or systematic manner the suggestions made in the theoretical chapters. This book is not a map or plan for how the field should be organized in all its various subspecializations and allied disciplines. I make no claim even to approach the ideal of the "organic intellectual" imagined by modern theorists. Instead, I offer my own work as that of a scholar trained originally in American literature and history who has developed in the direction of American Studies as a far more comprehensive field and who has found its challenges vital for my scholarship and teaching. If this book is not a systematic plan for the new American Studies, as my title suggests, then what claim does it make on the reader's attention? At one level, it is a sort of intellectual autobiography, omitting personal anecdotes and indulgences, in which I review my own education as a scholar who began his career with primary interests in American literature and moved increasingly toward American Studies, demonstrating thereby how an older conflict between these two fields might be overcome. At another level, it foregrounds my training in critical theory as a challenge and provocation to encourage American Studies to avoid the provincialism of an older exceptionalist model. In still another sense, this book identifies those points of intersection among theory, literary history, popular cultural analysis, and media and visual studies that strike me as some of the most important areas of emphasis for the new American Studies.

I am grateful to William Murphy, now of Random House, who first discussed with me the idea for this book while he was at the University of Minnesota Press, and to Richard Morrison for the continuing support that he has given it at Minnesota. Many colleagues in American Studies around the world gave me ideas for this book in countless ways, but I want to thank in particular Lindon Barrett, Suzanne Chávez-Silverman, Emory Elliott, Winfried Fluck, Thelma Foote, Giles Gunn, Heinz Ickstadt, Katherine Kinney, Paul Lauter, Frank Lentricchia, Günter Lenz, George Lipsitz, Steven Mailloux, Jay Mechling, Patrick O'Donnell, Donald Pease, Mark Poster, Gabriele Schwab, Shelley Streeby, Cheryl Walker, and Robyn Wiegman. Whether you know it or not, each of you contributed directly and substantially to the shape of this book.

Introduction

If we consider the diversity of topics and vitality of the discussions at recent conventions of the American Studies Association and other such professional organizations around the world, the formal founding of the International Association of American Studies at Bellagio in 2000, exciting new books and essays in the field, and Internet exchanges of scholarship and pedagogy on a global scale, we see American Studies as having a bright future as its scholars face the challenges of the new millennium. If we consider the number of American Studies programs and departments around the world that have been closed, merged with other academic units, been frustrated in their efforts to add Ph.D. or other graduate degrees or just generally underfunded and neglected by their respective colleges and universities, we see the institutional future of American Studies as far less secure. The academic job market for young specialists in American Studies seems to reflect the institutional rather than the scholarly realities of the field. Most of these young scholars will find positions not in American Studies programs or departments, but in history, English, women's studies, media studies and visual studies, ethnic studies, and new programs in cultural studies, with occasional opportunities in such social sciences areas as anthropology, folklore, and political science.

This disparity between the intellectual energy of American Studies scholarship and the embattled institutional situation of the field is cause for alarm, but, as I argue in the following chapters, the situation should not cause advocates of the discipline to become stubborn defenders of founding principles and basic methods. In 1979, Gene Wise claimed that American Studies "has been in decline" since "the demise of the Parrington paradigm" of the 1920s and 1930s, but today we should be careful not to mistake significant changes in methods and objects of study for disciplinary "decline."[1] Undoubtedly the consensus-based intellectual history that was once foundational for American Studies is no longer a possible or even desirable goal for the field, and new terms for intellectual debate and exchange are vitally needed to address such central issues as colonialism and postcolonialism, postnationalism, multiculturalism, cultural hybridity, postindustrial class divisions, neoregionalism, and subject positions determined by ethnicity, gender, and sexuality.

In addition, American Studies scholars should not allow institutional politics, often influenced by specific local circumstances with little relevance to the field, to cause us to compete in adversarial ways with other disciplines and methods that complement our own work. Our task should be to learn from these disciplines and methods at a time when American Studies is obviously undergoing significant and potentially valuable changes. How programs and departments of American Studies will be defined and situated in colleges and universities over the next few decades will depend crucially on how successfully its scholars and teachers forge intellectual, curricular, and pedagogical coalitions with like-minded colleagues in history, English and American literature, comparative literature, Latin American studies, African American studies, Asian American studies, Latino and Chicano studies, women's studies, anthropology, folklore, political science, popular culture, critical theory, media and visual studies, art history, and the programs in foreign languages and literatures relevant to the study of the western hemisphere, especially the many different Native American languages, Spanish, Portuguese, French, German, Dutch, Japanese, Chinese, Korean, and Vietnamese.

The "new" American Studies is already a comparative discipline that is reorganizing its scholarly projects and curricular designs at the same time specialists in comparative literature are challenging an older world literatures paradigm and trying out such ideas as "global cultures."[2] Both fields were founded upon the study of national cultures and their histories, perhaps understandably because of their development when the nation-state was considered the preeminent social form. As American Studies reconceives its intellectual project as the study of the many different societies of the western hemisphere and of the influences of the different border zones that constitute this large region, such as the Pacific

Rim and the African and European Atlantics, it will become a genuinely "postnationalist" discipline whose comparatist methods will overlap and thus benefit from the work of other comparatists. Such a positive development assumes, of course, that comparative literature will broaden its older Eurocentric model and recast its literary model to include global cultures and their different semiotic systems. To accomplish this postnationalist and transliterary work, both disciplines will have to rigorously criticize their own contributions to national mythologies and to the privileging of certain national cultures that often contributed to modern cultural imperialism.

Some critics will argue that this comparatist dimension has always been a crucial aspect of American Studies, as others will complain that comparative literature was never Eurocentric or structured around the study of different national literatures. At the outset, I want to say that the task of the "new" American Studies should not be to demonize the "old" American Studies, especially on the basis of generalizations about past or present approaches. There are many precedents for new interests in both the comparative approaches and the cultural studies of early practitioners and the movements with which they were associated.[3] If the discipline is to be successful in the future, it must include coalitions with complementary approaches and must respect previous efforts that contributed to greater social justice and understanding in their times and are thus precursors of our own era.[4] By the same token, we should not avoid the new or simply trivialize its claims as historically ignorant because we imagine it has been done before. History rarely repeats itself, even though there are important influences and analogies between different periods and crises that we may judiciously identify in the interests of improving the effectiveness of newer approaches.

A comparative American Studies will not only have to address the problems of understanding the many different societies of the western hemisphere and its strategic border zones or "rims"; it must also treat comparatively the internal social relations of whatever geopolitical units define themselves as nation, state, region, community, or group. The relationship between foreign and domestic social relations should be taken into account in terms of the historically established and continuing mythologies of such entities. What this means is that the postnationalist enterprise of American Studies should continue to take very seriously the histories of those nations that have helped determine the objects of study in the field. By the same token, the nation, especially the United States, can no longer be treated as the exclusive domain of American Studies. We should use terminological distinctions consistently to remind readers and students that the United States is not synonymous with America or the Americas and that the latter denotations also exclude such important nations and communities as those composing Canada.[5] We should be as attentive to the political consequences of frequently used terminologies as activists in the civil, gay, women's, and international labor rights movements have been in their related reform movements.

The comparative aspects of the new American Studies pose a number of intellectual and political problems. As I argue in several of the following chapters, comparative cultural study can often reinforce, rather than transform, national and cultural hierarchies and even contribute to the sort of cultural imperialism it is intended to criticize and overcome. In chapter 1 I discuss how Paul Lauter's otherwise laudable comparative approach to the different cultures of the United States can potentially distract us from the comparative study of the western hemisphere. Lauter's work obviously invites other cultural perspectives, but recent work by Lawrence Buell on the United States as "postcolonial" since the American Revolution helps obscure the simultaneous development of U.S. colonial ventures at home and abroad.[6] In an effort to compare France, Great Britain, and the United States as late modern nations, Julia Kristeva has reduced the complex history of U.S. multiculturalism to "problems of immigration," thereby utterly ignoring the rights struggles of native peoples and how diasporas, such as that resulting from slavery, differ from conventional immigration.[7] For Kristeva, U.S. multiculturalism is a case of immigration and national purpose gone awry, in which "new immigrant islands" exhibit "autistic withdrawal into their originary values."[8]

Citing the work of Ella Shohat, Ania Loomba has observed that "one negative implication of the very acceptability of the term 'postcolonial' in the Western academy" is that it "serves to keep at bay more sharply political terms such as 'imperialism,' or 'geopolitics.'"[9] Tempting as it may be to treat ethnic minorities in the United States as postcolonial subjects or merely as "immigrants," such approaches may also encourage us to neglect or trivialize the continuing effects of internal colonialism, as Gesa Mackethun has pointed out in her recent review of C. Richard King's collection *Post-Colonial America*: "An appreciation of the positive effect of taking a postcolonial *perspective* on the history of the United States . . . ought to be distinguished from historically unfounded claims that the United States [is] a postcolonial country."[10]

Postcolonial and cultural studies approaches that focus exclusively on the United States may also tend to ignore the polylingual realities of the new comparatism, even though we should know that today the study of U.S. cultures is necessarily multilingual.[11] Still another way in which American Studies and comparative literary and cultural studies (I prefer the term comparative cultural studies) should work together is in advocating foreign language and cultural curricula, as well as international exchanges of students and faculty, as integral to their respective fields. In the following chapters I rely on such heuristic models for comparative study as Mary Louise Pratt's "contact zone" and Paul Jay's revision of Edouard Glissant's "cultural zone," each of which fundamentally depends on the different languages and semiotics constituting the cultural locations and negotiations to be analyzed.[12] These theoretical models crucially rely on language as both the medium for and the obstacle to cultural understanding, and they remind us that comparative study of virtually any subject involves serious treatment of translation between different representational systems, ranging from specific languages to semiotic codes. Scholars of American Studies and comparative studies need to see the study of languages not simply as the acquisition of useful tools, but as an integral part of their disciplines.

Both my emphasis on the "language model" and my call for American Studies to cooperate with comparative cultural studies suggest the need for a much greater reliance on semiotic and poststructuralist approaches than has been the case among those doing traditional work in American Studies. Reflecting on changes in American Studies in the first half of the 1990s, Norman Yetman has observed that a new generation of scholars "self-consciously and prominently" displayed its "theoretical assumptions," drawing on such scholars as "Michel Foucault, Raymond Williams, Stuart Hall, Roland Barthes, [and] Julia Kristeva [who] were not even American in their backgrounds or in the substantive focus of their work."[13] Yetman notes that "earlier generations of American Studies scholars had certainly approached their substantive interests with certain theoretical assumptions," but he is right to conclude that such predecessors had often been wary of theoretical models, especially those drawn from scholars working outside the United States and on topics not directly related to the study of this country.[14] We should not generalize about an antitheoretical inclination in American Studies, because there are many different reasons why scholars in the field have rejected theoretical models with claims to transdisciplinary applicability. There were certainly excellent reasons, for example, why American Studies practitioners in the 1940s and 1950s avoided the theoretical claims of the Anglo-American New Critics, just as

American Studies in the 1930s attempted to "overcome the limitations of an aesthetic-philological . . . approach in the reading of literary texts and of the dominant political and socio-historical focus in history."[15]

In their efforts to avoid the limitations of other theoretical approaches, American Studies scholars have worked through a wide range of influential theoretical models while giving the appearance of being antitheoretical and concerned instead with historical particularities. One consequence of the challenge of those theoretical approaches now generally included under the headings of postmodern and postcolonial should be our reconsideration of American Studies' different theoretical claims, especially as they have been used in reaction against other theoretical models. At some level, there has been a nativist bias in American Studies for reasons tied both to the field of study and the subtler political work American Studies scholars have done on behalf of U.S. nationalism and globalization. Yet appeals for an autochthonous American Studies not only ignore the diverse and very different work done by international scholars in the field—a topic of central importance in the following chapters—but are also usually subject to criticism in their own rights, because many of the "native" traditions of American Studies are obviously borrowed from other cultural and intellectual traditions.

The liberal Emersonian tradition I have criticized elsewhere, for example, has strong roots in European romanticism, especially German idealist philosophy.[16] The approach of the Puritan Origins School associated with Perry Miller's work cannot be separated from the wider intellectual and religious history of the European Reformation, the rise of the middle class, and the role of industrial capitalism in European colonialism.[17] Exceptionalist as the Puritan Origins school claimed to be, its theoretical assumptions are inextricably bound up with the development of Euro-American ideas of modernity and the capitalist processes of modernization and expansion.[18] Similarly, the approach of the Myth-and-Symbol School of the 1950s and 1960s is unimaginable without reference to the theorization of the symbol by such English and Continental intellectuals as Coleridge, the Schlegels, Hegel, and Carlyle and to the syncretic mythography of Enlightenment intellectuals, which culminated in such Victorian scholarly monuments as Sir James George Frazer's *The Golden Bough.* Even American pragmatism, so vaunted as the only original U.S. philosophy in the writings of C. S. Peirce, William James, and John Dewey, finds its intellectual lineage in the Greek Sophists, Aristotle, Berkeley, Hume, German idealism, and a host of other nonnative sources and influences.

One of the aims of those scholars who attempted to adapt Continental theories to the study of U.S. culture in the 1970s and 1980s was to challenge the intellectual provincialism and artificiality of claims that nativist traditions were untheoretical formulations of essential U.S. traits.[19] To speak or write about the United States in any unified way was always already a fiction for poststructuralists, both on the basis of the illusion of the signified operating in any representational act and in the more particular case of the fiction of national consensus. Given its explicitly multicultural and transnational composition and the rapid national legitimation demanded by its revolutionary origins, the United States calls particular, albeit not unique, attention to the fabricated, imaginary qualities of its national coherence. It is interesting to recall that the poststructuralist avant-garde of the 1970s and 1980s often claimed, from both inside and outside the American Studies discipline, that U.S. culture and especially its literature best exemplified the key tenets of poststructuralist theory.[20]

Such arguments perpetuated a notion of American exceptionalism as false in its own right as the idea of native uniqueness claimed by some practitioners of American Studies. Recasting the United States as the site contested by modernists and postmodernists had another dangerous consequence, which was to equate the modernization process both with the United States and with its nation form. Taking his cue from several non-U.S. intellectuals, such as the Caribbean Edouard Glissant, the British cultural studies scholar Paul Gilroy, and the Mexican philosopher Edmundo O'Gorman, Paul Jay argues that modernity should be understood in terms of "the whole ensemble of ideologies, economies, and technologies that led to the 'discovery,' conquest, and colonization of the 'New World.'"[21] This reconceptualization of "American modernity" broadens this subject to include the several Americas and Canada, and it stretches the historical framework to encompass prenational colonial and imperial practices, as well as the Amerindian cultural processes they would confront and disrupt, in ways that make it impossible for scholars to ignore the relationships among mercantilism, imperialism, diaspora, modernization, and nationalism. No longer an abstract formulation of America as modernity, Jay's approach locates modernity in an unavoidably complex history: "Of course, this would revise the conventional approach to modernity that dates it from the Enlightenment, suggesting at once that the 'discovery' of the New World marks the epochal moment of modernity, *and* that the Old World gets redefined in the context of that discovery in ways that accelerate the emergence of modernity."[22]

Such a reconceptualization of the Americas' roles in the history of modernity cannot avoid being cast as a new American exceptionalism, but it may well be a version we should accept. Not all instances of American uniqueness need be condemned. The voyages of conquest by Europeans to the western hemisphere did in fact rely on certain technological developments that made expansion possible in the first place and initiated new transoceanic empires that are hallmarks of both modernity and nationalism. By understanding this modernity as "not just scientific, technological, and political progress," but "'catastrophe' and 'unsettlement'" as well, we might be able to resituate the more restricted understandings of traditional modernity—as industrialization and nationalism—and postmodernity—as the postindustrial, postcolonial, and postnational consequences of modernity's breakdown—in the larger history to which both still belong.[23] In these more expansive historical, cultural, and theoretical contexts, scholars certainly will face many challenges of intellectual focus, curricular coverage, and pedagogical effectiveness, but they will gain the possibility of new relations among previously discrete areas of knowledge.

Interpreting any of the numerous literary and aesthetic movements we accept today as "modernist" in this larger historical framework, scholars will have to consider the role played by such avant-gardists in a modernization process that often relied on the artificial binary Stuart Hall has termed "the West and the Rest": "Without the Rest (or its own internal 'others'), the West would not have been able to recognize and represent itself as the summit of human history. The figure of 'the Other,' banished to the edge of the conceptual world and constructed as the absolute opposite, the negation, of everything which the West stood for, reappeared at the very center of the discourse of civilization, refinement, modernity, and development in the West. 'The Other' was the 'dark' side—forgotten, repressed, and denied; the reverse image of enlightenment and modernity."[24] The study of the Americas in terms of how such modernization practices produced colonial, imperial, postcolonial, and neocolonial attitudes and values is itself an act of resistance to the bipolar construction of civilization and its "others" as described by Hall. Modernization cannot be understood without taking into account the peoples, cultures, and territories it claimed to subjugate, eliminate, and transform. Of course, if we treat this large and complex history from the exclusive perspective of "civilizing" impulses, no matter how critical of such purposes we may be, we will be inclined to reproduce Hall's binary. But if we take seriously the dialectical relationship between modernity and its others, the latter abstraction will assume cultural and historical specificities according to the varieties of resistance, adaptation, and alternative social formations identifiable in the long and complex histories of the western hemisphere and its relevant cultural zones.

Such an approach or suite of complementary approaches will also help us understand recent social and cultural phenomena in more historically grounded contexts. Globalization, for example, should no longer be understood as an exclusively postmodern phenomenon that is distinguished by new technologies of communication, new modes of production, and postnational corporate organization and affiliation. To be sure, postindustrial economic practices have had considerable impact on transnational capitalism and on the related hierarchies from first-world nations to those of the fourth world, but economic internationalization was one of the principal motives of the early modern European voyages of expansion and conquest.

Of course, American Studies scholars must be attentive to the important distinctions between modern and postmodern processes of globalization. Modern imperialisms often relied on international hierarchies based on competitive nations, whereas Frederick Buell has argued that "national cultures" have had to reconceive themselves "in order to persist in an era of intensified globalization" marked by the diminishing significance of national economies.[25] Buell points out that critics of postmodern globalization have redefined certain key concepts in the analysis of modern internationalization in order to recognize the continuity of these two modes while still taking into account their salient differences. Commenting on the critical work of the Kenyan writer Ngũgĩ wa Thiong'o, Buell writes: "Deterritorializing the category 'Third World,' abandoning the nation-state as the unit of analysis, and employing the rhetoric of boundary violation, Ngũgĩ has written that the Third World is 'all over the world.'"[26] Such strategies should not be undertaken without understanding the long history of the ideas of national progress and "development," especially as they are measured by economic and cultural expansion. As we attempt to transcend, rather than abandon, the "nation-state as the unit of analysis," we will still have to take into account the complex, often contradictory, forces of neonationalisms, other local claims to power, and global hegemony. We should certainly recognize the persistence of the nation form and criticize it "without selling off its assets," as Kristeva has written, but we should be cautious of her prediction that "within and through the nation . . . the economic, political, and cultural future of the coming century will be played out."[27] In the twenty-first century, the nation form will certainly undergo dramatic changes and other social, economic, and political organizations will challenge the nation's hegemony.

As we widen our critical perspectives, so should we consider a broader spectrum of social, political, and cultural alternatives to the nation. Frederick Buell concludes that the "use of borders, not to separate, but to connect has become the basis for assembling new coalitions to negotiate the postnationalist fragmentation and restructuring of the world system."[28] In another context, Donald Pease has argued that the "emergent discourse of 'global-localism' . . . argues against the colonizer's power to construct the 'other' out of figures within an ethnocentric unconscious," thus locating "imperialism . . . as a phase in the process of globalization that, in disrupting the coherence of the geopolitical entities called nation-states, thereby enabled their openness to interconnection with other nation-states."[29] These perspectives have already led to important new work on American Studies' role in the study of globalization, but we should also be wary of political coalitions based on abstract criteria. After all, such "border-crossings" and comparative connections, however attractive, may also contribute to the formation of homogenized ideas—"traveling theory" in its most banal form—that differ little from the commodities transnational corporations market globally, changing only their advertising slogans while producing the same product for vastly different markets. Boosters of globalism like Francis Fukuyama celebrate the promise of new social and political equalities while ignoring how transnational capitalism exacerbates enduring socioeconomic inequalities.[30] In the new global contexts, such inequalities are often rendered invisible or inconsequential precisely because they do not circulate in those international media whereby products and other representational signs achieve their primary values.

American Studies has traditionally claimed the mass and popular media as indispensable fields of study. For some scholars, broadly based studies of visual and electronic media often mean that special emphasis is placed on postmodern societies, in which the print media no longer determine the communicative and hermeneutic paradigms. Indeed, the strong emphasis in American Studies on the mass media and popular culture is yet another point of intersection and possible coalition with poststructuralist theory and postcolonial and cultural studies approaches. We should also recognize that the relatively recent scholarly interest in nonprint media derives in part from the central roles played by such media in contemporary processes of globalization. The social habitus is today everywhere conditioned both by the globalization of "brands and products" and by "global media," all of which encourage people to "increasingly 'dwell' in a global network."[31] By the same token, studies of the new global media should broaden the communicative and interpretive practices of print-dominated modernity to include such nonprint forms as orality, architecture, iconography (including painting and photography), music, dance, religious ritual, everyday performative and symbolic actions, and the many other semiotic modes that may assume new significance in relation to nonprint alternatives.

Such consequences have followed, I think, postmodern critiques of print-dominated Euro-American modernity, often leading artists and scholars to a new appreciation of previously marginalized oral and performative practices of Native American, African American, and Chicano peoples. Recent approaches to African American modernism by Houston Baker, Cary Nelson, Michael North, Sieglinde Lemke, and Lindon Barrett, for example, argue that the modernists' social critique and aesthetic experimentation appear differently when they include the performative aspects of music, dance, and the telling of folktales.[32] Native American specialists, like Gerald Vizenor and Arnold Krupat, have used postmodernist theory and practice to historically and culturally situate the Euro-American print media and thereby gain new credibility and validity for the orality, music, dance, and ceremony central to many Native American cultural traditions.[33] There are limitations to such retrospective approaches, including a tendency to confuse, even at times reductively equate, Native American traditional practices with those of postmodern avant-gardists, but such dangers may well be worth risking in the interests of representing in our curricula, teaching, and scholarship a greater diversity of the media that constitute lived reality in any historical era.

American Studies' traditional emphasis on the significance of nonprint media has not included sufficient treatment of telematic, computer, and Internet forms of communication. Of course, the broad social application of these technologies is relatively new, and we can expect future scholarship to build on the work of such leaders as Randy Bass, N. Katherine Hayles, and Mark Poster.[34] We should not expect simply to add the study of these new technologies to the customary repertoire of media associated with modernity, such as photography, telegraphy, telematics, sound recordings, film, television, and video. Mark Poster has argued that the postmodern technologies of the computer age often depend upon significant reconceptualizations of the philosophical and psychological subject, the public and private spaces it inhabits, and its sociopolitical relations with others. In Poster's view, the modernist intellectual's critique of the human-machine relationship in terms of alienation, dehumanization, commodification, and other related terms no longer accurately describes the new conditions of subject formation: "The goal is not to evaluate the quality of the subjects constituted by the media but to open an analysis of their forms and to do so in such a way that the inherent mechanisms of domination may be revealed."[35] Not only will American Studies scholars have to consider the methodological relevance of poststructuralist approaches for understanding postmodern conditions and technologies, but to do so we will have to broaden our research sources to include work by specialists in information and computer sciences, social sciences, communications, and media and visual studies.

As American Studies continues to widen its scope to include complementary fields and emphases, there will be even more reason to criticize the centrality of U.S. history and literature to the field. The Myth-and-Symbol School tended to overdetermine literary and aesthetic criteria in its various assessments of defining American myths, and the Puritan Origins School often strategically confused religious and literary utopianism, especially as later practitioners adapted the model to the study of the American Renaissance.[36] Insofar as the overdetermination of historical and literary issues by previous schools of American Studies led to serious omissions of economic, political, anthropological, and media forces in the shaping of U.S. society, we should work to broaden the disciplinary scope of the field to avoid such limitations. And insofar as this very widening of scholarly attention has already helped challenge the centrality of history and literature in American Studies, often by way of competitive interdisciplinary programs claiming to address the very areas ignored or marginalized by previous practitioners, we should consider how relevant work of scholars in women's, African American, Native American, Chicano, Asian American, Latin American, and Canadian studies helps us rethink American Studies as a multidisciplinary, rather than interdisciplinary, field.

By the same token, the changing institutional and scholarly situations of American Studies should not cause us to trivialize the significance of U.S. history and literature in any future American Studies project. Although no longer necessarily foundational, these two disciplines should continue to play integral roles in the field. In purely practical terms, many American Studies scholars hold appointments in history and English departments around the world, and such departments often are the largest and most influential in their divisions. U.S. historians and specialists in American literature often work directly with faculty in ethnic, gay, and women's studies programs as a consequence of joint appointments, team teaching, and cross-listed courses. Both U.S. history and U.S. literature have already undergone considerable revision in response to criticism of scholarly specializations based on national identities. Of course, this revision may have led in some quarters to vigorous, even strident, defenses of nationalist and exceptionalist aims, but in other cases such crises of disciplinary knowledge have produced important opportunities for new configurations of knowledge. In chapters 1, 3, and 4 I argue that the future of American Studies need not be built exclusively in the discipline's institutionally established fields; intellectual, curricular, and scholarly connections and coalitions are especially possible with faculty and programs in history and literary studies (including English and comparative literature), as well as in ethnic, women's, gay, Latin American, and Canadian studies.

My defense of scholarship in U.S. history and literature is motivated in part by my own training and work in these fields.[37] Of the textual examples that form part II of this book, three of the six chapters deal primarily with literary examples, albeit in such interdisciplinary contexts as the visual and plastic arts (chapter 5), changes in the mode of economic production (chapter 6), and the political role of avant-garde poetry in the 1930s Left (chapter 7) that meet the traditional criteria for work in American Studies. In a certain way, this book represents my personal effort to come to terms with the long-standing, often unspoken divisions among specialists in U.S. history, American literature, and American Studies. There are encouraging signs that these old animosities, many fueled by local, institutional politics, are diminishing, if not disappearing entirely. Historians have certainly been powerfully influenced by postmodern and poststructuralist theories, including those that have blurred conventional boundaries between literary and other forms of textuality.[38] Most historians today recognize the centrality of culture as a category of historical understanding. New Historicism, feminism, critical race theory, and postcolonial and cultural studies have radically transformed the study of American literature both by broadening its scope to include the several Americas and by treating literary functions other than the purely aesthetic.[39] By the same token, new anthropological approaches have helped American Studies scholars to appreciate the aesthetic functions of nominally nonliterary practices of everyday life.[40] New multidisciplinary and intersectional approaches have helped fray what were once established disciplinary boundaries and encouraged a new dialogism that crucially depends on "the corresponding refusal of analytic totalization, of retotalizing culture in a new way."[41]

The risks of such decentered, nontotalizable approaches to the broadened topics of American Studies cannot be ignored. The float and drift of disciplinary interests may be symptomatic of a lack of scholarly rigor or of the absence of theoretical frameworks.[42] Stubborn, purely theoretical insistence upon "nontotalization" may also diminish the authority of scholarly knowledge in its response to more insidious forms of political totalitarianism, including fascism, bureaucratic capitalism, and military and dynastic dictatorships. As Etienne Balibar and Immanuel Wallerstein as well as Masao Miyoshi have urged in different contexts, a revised conception of totality may be a crucial weapon in the struggle against the postmodern, decentered, flexible, and still cynical operation of transnational capitalism.[43] Otherwise, new forms of knowledge production, even in fields traditionally committed to social critique and reform, are likely to contribute to processes of globalization, together with their illusory claims of having fostered greater democracy and improved human rights, in ways contrary to their critical intentions. By the same token, the broadened scope of American Studies should warn us to be patient and allow new configurations of the disciplines to work toward theories of totality and utopia without resorting to older, outmoded paradigms. In this context, we may learn from postcolonial theorists, who call attention to the discrepant historical developments of emergent national and other postcolonial phenomena as evidence that "no one definition of the 'postcolonial' can claim to be correct at the expense of all others, and consequently a variety of interrelated models of identity, positionality, and cultural/critical practice are both possible and necessary."[44]

The interrelation of such different models will require considerable work, not just hope that a liberal plurality of approaches will magically produce new terms of coherence and analysis in an elusive future. Marxian and neo-Marxian theories, for example, must take into account postmodern conditions, including class divisions (and thus the terms of class struggle), labor and its relation to the production of value, and processes of commodification and reification. These key concepts and many others must be reconceptualized and their historical differences reconsidered as part of the project of imagining appropriate theories of totality and utopia to guide our critical practices. Older concepts may be redefined for new purposes, as some scholars have recently proposed new definitions and uses for cosmopolitanism. Bruce Robbins has argued that a new "cosmopolitics" might be developed out of the "common norms and mutual translatability" of a multicultural society while avoiding the universals we associate with modernist cosmopolitanism.[45]

We should also recognize that empirical evidence can help bring together disparate disciplines and practices, if not by itself provide a common ground for adjudicating competing claims and negotiating disciplinary differences. Empirical evidence must always be assessed according to the methods and models used to gather and organize such evidence; no datum is ever politically neutral or value free. Scientific data are textual and dependent on complex discursive practices in the sciences that we have only begun to interpret and understand. Nevertheless, we should acknowledge that a great deal of work in American Studies is conducted without statistical, clinical, demographic, and other forms of empirical evidence that would make this work both more convincing and more conversant with disciplines in the social, natural, physical, and health sciences. Other kinds of evidence might also encourage us to think critically about the textual evidence used so frequently by American Studies scholars. Historical and literary writing, as well as visual images, should not be taken as self-evidently representative of their eras or the issues they are used to clarify. Who were the readers or viewers of such works, and how many readers were there? How and where were they published, exhibited, or consumed? If such data are not available, perhaps collaborative research initiatives might help us answer these questions. Challenging our overdetermination of the textual archive by considering alternative forms of evidence, including scientific data, we might also begin to address more centrally such difficult theoretical questions as the role played by the popularity of certain ideas in the formation of enduring values. Does it matter, for example, that a television situation comedy is viewed by millions of people on a weekly basis and that important novels or influential poems have been read by only a few thousand people over many years?

I cannot claim to have addressed all of these issues in the following chapters. No single scholar is capable of responding to the many different demands that a future American Studies will have to meet by way of collaborative research, related curricula in the discipline and collateral fields, professional organizations on an international scale, and political advocacy regarding liberal education that increasingly will have to work at macropolitical levels outside the academy. My theoretical essays in part I of this book are intended to provoke and challenge colleagues also committed to broadening the scope of American Studies and articulating its relationship with complementary fields. My textual examples in part II of the book are intended not to provide a proper map or guide to the new American Studies, but instead to illustrate how an individual scholar has tried to engage some of the larger issues raised in this introduction and in the theoretical chapters of part I.

I have organized part II of the book according to the historical order of my textual examples, so that the reader begins in the nineteenth century with Hawthorne's and Henry James's anxious responses to sexuality in the visual and verbal arts and concludes with mass media and popular responses to one of our recent political crises: the international and familial custody fight over Elián González. The simple historical arrangement of the chapters also reinforces the development of my work from primarily literary scholarship to more broadly conceived analyses of the many different media contributing to significant cultural events and values. Chapters 5, 6, and 7 deal with American culture primarily in terms of literary case studies, whereas chapters 8 and 9 deal with television and film, respectively, and chapter 10 with the news media, the Internet, foreign policy, and the law. This narrative development does not, however, follow my own personal history. The chapters on Hawthorne, Henry James, and Muriel Rukeyser were written in the past two years; the chapters on television and film were written in the late 1980s. More traditional interdisciplinary work on literary and visual culture can and should coexist with studies of other media. Indeed, American Studies makes possible communication among these different media, which otherwise might be circulated in completely different professional fields and thus be consumed by different audiences.

The future of American Studies should build upon and give new significance to traditional approaches, even when we are critical of our intellectual heritage. For some of these reasons, I have avoided beginning this volume with a history of the discipline in which I would make critical judgments of predecessors and contemporaries without being able to treat the full contexts and specific historical urgencies in which their works were produced. In the following chapters I do not attempt to analyze this history, though such analysis is important; rather, I allow the reader to see how these works extend that history.

Part I.
Theoretical Approaches

1.

A Future for American Studies

The Comparative U.S. Cultures Model

I am a border woman. I grew up between two cultures, the Mexican (with a heavy Indian influence) and the Anglo (as a member of a colonized people in our own territory). I have been straddling that *tejas*-Mexican border, and others, all my life. It's not a comfortable territory to live in, this place of contradictions. Hatred, anger, and exploitation are the prominent features of this landscape. However, there have been compensations for this *mestiza,* and certain joys. Living on borders and in margins, keeping intact one's shifting and multiple identity and integrity, is like trying to swim in a new element, an "alien" element. There is an exhilaration in being a participant in the further evolution of human-kind, in being "worked" on. I have the sense that certain "faculties"—not just in me but in every border resident, colored or non-colored—and dormant areas of consciousness are being activated, awakened. Strange, huh?

—Gloria Anzaldúa, *Borderlands/La Frontera: The New Mestiza*

The international community of scholars committed to the study of American Studies must work to transform the traditionally nationalist concerns of the field to address the several ways in which "America" sig-nifies in the new global political, economic, technological, and cultural circumstances that inform our postmodern and, one hopes, postnational future. Given the long traditions of study systematically devoted to "American identity" or "national character," we must continue the critical work of the past two decades, in which just such a provincial nationalism has been subjected to successful criticism in terms of its ideological consequences. In the coming decades, however, we must complement this work of criticism by constructing the terms of intracultural and intercultural affiliation by means of which we can transcend successfully the monolingual and monocultural myth of "America" that is both a political and an intellectual anachronism.

If we are to address the diverse inter- and intracultural areas of the new American Studies, we will have to revise the traditional interdisciplinary methods of the field to be more comparative in scope. In this regard, scholars in the United States have much to learn from non-U.S. scholars of American Studies, and I want to call for closer working relations between international professional organizations related to American Studies and the United States' American Studies Association. The new International Association of American Studies should consider such cooperation and coordination one of its principal tasks, and it should use the many technological means now available to facilitate communication and advance planning among such professional groups and research centers. My appeal to improve intellectual and professional relations between international and U.S. scholars in American Studies is made to intellectuals in fields including American, Latin American, Luso-American, Caribbean, and Canadian studies.

The challenging prospect of a new American Studies that is more attentive and sensitive to the global community in which it participates also involves some serious dangers, not the least of which are the enormous difficulties that will confront us in the development of practical curricula in the many cultural and theoretical fields that must compose a postnational and comparative "American Studies." Because the new American Studies is central to changes in the conduct and organization of liberal education, our changing field has come under increasing attack from political conservatives. We must not ignore these attacks, as some have proposed we do; they will not vanish with changes in governments. The culture wars are not over; they are simply being fought on different battlefields. The resistance of intellectuals to the changes so necessary for an American Studies that will address and encourage the multiculture of the United States and the western hemisphere is deep and profound, even if it is often based on ignorance and willful misinterpretation. I propose that we work together as intellectuals committed to a new and comparative American Studies that will help educate both our students and our most resistant critics. Since William Bennett published *To Reclaim a Legacy* in 1984, initiating what has come to be known as the campaign against "political correctness," the scholarly and instructional aims of the new American Studies have been central, at times exclusive, targets. Dinesh D'Souza's *Illiberal Education* (1991) specifically targets new curricula in ethnic and gender studies that are closely allied with the traditional aims of American Studies.[1] To be sure, conservative criticisms by nonacademics like Bennett and Dinesh D'Souza are so misinformed about the actual changes taking place in the U.S. academy as to have little immediate impact on reforms that seem at the moment necessitated by student demographics and the rapid "globalization" of the humanities and social experience. Bennett and D'Souza are not cited often in curriculum committees or at American Studies Association meetings in support of more traditional models for U.S. literary and cultural studies. Their influence has been felt, however, in a more indirect and finally more insidious manner: that is, in the frequent appeal to an educational pragmatics and the usually implicit, but increasingly explicit, critique of the incoherence of multiculturalism as the conceptual, curricular, and methodological horizon for the study of U.S. cultures.[2]

However appealing ideals of radical democracy may be in what promises to be a postnationalist era, they remain subject to criticism that they are inchoate and impractical. The theories of radical democracy that are available often build upon a rhetoric of marginality and liminality, sometimes identified collectively as border discourses, that has in large part been *produced* by the monologic (and often explicitly monolingual) myths and narratives of U.S. national identity. Therefore, they often unwittingly support conservative criticisms that the social utopias projected and the curricular and scholarly plans supporting them are themselves mere effects of an increasingly schizophrenic, fractured, and overspecialized postmodern age in desperate need of reorganization by way of a return to traditional values.

In an essay that is both infuriating and brilliant, Homi Bhabha tries to open rather than conclude the various cultural and disciplinary crossings collected in his *Nation and Narration* (Routledge, 1990). In "DissemiNation: Time, Narrative, and the Margins of the Modern Nation" he grafts deconstructive theory onto the cultures of the "postmodern migrations" associated with the history of decolonization. In a deliberately antisystematic and rhetorically playful manner, Bhabha approximates in the intertextuality of his essay (and, of course, in the edited volume in general) a notion of "cultural hybridity" that would provide both the social utopia and the hermeneutic model for postnational communities: "The frontiers of cultural difference are always belated or secondary in the sense that their hybridity is never simply a question of the ad-mixture of pre-given identities or essences. Hybridity is the perplexity of living as it interrupts the representation of the fullness of life; it is an instance of iteration, in the minority discourse, of the time of the arbitrary sign—'the minus in the origin'—through which all forms of cultural meaning are open to translation because their enunciation resists totalization. . . . In the restless drive for cultural translation, hybrid sites of meaning open up a cleavage in the language of culture which suggests that the similitude of the *symbol* as it plays across cultural sites must not obscure the fact that repetition of the *sign* is, in each specific social practice, both different and differential."[3] If we are to take seriously such a notion of cultural hybridity, especially in its nontotalizable and ceaselessly performative dimensions, we must conclude that curricular planning or design can reveal only the limitations of the modern Euro-American university and its Enlightenment model of rationality. What Bhabha implies is that postmodern critical theories and the literatures and cultures marginalized, if not traditionally excluded, from that Enlightenment model of Euro-American reason, simply practice in coordination the sorts of disciplinary and cultural transgressions that will at once deconstruct the Enlightenment model (together with its departmental and discipline-specific boundaries) and realize in their own practices new and hybrid modes of knowing and communication for which we at present have only the most rudimentary versions, sometimes classified inadequately as critical theories, cultural studies, or minority literatures. The limitations of the Euro-American educational model are not restricted simply to the United States and Europe, because many postcolonial states still rely on educational systems organized by their former colonizers. Bhabha's intellectual revolution will require transformations not only in the first-world institutions of learning but in second- and third-world educational institutions still dependent, often quite invisibly, on Enlightenment assumptions and everyday pedagogies.

Bhabha may well be right, but the consequences of such knowledge at this moment in the history of the academy in the United States, if not that of higher education globally understood, could be devastating. In order to respond to critics who complain on reasonable grounds and by appeal to the pragmatics of education that the multiculture of the United States cannot be taught effectively or responsibly in a four-year college program (of which only two years may be devoted to a specialization), we must offer plans that rely on more articulable postnational concepts of community without resorting to now outmoded notions of ethnic or gender essentialism.

I want to explore two other models for developing a postnational curriculum for American Studies, one of which compares different cultures within the United States and another that allows us to situate U.S. multiculturalism within international, transnational, and potentially postnational contexts. The first is Paul Lauter's conception of "the literatures of America" as a fundamentally "comparative discipline," which first appeared in the opening essay of the Modern Language Association volume *Redefining American Literary History*.[4] This essay is a condensation of the arguments in his book *Canons and Contexts*, as well as in the equally important new Heath anthology of American Literature, which makes undergraduate instruction in the "multiculture" that is the United States possible for virtually the first time.[5] The second is Mary Louise Pratt's theorization in *Profession 91* of what she terms the "arts of the contact zone," which applies the linguistic model developed in her 1987 essay "Linguistic Utopias" to the curricular and pedagogical issues she has experienced in her participation in the "Cultures, Ideas, Values" course at Stanford—the new core course that was the eventual product of the institutional and then national debates concerning Stanford's revision of its traditional introductory course in Western civilization. Indeed, it was William Bennett's criticism of proposals at Stanford for a more culturally diverse core course that many identify with the beginnings of what is now an international debate concerning "political correctness" in education.[6]

Before adapting Pratt's arts of the contact zone to the reasonable, but finally still nationalist, comparative model offered by Lauter, I want to say explicitly that my aim is not simply to use these two theorists to dismiss Bhabha's poststructuralist model, but finally to identify the limitations of each of these approaches in order to come up with a more articulable program for the comparative study of U.S. cultures in a postnationalist era. For all three, despite their very distinct theoretical differences, share a commitment to multicultural topics (as well as the radical democracy inherent in such an educational model), necessarily collaborative research in a field that clearly consists of a suite of disciplines and cultures that cannot be commanded by a single scholar, and a new concern for the relation of our research to the theories and practices of teaching.

Few of us today would disagree with Paul Lauter's view that the "severely limited canon of 'major writers'"—whether or not these major writers happen to be white males from New England—must be replaced by a culturally diverse and thus fundamentally comparative approach to the literatures and cultures of the United States.[7] Lauter's comparatist model, however, follows older approaches to world literature and their admirable but impractical goal of representing "differing literary traditions and thus of differing (and changing) social realities" (12). Such a comparative model, whether applied to world literatures or to the microcosm of U.S. cultures, accepts the discreteness of different cultures and then articulates resemblances and differences according to structuralist binaries. As long as the self-sufficiency of the culture represented by a few texts can be predicated with some confidence, there is nothing wrong with this model beyond the inherent limitations of its synecdochical—in which part is taken for the whole—rhetoric, which is necessitated in its turn by the impossible variety of discrete cultures to be represented.[8]

Lauter makes no explicit connection between his proposal for a comparative study of the literatures of America and the now outmoded world literatures model, perhaps in part because he knows that the latter tended to stress Euro-American traditions and national literatures at the expense of the many other cultural influences that have demonstrably shaped the United States and the several Americas of the western hemisphere. Indeed, one of the great attractions of Lauter's comparative model is its focus on different cultural backgrounds and influences in the shaping of the different literatures and cultural practices of Native Americans, African Americans, Chicanos and Chicanas, Euro-Americans, Chinese Americans, Japanese Americans, and others. For Lauter, the European traditions so fundamental to nation building play only one part among many different cultural traditions in the formation and transformation of a complex society.

Nevertheless, Lauter's comparative method, insofar as it merely acknowledges the heterogeneity of cultures represented in the United States and the differences in their historical development (and thus in the corresponding development of their cultural forms), implies a curriculum of representative courses and even more highly selective representative texts arranged in a cumulative (or additive) manner. It is just this notion of the academic sample of different U.S. cultures that has prompted critics of political correctness to criticize the "irresponsible" curricular designs of the new multiculturalism. To be sure, these critics may cite the extraordinarily refined (albeit exclusive) curricula of the Western canon in comparison with the still developing curricula of multicultural literary study, and we might defend ourselves by quoting Lauter: "A full literary history of this country requires both parallel and integrated accounts of differing literary traditions and thus of differing (and changing) social realities. We are only at the beginning of the creation of such a complex history" (12). In fact, Lauter offers us primarily the comparative methods for articulating the parallel accounts of those "differing literary traditions," and what we need rather urgently at the moment are better comparative methods for articulating "integrated accounts of differing literary traditions."

In effect, the new multiculturalism needs its own code of knowledge with its own narrative logics, and yet such an "integrated" account, together with the canon or canons it will project explicitly or simply by implication, must avoid the dangers of a superficial pluralism or a deceptive assimilationism. Lauter's comparative model risks adopting as its social ideal a simplistic pluralism—every discrete cultural group in the United States deserves its own recognition and study. Lauter assumes that what makes a group identifiable depends largely on its own practices of cultural narration. The oppression, marginalization, or mere neglect of that community by the ruling class may have impeded that cultural development, but it is not an integral part of the group's cultural specificity. Thus there is an "uneven cultural development" in the United States of different cultural groups that Lauter proposes we take into account in order to acknowledge how, for example, the prohibitions against literacy among slaves in the antebellum South might account for the "painfully underdeveloped, in places even crude and propagandistic" qualities of such early African American novels as "William Wells Brown's *Clotel* (1853), Frank Webb's *Garies and Their Friends* (1857), Martin Delany's *Blake* (1859), and Harriet Wilson's *Our Nig* (1859)" (13).

Lauter claims that reading these African American novels in terms of the great tradition of the Euro-American novel is bound to find the African American examples secondary, if not demonstrably inferior to such contemporary works as *The Scarlet Letter* and *Moby-Dick* or to other works that are more obviously descended from Euro-American cultural traditions. Lauter thus argues that the effort to expand the Euro-American canon of the novel by adding Brown, Webb, Delany, and Wilson obscures "what were undoubtedly the major cultural influences on these books: the well-established tradition of black slave narratives, the African American oral tradition of tales and legends, and the publication of *Uncle Tom's Cabin* (1852)" (13). Lauter is certainly right that reading these "first black novelists" in terms of Douglass's *Narrative* (1845), Jacobs's *Incidents in the Life of a Slave Girl* (1861), and the folklore traditions ranging from West Africa and the Caribbean to the antebellum South makes far more sense than interpreting them according to literary traditions ranging from the Elizabethan picaresque to the rise of the novel associated with Defoe and Fielding.

Lauter's passing reference to Stowe's *Uncle Tom's Cabin* suggests a way out of a comparatist method that would remain fully tied to the specificity of discrete cultures in the United States and their uneven cultural developments. Lauter argues that the slave "narratives and Stowe's novel helped establish and broaden an audience for which reading and writing was integrated with social activism; an audience that responded to images of heroic and adventurous black men and women and was willing to confront the complex realities of the oppression, particularly sexual, of black women; that also accepted the very idea of a black *writer*—a problematic conception for many people, even some blacks, in antebellum America" (13). Insofar as the writings of Douglass, Stowe, Jacobs, and similar writers constitute an integrated account of the complex issues of race and gender in the political activism of the abolitionist movement, as well as the political and historical purposes served by literary and other belletristic acts by white and African American men and women, often under conditions of historical crisis and personal risk, we have a model for an integrated comparative approach in these three works and writers.

This is a bare hint of a way to escape the fragmentation of a comparatism that does its work *within* the cultural specificities of the many different cultures of the United States. With the help of Mary Louise Pratt's concept of the "contact zone," I want to suggest how we might develop an integrated comparative study of U.S. literatures and cultures that would avoid the traps of multicultural pluralism and melting-pot assimilation. The model I am proposing also has the virtue of suggesting a number of common issues for theoretical resolution rather than accepting Lauter's notion that multicultural studies always require different aesthetic and cultural theories for each of the different communities studied. To be sure, different cultures develop different heremeneutical and philosophical paradigms, but it may be possible to develop some common terms for understanding the intersection of such paradigms—terms not thoroughly saturated with the ideological purposes of psychically or rhetorically colonizing the Other.

Pratt defines contact zones as "social spaces where cultures meet, clash, and grapple with each other, often in contexts of highly asymmetrical relations of power, such as colonialism, slavery, or their aftermaths as they are lived out in many parts of the world today."[9] Pratt develops her notion of the "contact zone" by way of an actual text, *El primer nueva corónica y buen gobierno* [The first new chronicle and good government], which was "dated in the city of Cuzco in Peru, in the year 1613, some forty years after the final fall of the Inca empire to the Spanish," was "signed with an unmistakably Andean indigenous name: Felipe Guaman Poma de Ayala," and was written "in a mixture of Quechua and ungrammatical, expressive Spanish" in the form of a letter "addressed by an unknown but apparently literate Andean to King Philip III of Spain"—a "letter" of "eight hundred pages of written text and four hundred of captioned line drawings" (34).[10]

Pratt believes that the intertextual character of Guaman de Poma's text belongs not so much to the literariness of the work itself as to the social and historical conditions that produced it. By this I mean not only its actual composition and material reproduction, but also its reception—or, in the case of *El nueva corónica*, its neglect.[11] Within this text, Pratt argues, we find "autoethnography, transculturation, critique, collaboration, bilingualism, mediation, parody, denunciation, imaginary dialogue, vernacular expression" along with "miscomprehension, incomprehension, dead letters, unread masterpieces, absolute heterogeneity of meaning"— both the "arts" and the "perils" of the contact zone (37). As Pratt points out, these are the very contraries that "live among us today in the transnationalized metropolis of the United States," thereby connecting the multicultural issues of seventeenth-century Spanish colonialism and those of our own postcolonial and postmodern era.

Pratt generalizes the contact zone as an alternative to the monolingual and profoundly ideal space of the imagined community of the nation. In her adaptation of Benedict Anderson's *Imagined Communities: Reflections on the Origins and Spread of Nationalism* (1984), Pratt argues: "The prototype of the modern nation as imagined community was . . . mirrored in ways people thought about language and the speech community. Many commentators have pointed out how modern views of language as code and competence assume a unified and homogeneous social world in which language exists as a shared patrimony—as a device, precisely, for imagining community. An image of a universally shared literacy is also part of the picture. The prototypical manifestation of language is generally taken to be the speech of individual adult native speakers face-to-face (as in Saussure's famous diagram) in monolingual, even monodialectical situations—in short, the most homogenous case linguistically and socially" (38). Pratt criticizes this model in ways that have immediate relevance (which Pratt does not develop) to the conservative call by E. D. Hirsch Jr., in *Cultural Literacy,* both for a return to the standards of monolingual education and for the centralization of educational testing.[12] Hirsch's rear-guard action, however, is not likely to do much except slow down, albeit in unpredictable, dangerous, and potentially very violent ways, the polyglot, intertextual, heteroglossic "cultural speech-act situation" that increasingly dominates everyday experience in the course of globalization.[13]

I propose that we begin to construct a new comparative U.S. cultures curriculum and canon around an elaborated and developed theory of the contact zone. I am not daring and foolish enough to try to work out such a history in precise detail here or even to name the appropriate texts, but I will offer a few examples. Pratt insists that the arts of the contact zone involve a rethinking not only of the basic speech-act situation of communication and the character of the formally coherent text, but also of the very idea and purpose of teaching. The conclusion of Pratt's essay in *Profession 91* focuses on her translation of the colonial contact zone in Guaman de Poma's text into the contact zone of the contemporary humanities classroom at Stanford.

All three of Pratt's translations are important for my purposes, because the cultural speech act for the new American Studies will have to be multidisciplinary and multicultural in ways that will involve new communicative models and thereby rely on broader, less aesthetic, conceptions of textuality. If so, the teaching situation will have to take this into account, not merely attempt to analyze and subject to rational understanding—Enlightenment methods whose ideological effects have often enough been deconstructed—aspects of social and cultural experience that students are likely to use in their everyday lives, if the hybridized culture described earlier by Homi Bhabha is to become the ethos of the postnational multiculturalism. The texts or textual effects that we choose, then, must identify in particularly effective ways the sites of social confrontation and negotiation that have defined U.S. history and are likely to confront students in the future.

Reconceived in terms of the contact zone as the liminal region or border zone in which different cultures meet and negotiate—violently or otherwise—their neighborhood, the "literary" texts studied in traditional American Studies are suddenly seen to have immediate affinities with other nonliterary modes of social and cultural expression. Consider a captivity narrative like Mary Rowlandson's *A Narrative of the Captivity and Restauration* [sic] *of Mrs. Mary Rowlandson* (1682), so often treated as a textbook example of the invocation of religious rhetoric and theology to rationalize the experiences of suffering in captivity. Ignored within this text of the contact zone, however, are many instances of food exchange, food preparation, shared meals, and the like through which Mary Rowlandson comes to understand her captors and their own sufferings after colonial troops have destroyed Narragansett food supplies. Despite its overdetermination by countless U.S. legends, John Smith's account of his first meeting with Powhatan displays extraordinary discursive indeterminacy or disparity. Many narratives of conquest and colonization seem to be almost generically describable in terms of such moments of cultural difference, discursive and symbolic conflict and contest. Of course, such disparities and contradictions are often utterly repressed by the conquerors or brutally negotiated by the force of arms or the planting of a conventional sign of imperial power. Myra Jehlen generalizes from the colonial encounter between the Aztecs and Cortés a "common denominator which is precisely the commonality of their encounter, the common ground they construct, new to both, and on which they are neither the same nor different but only inextricably related; indeed neither the same nor different *through* their relation."[14]

These transcultural confrontations, treated so often in strictly anthropological terms, have obvious relevance to other defining moments in virtually any history of any imagined community. What should be a criterion for the selection of texts to represent and thus distinguish important moments of contact need not be the self-evidence of historical events, although it is likely that some will take the established events of conquest, colonization, revolution, abolition, reconstruction, Manifest Destiny, Indian removal, modernization, and so forth as the familiar mythemes of a new cultural history. But the quest for interesting problem texts that represent certain difficult contact zones might also take us beyond the customary categories of this history. Melville's *Typee,* rather than being the first publication of the famous American romantic, becomes an effort to engage the first quixotic efforts of U.S. colonialism, in this case in concert with the French and the British in the Marquesas (and the South Pacific in general).

Because the conflicts and disparities belong not so much to the specific text taught as to the social situation, we are not restricted in our selection of texts to those that are formally coherent, represent particularly successful solutions for their time or all time, or otherwise suggest imaginative resolutions. To be sure, some of our texts ought to be chosen with some of these notions in mind, because we need them to serve our students as models (rather than exempla) for negotiating their own multicultural contact zones. Certainly those texts that offer historically credible solutions and alternatives will tend to be valorized, even if they must be contextualized. Douglass's 1845 *Narrative* offers viable alternatives in literacy and laissez-faire northern capitalism to the systematic exploitation and domination of southern slavery. In crossing the borders of South and North, of slavery and freedom, of subordination and political activism, it "negotiates" the contact zone in ways appropriate for its time, albeit limited and limiting in its relative neglect of gender differences and in its ambivalence regarding northern capitalism. Such limitations, however, may well enable us to construct better curricular narratives of these arts of the contact zone, because the very limitations of Douglass's 1845 negotiation of the border between freedom and slavery, between racism and democracy, calls to mind texts like Harriet Jacobs's *Incidents in the Life of a Slave Girl*, which makes up for precisely the limitations that are found in Douglass's work. Thus the contact zone may be refined to include, as in this instance, the disparity or conflict not only between white owner and African American slave, but between man and woman.

Actual texts and courses, as well as curricula, ought then to be designed in view of such contact zones through which cultural confrontations have been negotiated historically in the United States. In my view, such courses ought to be conceived primarily as theory and methods courses, in which various modes of discursive negotiation might be drawn from the different cultures involved in order to offer hypothetical as well as historically demonstrable solutions to such problems. Crucial to such theory and methods courses is not so much their placement in undergraduate majors or the catalog of graduate programs—such debates about a priori or a posteriori placement of theory have a way of deferring more important issues—as their minimally bicultural scope. Equally important, of course, would be the customary interdisciplinary aims of American Studies programs; the intertextual site of the contact zone is itself already one demanding the approaches of several different disciplines. Of course, such disciplines should be chosen from all the cultures involved, which is contrary to what we see in so many of our applications of theories developed in the United States or Europe to cultures in which these same theories may well exercise their own subtle colonial influences.

I do not think that such approaches to contact zones should take the places of courses devoted to the historical specificity and internal development of the diverse communities in the United States, except in those cases where such a comparative approach better represents a specific cul-

ture. It is interesting to note just how many communities might be studied rather thoroughly in terms of the several contact zones involved in
their historical constructions. Henry Louis Gates Jr. has argued persuasively that such is the case with African American culture, insofar as no
Afrocentric or even African American nationalist approach adequately
represents the diversity, intertextuality, and bricolage of African American culture. Gloria Anzaldúa has argued in a similar manner for Chicana/
mestiza communities of the Southwestern U.S.–Mexican borderlands in
her book *Borderlands/La Frontera: The New Mestiza* (1987), as have other
Chicana artists and critics in the collection *This Bridge Called My Back*.
Lisa Lowe's conception of Asian American "immigrant acts" suggests another way in which the minority subject identifies himself or herself by
way of hybridities, creolizations, and intertextualities that generally fall
under the heading of the contact zone.[15]

In fact, the most persuasive arguments for hybrid cultures in the
United States have often come from those communities' finest expressive
and critical writers, who thus give special credibility to the study of
many different communities in terms of their own arts of the contact
zone. Writers like Maxine Hong Kingston and Amy Tan are among the
best examples of "intercultural" writers who also claim to constitute the
special intracultural identity of Chinese American. In a similar manner,
LeLy Hayslip's *When Heaven and Earth Changed Places: A Vietnamese
Woman's Odyssey* speaks eloquently of the special divisions, crossings, and
hybridizations required of so many Vietnamese Americans since their
emigration.

Even those communities whose cultural specificity is not fairly represented exclusively by means of the contact zone and the modes of historical hybridization suggested by Bhabha are likely to benefit from the comparative perspectives proposed in this model. To study Native American
peoples primarily in terms of the contact zones that certainly have defined their historical experience over the past four hundred years would
nevertheless neglect the millennia-old cultural traditions of specific
Amerindian peoples, as well as their different media for the transmission
and preservation of such traditions. But there is little question that
pre-Columbian cultures may be studied in terms of their mutual contact
zones. Recalling how the Aztecs ruthlessly colonized other peoples in
their own conquest of Mexico helps us better understand how five hundred poorly equipped and fed Spaniards could recruit so many tribal
warriors to lay siege to Tenochtitlán. To be sure, the contact zones between native peoples in the Americas often included modes of peaceful

coexistence and territorial integrity that are worthy of study, insofar as they might offer us and our students other ways to live in neighborhoods. And within that five hundred-year history of Euro-American colonial domination and efforts to destroy native peoples of the western hemisphere, the opportunities for studying the ethical lessons to be learned from these contact zones hardly need to be detailed. Once again, however, we see that it is just such cultural contact and negotiation that are the distinctive features of some of the finest expressive literature to be produced in recent years by American Indians, as the writings of Scott Momaday, Louise Erdrich, Louis Owens, Gerald Vizenor, James Welch, and Leslie Silko suggest in their various intertextualities.

Such an approach lends itself quite readily, of course, to the borderlands dividing the "America" of traditional "American Studies" from the several Americas so often ignored and thus trivialized by that disciplinary title, as well as the territories defined to the west, north, and east of the United States, drawing again into view Asian, Canadian, African, and European borderlands in the construction of the imagined and utopian community of a U.S. multiculture. In this regard, the comparatist approach I have adapted from Bhabha, Lauter, and Pratt has the advantage of being considerably flexible in its expansions and constrictions. Insofar as this comparatist approach lends itself to the more established methods of Latin American and European scholars and critics, there is some likelihood that the curriculum in "comparative U.S. cultures" might develop actual connections with curricula in Latin American and European cultures. There is nothing about this model that discourages the work of traditional scholars of Euro-American immigration, for example; in fact, there is much that would enable such scholars to work in concert with those studying African American and Asian American immigration.

Perhaps these arts of the contact zone will help us develop the terms for living in each other's neighborhoods in our postnationalist era. Donna Haraway argues that we are by this late date, in the early decades of the truly postindustrial age, cyborgs, "chimeras, theorized and fabricated hybrids of machine and organism." She writes: "The cyborg is our ontology; it gives us our politics. The cyborg is a condensed image of both imagination and material reality, the two joined centers structuring any possibility of historical transformation."[16] I suspect that she is right, that we had better accept not only the conditions but also the possibilities of our fictionalized identities and communities. The cyborg certainly speaks to our postmodern age, perhaps frightening us to try at least to awaken to a better name for what we have made of ourselves.[17]

2.

Postmodernity and the New American Studies

Despite an enormous amount of recent American Studies scholarship and criticism that could be characterized as postmodern in method or concerned with "postmodern" cultural schools and movements—from postmodern literary experimentalism to architecture, music, dance, visual art, and performance art—the field has not yet come to terms with postmodernity in a central way. Whether as one of several useful methods or as one of the many historical eras American Studies treats, postmodernity has been treated simply as an addition to the repertoire of traditional methods and objects of study. But "postmodernity" describes in general terms the socioeconomic circumstances in which we do our work as American Studies scholars, especially when we understand this term as designating a historical period characterized by significant changes in social, political, economic, and cultural definition. "Postindustrialism" may not cover all of these changes, but it indicates very directly what is missing from many critiques of postmodern and poststructuralist methodologies and from many scholarly celebrations of the emancipatory possibilities of postmodern cultural practices as alternatives to middle-class U.S. society. By the same token, the very characteristics of postmodernity as a distinctive social, economic, and cultural order make conventional economic analyses also seem inadequate. It may well be that what is needed is a more coordinated, transdisciplinary approach to postmodernity. If so, such an analysis may well be an excellent test case for the claims of

17

the new American Studies that it offers transdisciplinary and multidisci-plinary accounts of complex historical phenomena. As an indicator of socioeconomic transformation, postmodernity also implies postnation-alist concerns usually identified with processes of transnational capital-ism and the waning of communist internationalism, which may now be understood principally as a modernist phenomenon.

In this chapter, however, I focus on postmodernity in the United States and on its postnationalist consequences, both because some focus is necessary in the discussion of such a notoriously elusive topic and be-cause I do not have the expertise necessary to discuss postmodernity on a global scale. I address three different aspects of postmodernity in the United States: the literary experimentation that came to dominate U.S. fiction between 1965 and 1975; poststructuralist and deconstructive scholarly approaches in the United States between 1975 and 1985; and the general outlines of a "postindustrial society," increasingly dominated by service- and information-related industries, that has begun to visibly change social and personal behavior from the 1950s to the present. There is considerable arbitrariness in any such dating, and my particular peri-odization tends to emphasize the discreteness of literary, critical, and socioeconomic postmodernisms. Let me write at the outset, then, that my periodization of these discrete versions of postmodernism is de-signed ultimately to construct a working relation among them without succumbing to the usual dodge that "postmodernity" is by the very terms of its own radical ambiguity or strategic undecidability an indefinable concept.

Postmodern writers in the late 1960s and early 1970s accepted the charge that the novel was dead, and they bid it good riddance. The most notable and vocal postmoderns worked primarily in prose fiction, and they generally preferred the term "fiction" to "novel." The title of Ronald Sukenick's *The Death of the Novel and Other Stories* (1969) implies an abandonment of the traditional concerns of the novel to represent social reality, the complex relation between psychological and social experi-ence, and the essential terms governing our lived realities. "Reality" and "realism" were attacked by the postmoderns as mystified terms. The moderns had attempted to criticize the accepted conventions of everyday life, proper behavior, and thus the consensually established terms for re-ality; the postmoderns claimed to go beyond their modernist ancestors by abandoning reality altogether. "Reality is a nice place to visit," John Barth said in an interview in 1967, "but I wouldn't like to live there—at least not for very long."[1] "Antirealism" and "counter-realism" (John

Barth), "fabulation" (Robert Scholes), "the fantastic" (Tzvetan Todorov), and "surfiction" (Raymond Federman) were only some of the terms used to describe the postmodernists' rebellion against literary realism and social reality.

Literature itself had been "exhausted," as Barth argued in his famous 1967 essay "The Literature of Exhaustion."[2] The great plots had been used again and again; centuries of stylistic innovation and formal experimentation had left contemporary writers with nothing new to say or do. That "nothing," of course, was the starting point for the postmoderns, itself the "key to the treasure" of a new literature, what Barth would subsequently call "the literature of replenishment."[3] Postmodern literature took the very terms used to criticize literature and transformed them into the slogans for its revolution. Literature is nothing, and that nothing can save us from a world too insistently material; the existential abyss was turned into a virtual geography of the literary imagination. Ronald Sukenick's *Out* (1973) was composed of "self-obliterating" characters, and the narrative moved literally to the "blank space," the "virginal" white page of Mallarmé's "pure poetry." Thomas Pynchon's *V.* (1960) focused on the quest for an elusive feminine figure who was narratively transformed into a machine that was dismantled toward the end of the text. John Barth's *Lost in the Funhouse* (1968) begins with a "Frame-Tale" that consists solely of "Once upon a time there," printed vertically on the first page, and "was a story that began," printed vertically on the next page. The corners of this literary Moebius strip were lettered, and the "Frame-Tale" consisted of these convenient directions: "Cut on dotted line. Twist end once and fasten *AB* to *ab, CD* to *cd*."[4] The "contents" of the rest of the collection of Barth's "Fiction for print, tape, live voice" were virtually "wrapped" in the endless Moebius loop of storytelling.

"Man would sooner have the void for his purpose than be void of purpose," Nietzsche wrote at the end of *The Genealogy of Morals* (1887), and it is as good a slogan as any for the postmoderns' obsessive fixation on nothingness, absence, triviality, exhaustion, entropy, and blankness.[5] The social and historical alienation of the individual that had been a central theme for the moderns became a formal building block, a fictional donnée, for the postmoderns. The moderns had focused on the social disintegration of modern industrial societies. They had used the literary themes of fragmentation, alienation, and decadence to represent the failure of social reality and everyday life; there was still that residual commitment to literary "realism" in their works. Postmodern writers attempted to turn the conditions of modern urban life into possibilities for literary creation and an ultimate transvaluation of those oppressive circumstances. They seemed intent upon "negating negation," or so dwelling upon the insignificance of literature and the marginalization of the artist as to turn these negative qualities into positive virtues. The result was an intensely self-conscious style carried to the virtual limits of language. The hallmark of postmodern literature was its obsessive concern with its own possibility of production. The questions writ large at the entrance to every postmodern fiction were, Why write and Why read?

Postmodern literature had answers to those questions, and they seemed exhilaratingly revolutionary at the time: We write because we are defined by our use of language; man, *homo faber,* is nothing other than his representation of himself. Self-conscious use of language is a liberation from the bonds of convention, from habitual and unreflective speech. How we express ourselves defines us, for better or for worse, and thus literary technique is not simply a minor category of literary study but a key to human knowledge. How we know is finally more important than what we know; or, in another version, what we know is nothing but a function of how we know. Because literature, unlike other modes of production, begins with the raw materials of existing language, the literary author must be especially attentive to the ways in which everyday language works, as well as to the more specific literary uses of language prompting any avant-garde aesthetic movement. In effect, the literary author is a specialist in linguistics, but of a fundamentally different kind than the academic linguist who is intent upon analyzing the basic rules by which languages function. The literary author knows language only by using it, and he knows the conventions of language only by violating them with unconventional styles and avant-garde forms.

Like their modern predecessors, postmodern writers insisted upon the special qualities of literary language to defamiliarize the ordinary, thus offering an opportunity to combat the automatization of individual existences in the urban mass. It is no surprise that the protagonists of modern and postmodern narratives are generally artists or at least "poetically" sensitive figures. But postmodern writers were often more ambivalent than the moderns about the power of literature to effect large-scale social transformations. The utopian dimensions of modernism are commensurate with the ambitions of its major works. Pound's *Cantos,* Williams's *Paterson,* Eliot's *Four Quartets,* and Faulkner's Yoknapatawpha narratives, for example, argue variously for major social changes initiated by literary works that address economic, political, scientific, religious, psychological, and philosophical issues. Much as they differ from traditional epics, many modern narratives in both verse and prose share the epic's utopian vision of a redeemed or ideal social order.

Postmodern writers were more modest, in part because they had witnessed the dramatic failure of the modernists' social ambitions. The Frankfurt School writer, Theodor Adorno, wrote shortly after World War II: "To write a poem after Auschwitz is obscene."[6] Moderns like Yeats, Thomas Mann, and Eliot had obliquely "predicted" some reign of terror and destruction in the aftermath of the First World War, but none had anticipated the mass murder of the Holocaust. In their literary efforts to save Western societies from their own destructive potential, moderns like Ezra Pound and Wyndham Lewis had found a certain appeal in fascist "solutions." Postmodern writers in the United States therefore trivialized the political functions and contents of literature, even though their most provocative works appeared in a period—roughly 1965 to 1975—when "not to be part of the solution [was] to be part of the problem," as Huey Newton had insisted. The great issues of that period—civil rights, women's rights, and the Vietnam War—helped produce a powerful New Left political coalition. Yet postmodern experimentalists marginalized these issues in their works. John Barth, John Hawkes, William Gass, William Gaddis, J. P. Donleavy, and Ronald Sukenick, to mention only some of the familiar names, had nothing to say in this period about the Vietnam, women's and minority rights, the urban war waged in America against African Americans ("race riots"), and antiwar activism. The few exceptions were writers like Norman Mailer and Philip Roth, who had established their careers in the 1950s, when existential realism, despite its bourgeois obsession with the absurd and the alienated individual, had retained some of the commitment to the representation of social and political realities that had characterized its European models, notably the writings of Sartre and Camus.

Even these exceptions to the apolitical rule for postmodern literature used the techniques of the postmoderns to render concrete political issues in oblique, often equivocal, ways. Mailer's *The Armies of the Night* (1968) took the 1967 antiwar march on Washington as its subject, and his *Why Are We in Vietnam?* (1967) took the war as at least a titular topic. In both works, however, Mailer argued that it was our failure to comprehend the entanglement of our deepest psychic drives with our most visible cultural myths that had led us to war in Southeast Asia and at home. In his insistence that such understanding could be achieved first by literary means, through the metaphoric connections possible only through poetic logics, Mailer adapted postmodern techniques to modernist literary

ambitions and utopianism. By the same token, Mailer mocked and parodied liberal reformers and intellectuals, including one of his several alter
egos, for their superficial grasp of much deeper and more complicated issues. In this regard, he resembled many of his postmodern contemporaries, who viewed direct political activism with skepticism while preserving literature as a means of patiently investigating our nearly hopeless
social and political circumstances.

One reason for this caution was that postmodern experimentalists
were often hard pressed to compete with the growing influence of the
mass media. Television and film declared themselves players in, not just
observers of, the Vietnam War and the antiwar movement. Antiwar
demonstrators unfurled the North Vietnamese flag during protests, and
news photographs of Jane Fonda in Hanoi, the Saigon chief of police
executing a Vietcong suspect, and a naked Vietnamese girl burned by
Napalm assumed much more than merely reportorial significance. Both
the demonstrators and the news media, often in very contrary ways, employed the mass media to capture and economically express the historical
moment and specific political issues; this use of the mass media in itself
constituted a mode of symbolic action often claimed by literary artists.
One of the consequences was that the literary response to contemporary
political and social issues frequently insisted upon more complex ge-
nealogies for current events. Thomas Pynchon's *Gravity's Rainbow* (1973)
and Robert Coover's *The Public Burning* (1976) are familiar examples of
the postmodern literary effort to explain the Vietnam War. It is not
enough to argue simply that these highly political and arguably leftist
works arrived too late to make a literary difference in the New Left political coalition. Nominally about World War II, *Gravity's Rainbow* may be
the great work about how we got into Vietnam, but the political and historical issues are represented as so complex, so intertwined with our psychic lives, that resistance, or the "counter-force" of Pynchon's final section heading, seems at best elusive and at worst conventionally literary. In
a similar sense, Coover uses *The Public Burning* to trace Richard Nixon's
rise to political power to the virulent anticommunism of the McCarthy
era. The witch-hunt that culminates in the electrocution of Julius and
Ethel Rosenberg as convicted spies anticipates our special brand of imperialism in Southeast Asia. In the works of both Pynchon and Coover,
however, the specific events of the Vietnam era are barely mentioned, as
if the consequences of the historical motives analyzed in these novels—
the Vietnam War, racism, sexism, and the increasingly rigid class distinctions of the 1970s—can virtually be left unspoken.

Wary of the moderns' unrealized ambitions for literature to bring about the transvaluation of the age, the postmoderns claimed instead to provide a more detailed critical understanding of our social situation. Some creative writers became academic, insofar as they made special claims on a growing number of intellectual disciplines and often their specialized languages. Undoubtedly, the academic interests of some experimental writers can be traced to the growing number of such writers who held college and university positions, but this can be considered only one factor. The multidisciplinary interest of much contemporary work in the humanities has at least one of its recent origins in postmodern literary experimentation. The postmoderns' claims to understand that language functions by means of the strategic deformation of verbal conventions implied that any significant social change would depend upon our knowledge of language and its determination of thought and values. By the same token, this knowledge led to a familiar intellectual skepticism with regard to the bases for specific social and political praxes. The rhetorical complement of such skepticism was irony, which is the distinctive stylistic characteristic of postmodern literary experimentation.

The moderns attempted to redefine, even redeem, the individualism destroyed by urban and industrial life. However protean, contradictory, or pluralistic, the modern artist precariously clung to the special integrity of his consciousness or his style. The postmoderns no longer had such confidence in the redemptive powers of individualism, although their responses to and diagnoses of the "death of the subject" are extremely various. In philosophical terms, the postmodern subject is a verbal or semiotic fiction, constructed in part by the language acquired through normal development and acculturation and in part by the specific employment of language in concrete situations—speech acts. Self-expression thus offers only limited freedom and paradoxical identity. Characters in Donald Barthelme's stories speak in popular clichés, the "dreck" of contemporary society, and thus are defined ontologically as waste products. Characters in Pynchon's fictions are named for idioms, as is the protagonist's former husband in *The Crying of Lot 49* (1967), Mucho Maas, or for consumer commodities, as is another character in that novel, Stanley Kotecks. Characters in Barth's *Chimera* are drawn from familiar myths—Scheherazade, Perseus, Bellerophon—to suggest how dependent identity is upon the mythic narratives that tell *us*. Barth himself appears as the genie of *1001 Nights*, in keeping with the postmodern assumption that the author is merely another character in the ultimate novel, the narrative of history. Characters like Malcolm in James Purdy's *Malcolm* (1959) or the gardener,

Chance, in Jerzy Kosinki's *Being There* (1971) are simply blanks or radical innocents, determined entirely by the historical fictions they encounter.

The negative consequence of such historicism was a trivialization of history, in part because postmodern aesthetics seemed to comprehend the entire historical process abstractly. The details were uninteresting. On the other hand, such historicism motivated a nearly scholastic commitment to accurately represent historical stories, even in the midst of the most playful literary experiments. Scholars are still finding historically accurate material incorporated into *Gravity's Rainbow,* and such material constitutes some of the most fantastic of Pynchon's stories in that work. Barth's fictional variations on the *1001 Nights* and on Greek myths in *Chimera* are by no means purely fanciful, but rely on legitimate scholarly versions of these narratives. Ishmael Reed's *Mumbo Jumbo* (1972) uses footnotes, photographs, and bibliography to argue that his fictional history of jazz, the Harlem renaissance, the U.S. occupation of Haiti, and the persecution and eventual deportation of Marcus Garvey by the federal government, for example, constitutes a way for the repressed history of African Americans to be made readable.

Reed's suggestion that one function of a postmodern author is to reveal an otherwise repressed history is shared by a number of other postmodern experimentalists. The novel, of course, has always claimed a special historical function, generally to represent those aspects of history ignored by professional historians. The historiographical assumption of postmodernist aesthetics, however, was that the textual characteristics of history made it malleable and thus available for literary revision and adaptation. Not only did this notion considerably exaggerate the actual historical authority of creative writers between 1965 and 1975; it also prompted investigations of the literary infrastructure of history in the place of more concrete, politically relevant reinterpretations of modern history. Like so many avant-garde movements, postmodernism seemed intent on demonstrating the universality of its own aesthetic tenets. Barth argued in "The Literature of Exhaustion" that the noted self-consciousness of postmodern literature is characteristic of all literature and myth and thus of the origin of all storytelling. Postmoderns became adept at recycling familiar myths, often in order to recall us to the mythopoetic sources of all human experience. With certain exceptions, such as Reed's account of how and why modern African American history has been repressed by a white ruling class (Reed's "Atonists"), many postmoderns stressed the mythic dimensions of history for the sake of two finally banal conclusions: our daily lives are governed by fictions we accept as real and true; we can play with those stories to find some limited self-expression in an otherwise deterministic history. The distinction between good and bad myths was based on a clear, albeit questionable, ethical claim: good myths announce their human and thus fictional origins; bad myths disguise such origins and insist upon their truth and reality. Good myths invite further elaborations and versions, thus remaining adaptable to historical and human changes; bad myths discourage revision and insist upon universality. At root, this was postmodern literature's defense against the charge that its own aesthetic principles made it difficult to distinguish between literature and propaganda. Propaganda, the postmoderns argued, is bad literature.

Not all the uses of history have been so curiously aestheticized or de-historicized by postmodern writers, of course. After roughly 1975, there was a return to neglected historical topics and issues that has informed a wide variety of literary, historical, televisual, and cinematic work in the United States. A great deal of this work belongs to versions of film and television documentary and docudrama, traumatic witness, and autobiography, among many new and revived genres that belong to a new realism. A great deal of this cultural work, however, is inflected by a certain awareness of postmodern socioeconomic circumstances, so that the styles and rhetorics of such realism have more in common with the postmodern avant-garde than with late nineteenth-century Anglo American literary naturalism and realism. Maxine Hong Kingston's *Woman Warrior* (1976) and *China Men* (1980) represent Chinese American experience in terms that are both historically accurate and demonstrably fantastic, suggesting the conflicting realities of growing up in at least three different and overlapping cultures. Louise Erdrich's fiction about Ojibwa people on and off the reservation in North Dakota and Minnesota, especially *Love Medicine* (1984) and *Tracks* (1988), also locates the fantastic aspects of everyday life in the political, social, and cultural conflicts between Native Americans and Euro-Americans, but Erdrich did this literary work in a thoroughly historical fashion. Don DeLillo's fiction is also distinguished by his defense of literature as a special mode of historical knowledge. DeLillo's *Libra* (1988) satirizes efforts by the Warren Commission and by Nicholas Branch to solve the mystery of John F. Kennedy's assassination, but his novel is an alternative form of explanation in which actual and possible relations among the important historical figures provide an imaginative history of the assassination. Hollywood films like *The Deer Hunter* (1978), *Coming Home* (1979), and *Apocalypse Now* (1980) offer alternative historical "explanations" of the Vietnam War in styles recognizably postmodern by calling attention to the postmodern factors contributing to the war.

The postmodern literary claim to historical authority is not the only basis for the noted multigeneric and multidisciplinary characteristics of postmodern fiction. Avant-garde literary movements generally reject traditional genres and canons, claiming to overcome their limitations. The moderns in particular had deliberately transgressed conventional generic boundaries. Pound claimed that Flaubert was his "true Penelope," and Stevens insisted upon the "elemental prose" of poetry. Williams chose deliberately "antipoetic" subjects for his poetry, and Eliot's *The Waste Land* parodied the footnotes and commentary of scholarship, such as Jesse Weston's *From Ritual to Romance*. The postmoderns also mixed and transgressed genres, but prose fiction was given special privilege. Whereas the Anglo-American New Critics often claimed that the lyric was the fundamental literary form upon which other poetic and even prose genres built, postmodern experimentalists considered the lyric's celebration of the individual poetic voice both a literary and a philosophical anachronism. Among contemporary poets identified as postmodern, such as John Ashbery and A. R. Ammons, the lyric became a poetry of loss and mourning, most often for the poetic voice itself. The dominant mode of postmodern writing would have to be characterized as pastiche, in which the limitations of previously dominant genres such as lyric, epic, and the realistic novel were identified.[7]

The postmoderns' interests in philosophy and linguistics—or "theories of language"—were far more central, in many instances shaping the historical subjects and themes of many of their literary works. Postmodern writers produced a wide range of nonfictional works in these academic disciplines. William Gass's *On Being Blue: A Philosophical Inquiry* (1976) and Walker Percy's *The Message in the Bottle* (1975) are typical. Of course, literary authors of many different periods have also written criticism and nonfictional prose, and avant-garde literary movements are particularly noted for aesthetic manifestoes, anthologies of "new writing," critical readings of previous literary movements, and assessments of contemporaries. The moderns produced a great volume of such work, much of which helped establish twentieth-century academic practices and institutions of literary criticism. The postmoderns, however, claimed a special coordination of their theoretical and practical work, often constructing fictional works around theoretical problems and issues. John Barth's *Chimera* is an extended reflection on the relations among myth, literary narratives, and ordinary language use. Robert Coover's *Universal*

Baseball Association, J. Henry Waugh, Proprietor (1968) can be read as a contribution to sociological game theory, especially as such theories have developed in the wake of Wittgenstein's efforts to establish human knowledge on the basis of the language game. Pynchon's fiction reexamines the possible intersections of thermodynamic entropy, informational entropy, and figurative or literary language. Much of the fiction of John Hawkes and Walker Percy reassesses the authority of such crucial Freudian concepts as Oedipal triangulation, the symbiotic relation of eros and thanatos, and sublimation.

In this context, the popular cliché that postmodern writing tends to be "academic" makes considerably more sense. Despite their literary criticism and nonfictional prose, the moderns were suspicious of academic writing they associated with what Williams called "the Traditionalists of Plagiarism" in *Spring and All* (1925). The postmoderns showed special respect for scholarly and critical modes of writing, even when they satirized and parodied the seriousness or narrowness of academic writing. On the one hand, the postmoderns were attracted to academic issues as a defense against their reluctance to write more politically specific work. Russell Jacoby's argument about the transformation of the U.S. intellectual from political activist to academic specialist may be flawed by his nostalgia for the 1930s Left, but there is a measure of truth to the argument that the U.S. university has more often been the means of containing and controlling dissent than of producing it.[8]

There is, however, a somewhat more positive way to understand the closer working relations between postmodern writers and the academy. Virtually contemporary with the emergence of postmodern literature as a coherent movement—that is, from 1965 to 1975—the humanistic disciplines in this country were undergoing profound changes that were attributable primarily to the influences of structuralist and poststructuralist theories developed in Europe. The date customarily assigned to the introduction of structuralism and poststructuralism to the United States was October 1966, the month that a conference was held at Johns Hopkins University, entitled "The Languages of Criticism and the Sciences of Man: The Structuralist Controversy." Although the conference focused on the work of structuralists in the several disciplines constituting the "sciences of man," the "controversy" of its title actually centered on two poststructuralist papers, one by Eugenio Donato, "The Two Languages of Criticism," and the other by Jacques Derrida, "Structure, Sign, and Play in the Discourse of the Human Sciences."[9]

By the middle of the 1980s, the poststructuralist methods we identify with Jacques Derrida's deconstruction were referred to generally as "post-modern writing," but in 1966 there was no direct relation between the postmodern literary avant-garde and poststructuralist theory. There were, however, several indirect connections worth considering. The post-modern experimentalists followed their modern predecessors' special regard for a comparative approach to literary history that stressed cosmopolitan over national traditions. The works the postmoderns considered influential rarely fit the prevailing definitions of the U.S. literary canon. John Barth's pastiche of the eighteenth-century picaresque narrative, *The Sot-Weed Factor,* is based on the actual writings of Ebenezer Cooke, a minor poet in colonial Maryland, but the novel quite self-consciously draws on Cervantes, Smollett, Swift, and Fielding in developing a distinctly American plot that is curiously European in its telling. In a similar fashion, John Hawkes relied on influences as diverse as Flannery O'Connor, Quevedo, Huysmans, and Céline. In writing *Gravity's Rainbow,* Pynchon relied on influences ranging from Jacobean drama to Henry Adams and German films of the Weimar period. Nevertheless, the literary influences and thus the alternative canon of the postmoderns tended to be predominantly European, and it often focused on just those works and movements that had comparable significance for the poststructuralists: the symbolists, decadents, and high moderns. To be sure, the writers of the Latin American "boom" also had a strong influence on postmodern experimentalists in the United States, but often because they shared with them aesthetic ideas and styles derived from European models.

Poststructuralism helped move the humanities, especially the study of literature, closer to the practices of literature itself, for some hopelessly confusing the traditional boundaries distinguishing literary production (e.g., creativity) and literary reception and understanding (reading and interpretation, professional or casual). Like the postmodern experimentalists, the poststructuralists insisted upon the fundamentally linguistic construction of social and psychic reality. Jacques Lacan's famous declaration, "The Unconscious is structured like a language," was effectively revised to read, "The Unconscious *is* a language," a claim for which there was much evidence not only in Lacan, but also in Freud's own works.[10] Poststructuralists believe that language determines and shapes thought; both truth and reality are comprehensible only in terms of the signifying practices that make their conceptualization possible. The building block of structural linguistics had been Ferdinand de Saussure's thesis that language functions by means of signs, and that each sign is composed of an acoustic image, or material means of transmission—the signifier—and a conceptual image or intellectual referent—the signified. The differential relation of signifier and signified was revised by Derrida to the irreducible *différance* of signifiers, so that the conceptual or intellectual "reference" of any speech act was understandable only as the repression or condensation of a potentially endless chain of signifiers. Thus "ideas" and "concepts" had to be reinterpreted as "compositions" of signifiers, and the analytical procedures established by philosophers (especially in the Anglo-American analytical tradition) for "understanding" complex ideas were transformed at a stroke into rhetorical strategies.

Given the strong and still current criticism that poststructuralism and, more specifically, deconstruction revolve around an ahistorical paradigm of language, we should remember that poststructuralism attacked structuralism on the very grounds that it ignored the complexities of historical language use. Theoretically, Derrida's translation of the structuralist sign into what he termed the "trace" or *"différance"* was motivated by a fundamentally historical understanding of language. In effect, poststructuralism argued that thought, truth, reality, and meaning itself could never be comprehended properly outside the sociohistorical conditions of their production. And this condition applied as well to the act of comprehension or analysis. Every aspect of human experience became a "text"—that is, a signifying system—including the acts of reading and interpretation by which we receive such texts. Understanding is actually an act of interpretation, and analysis always produces supplementary meaning.

Often accused of being ethically relativist or radically skeptical, as was the postmodern literary avant-garde, poststructuralism actually gave academic credibility to the moral conviction that the more self-conscious we are about the ways we use language, the more likely we are to improve our social and human relations. Poststructuralism thus seemed to offer a moral justification compatible with the ethics of literary postmoderns, but there is a very significant difference between the two movements in this regard. By insisting upon the inevitability of repression in any act of communication, deconstructive theorists exposed the naïveté of the postmodern literary distinction between good and bad myths. No writer can effectively control the reception and uses of his or her work; every text, however radical, remains indebted to the very language (and thus the social order) that has motivated its rebellion. Even with such knowledge, the canniest deconstructive writer still clings to the "intention" of his or her message, and "self-deconstruction" becomes a logical impossibility. Deconstruction thus rejected postmodern literature's neat distinction between literature and propaganda and challenged the very possibility of postmodern literature's moral insistence upon rigorous self-consciousness. Not only did this call into question the very possibility of self-consciousness; it treated self-consciousness as yet another mystification with a very specific sociohistorical locus—modern bourgeois culture.

To be sure, the most influential poststructuralists—Derrida, Lacan, and Foucault—wrote in profoundly literary styles, even though their subjects were philosophy, psychoanalysis, and intellectual history. Their forms also radically challenged the traditions of scholarly writing in their nominal disciplines. Derrida's *Glas* (1974), printed in double columns, the left-hand column consisting of a commentary on Hegel and the right-hand column on Genet, is often read as an example of postmodern literature. The title, *Glas*, "knell" in French, suggests the death knell of our Western modernity, "tolling" as it does the historical passage from Hegel to Genet. More than just a book printed in double columns, *Glas* is an effort to deconstruct the customary linearity of writing and reading in Western languages, and it accomplishes this task in a number of related ways. Quotations and footnotes are inserted into the columns and printed in smaller type; comments are printed as marginal glosses in larger type between the columns. Gaps, ellipses, and other verbal and formal suspensions further accentuate the nonlinearity of a text that is multiple, intertextual. *Glas* is a remarkable 1970s anticipation of what we now call a computer hypertext, on which music, imagery, and writing can be composed by means of laser disk technology, but other poststructuralist theorists accomplished such multimedia, intertextual work in less graphically visible ways. Lacan replaced the analytical categories of Freudian psychoanalysis with successive displacing metaphors that cannot be read in the customary cumulative fashion of scholarly arguments. Foucault combined texts from literature, the visual arts, medicine, the sciences, anthropology, linguistics, politics, and psychoanalytical case studies, commonly interpreting their rhetorical subtexts and secret affinities to each other. By the end of the 1970s and early 1980s, books like Elizabeth Bruss's *Beautiful Theories: The Spectacle of Discourse in Contemporary Criticism* (1982) were written on the poetic and literary values of what began to be called "postmodern theory."[11]

Poststructuralism's insistence upon the textuality of human reality and thus upon its fundamental historicality was actually a profound challenge to literary study as an academic discipline. Literature exists as a special discourse precisely because we choose to ignore the highly stylized characteristics of all language use. For literature to exist as a discipline, we must make distinctions between instrumental and figurative languages, together with such discriminations as denotative versus connotative meanings and literal versus figurative, nonfiction versus fiction, creative versus expressive, and scholarly versus expository writing. If literature is simply a function of all language use, relatively foregrounded or backgrounded in any given speech act, the existing institutions of literature and its study must be deconstructed in order to reveal the ways they have served to legitimize the false distinctions and dangerous hierarchies of high art over popular culture and folk art; enduring classics over journalistic, protest, and didactic writing; the original and avant-garde over the conventional.

In theory, poststructuralism criticized the dominant literary canons that governed twentieth-century curricula for literary study, and also criticized their exclusion or trivialization of popular and mass culture. By insisting upon the inevitably political motives for and consequences of any act of communication, poststructuralism abstractly supported the claims of minorities, women, and other marginalized social groups for voices, writings, and literatures of their own. If deconstruction helped expose social repressions in and through the normative discourse of that society, it was thought, those repressed and excluded would speak in ways theoretically compatible with the larger sociopolitical aims of deconstruction. There is still a poststructuralist logic to such desirable coalitions with marginal social and political groups that strikes me as too tidy and academic. If deconstruction makes the otherness of the text speak, the speech of the Other seems to be a logical consequence of deconstruction. Deconstruction itself teaches that no such logical necessity (a category, after all, of analytical philosophy) can be the basis for political coalitions among different groups in real historical circumstances. The slippage from the otherness of what is repressed in ordinary acts of communication to the Other obscures the specificity of actual social others. The very generality of the Other suggests a totalizing system likely to disregard differences of race, gender, class, culture, and history.

Between 1966 and 1975, this suspicion of deconstruction and poststructuralism in general was shared by feminists, scholars of ethnicity and minority cultures, and scholars of popular culture and the mass media—indeed, many of the fields and methods encompassed by American Studies. Many American Studies scholars rejected poststructuralist approaches as Eurocentric while themselves defending the exceptionalist assumptions of much of American Studies in that period, but there were other, more compelling reasons for the critique of poststructuralism in this country. U.S. feminists were particularly wary of poststructuralist theory because it claimed as a predecessor yet another venerable tradition of masculine theorists from Hegel and Nietzsche through Freud and de Saussure to Lacan and Heidegger. By this I do not mean that U.S. feminists criticized simply the fact that the major predecessors of deconstruction happened to be men, although this case was sometimes made. Feminists argued instead that the assumptions of these thinkers had been shaped by their European cultures and inevitably reflected the patriarchal values of those cultures. Lacan's revisionary interpretations of Freud still relied on the centrality of the phallus (the Oedipal paradigm) in the process of social acculturation. Derrida's productive deconstructions of Hegel and de Saussure paid little attention to questions of gender, even though Hegel had offered repeated justifications for bourgeois gender hierarchies and de Saussure had treated highly gendered languages, such as French, as if "masculine" and "feminine" were simply grammatical, rather than also political, cases.

By the same token, scholars of ethnicity and minority cultures considered poststructuralist treatments of repression and exclusion largely esoteric, often excessively psycholinguistic, issues rather than concepts designed to address explicitly the continuing effects of racism and internal and external colonialisms. Like the feminists, these scholars noted that the intellectual genealogy of poststructuralism consisted primarily of white European thinkers, who had often written in the midst of Europe's colonial expansion. The Eurocentrism of Hegel, the bourgeois orientation of Freudian analysis, and the inevitable ethnocentrism of structural linguistics were not sufficiently deconstructed by the poststructuralists to give voice in any genuine way to the thoughts and writings of peoples of color.

The dominant academic applications of deconstruction between roughly 1975 and 1985 did not do much to challenge these suspicions of feminists and scholars of minority and non-European cultures. Especially as it was practiced in literary studies in this country, deconstruction did not abandon the established literary canons and authors, but instead embarked on revisionary readings of these canonical figures, together with complementary interpretations of minor works and authors. Acknowledging the power of such canons and thus the impossibility of simply dismissing their values and works, poststructuralist theorists argued that they would have to be deconstructed to reveal their ideological assumptions. Just who "they" were was often at issue, because many deconstructive readings of authors as canonical as Emerson and Melville, Shelley and Trollope, Shakespeare and Henry James implicitly saved these authors from critical and scholarly traditions that had conventionalized their works. Often enough, these writers were liberated from such traditional constraints just insofar as they could be read as modern or postmodern in their interests.

Literary deconstruction or the aestheticization of deconstruction is commonly associated with the Yale School that flourished between 1975 and 1985, so called because of the prominence at Yale of such deconstructive critics as Geoffrey Hartman, J. Hillis Miller, Paul de Man, and Harold Bloom. Derrida became a regular visitor to Yale in 1975, and the Yale School declared itself in a manifesto of sorts published in 1979, *Deconstruction and Criticism*. Yet the identification of "deconstruction in America" with the Yale School and the critical tendency to treat even those five theorists at Yale as virtually equivalent have too often been means of containing and controlling poststructuralist theories.[12]

After 1979, if I may use the publication of *Deconstruction and Criticism* as a heuristic turning point, deconstruction divided into literary and political versions. In the second decade of deconstruction's influence on scholarship in the humanities in this country, "literary deconstruction" achieved the greatest popularity, even though political deconstruction, especially in its feminist versions, was significantly changing the traditional study and practice of the humanities, especially by developing women's and gender studies curricula and thereby establishing independent academic units. Such programs were often founded in response to the lack of attention paid to these issues in English, history, and American Studies. Often attracting large enrollments and a lot of student interest by teaching subjects of immediate social and political importance, women's and gender studies challenged the established structure of the university and the aims (and exclusions) of traditional liberal education. Ethnic and minority scholarship and pedagogy often had similar aims for changing education and the university as an institution. Such programs usually insisted upon interdisciplinary work and challenged the very foundations of discrete disciplines such as literary studies, history, philosophy, linguistics, psychology, sociology, and anthropology.

On the other hand, deconstruction in its aestheticized version was relatively easy to understand and to practice, and in this form served specific, often conservative, purposes in the micropolitics of U.S. universities. Any literary text calls attention to its figurative dimensions, its explicit style, and in so doing often challenges the referential functions of ordinary language. The literary author characteristically resists critical paraphrase and

insists upon a literary excess that is often at the basis of claims for originality and genius. In this regard, literature has always read critically, if
not precisely deconstructively, the language of the marketplace. The
adaptability of deconstruction to customary literary values was also motivated by the socioeconomic situation of professional literary studies in
the United States between 1975 and 1985. In its aestheticized version, deconstruction helped relegitimate literary study—departments, faculties,
and curricula—at the very moment that most formal disciplines in the
humanities in this country were faced with declining undergraduate enrollments and majors and their customary complements: decreased
graduate enrollments, fewer academic jobs, and reduced funding for all
activities. Exciting new programs in women's and ethnic studies, for example, often departing from more traditional curricula in American
Studies, English, or history, found themselves struggling for limited
"start-up funds" and otherwise competing with established departments
and programs capable of defending their budgets and institutional power,
even if they did not always hold onto their enrollments.

It is quite clear that deconstruction brought new interest to literary
texts and authors that by the middle of the 1970s had in many ways been
exhausted by previous historical and formal methods of study. This renewed interest often resembled that claimed by the postmodern literary
avant-garde. Both postmodern writers and deconstructors found cultural evidence all around them that literature was declining as a central element of social discourse. Just as postmodern experimentalists had accepted "the literature of exhaustion" as the paradoxical basis for a "new
literature," so literary deconstruction argued that the exhaustion of
canonical texts called for drastically revisionary approaches. Deconstructive critics generally attributed such scholarly exhaustion to the narrowness of previous critical approaches and offered to revitalize traditional
texts with an intertextuality that engaged literature, philosophy, history,
and linguistics in a much wider conversation.

The specific historical situation of literature in the West was not treated very seriously by these scholars; reports of the novel's demise were
often considered exaggerated by literary defenders armed with statistics
documenting rapid increases in the sales of popular and serious fiction,
as well as studies of growing literacy and comparative demographic figures that seemed to prove that there had been steady increases in the
reading population since the nineteenth century. In fact, few deconstructive critics had much interest in statistical studies of declines or increases
either in enrollments or the reading population. To them, the only fact

that mattered much was that human beings used signs to function in the world and were always likely to do so. Thus how we read and interpret those signs, whether they come to us in the form of literary texts or bank statements, determines our very modes of knowing and being. Versions of literature have changed and will change, but the essentially literary reflection on the nature and function of language will remain and explain.

But the argument that literature was dying had little to do with the statistics and much to do with how literature was received and used. One of the consequences of the Vietnam War, often termed the "living-room war," was the transformation of television into the principal medium of social debate. Not only television news, but also melodramas, situation comedies, and police shows engaged major social and political issues in the "new realism" of television in the late 1960s and early 1970s. Popular film had also assumed growing authority to address social and political issues in the 1970s. New technologies, such as the portable mini-cam developed during the Vietnam War, helped expand and speed the news coverage of world events. Television and film documentaries and docudramas became increasingly popular in this same period.[13]

Television and film also changed our assessment of the popularity of all kinds of cultural works. Rather than just counting readers or viewers, evaluators of any text's relative success must also take into account the viewing or reading time involved. On the other hand, statistics regarding market shares, target audiences, and viewing time fail to measure what influence literary works had on the lives and behaviors of those who read them. For the gloomiest cultural prophets, the decline of literary influence was reflected in the deterioration of literacy skills. As Neal Postman argued in *Amusing Ourselves to Death: Public Discourse in the Age of Show Business* (1985), the very media of television and film discourage complex rhetoric and profound discussion. Despite a new age of television interpretations of everything from presidential addresses to significant sports events, Postman and others insisted that our very capacities for knowledge were being conditioned by television's demand for condensed statement rather than extended discussion and debate.

Both traditional intellectuals like Postman and literary deconstructionists maintained that reading and interpretation require intellectual effort—*hard work*—that is implicitly discouraged by the forms of television and popular film. In a similar manner, many poststructuralists argued that such diligent labor would be rewarded with a certain empowerment of the reader that ultimately would mean greater political power. Postman's notion of such empowerment was rather modest and conventional: the educated citizen is a good citizen, because he or she can make intelligent decisions. Literary deconstruction often offered a more ambitious, albeit elusive, political reward: to understand how a culture represents itself gives one access to culture's secret authority, transforming one into the poet of Shelley's fantasy, "unacknowledged legislator of the world."

Between 1965 and 1985, however, neither postmodern literature nor postmodern theory realized such bids for political empowerment when measured against the influence of the mass media. Quite the contrary; the mass media increasingly encroached upon established intellectual and academic territories. By the mid-1970s, the talk show had changed from a forum primarily for promoting new films, books, and television programs—that is, from its primary advertising function—to yet another forum for the public discussion of social issues. Admittedly, this new form evolved into culturally hysterical modes, such as the *Geraldo* show of that period or the recent *Jenny Jones* and *Jerry Springer* shows, which focus on social pathologies of all sorts, and the confrontational "town hall" shows of Morton Downey Jr. But more modest programs of the 1980s, ranging from the *Merv Griffin* show to *Donahue,* refunctioned today in *Oprah!* and *The Rosie O'Donnell Show,* effected an interesting media transition from show-business promotion to social forum. What is still interesting about these transitional talk shows is that the combination of show-business promotion and social debate helped lend even greater credibility to Hollywood's authority on matters of great social concern. As a consequence, the viewing public looked increasingly to film and television for the discussion of those topics traditionally addressed by serious fiction and by professional historians and political scientists.

Another consequence of the boom in television's claim to social relevance and value was that American Studies, along with film studies programs, had to include television as a more central field of study. Although many English and comparative literature programs began to include more courses dealing with film, television, and video, most retained core curricula built on print-based media and on theoretical approaches, however nominally radical, that were well suited to print textuality. It is too soon to judge what transformations the study of new electronic media will have on these and related disciplines, but it seems clear that most curricula in literary studies have changed little in assessing the influence of new media, whereas the influence of media studies on American Studies' curricula and scholars has radically transformed both the scope of the field and its sense of obligation to political criticism and public policy issues.

Even in its narrowly literary mode, deconstruction resulted in micro-political changes in the teaching and study of literature in the U.S. university, not all of which should be treated cynically as defenses against the embattled situation of literature and humanistic study. Often criticized for intensifying academic specialization by insisting upon the essentially infinite signifying potential of any given text and thus demanding intricate, even baroque, interpretations of even the briefest works, deconstruction actually worked more decisively against the sorts of subspecializations that had accompanied the twentieth-century professionalization of literary study. Postmodern theory relied upon a limited number of theoretical texts that generally challenged their respective disciplines. By a limited number, I do not mean to endorse the common criticism of deconstruction that it builds primarily on the writings of Hegel, Nietzsche, Freud, de Saussure, Husserl, and Heidegger: that is, the tradition of modern and masculine philosophy, adjusted to include the challenges of psychoanalysis and linguistics to the traditional aims of philosophical understanding. Any list of the major figures for deconstruction would be very long indeed and by no means would be governed by these six moderns, but despite many variations there was a "reading list" of sorts that cut across disciplinary and historical specializations.

Although subspecialization in literary studies continues to this day, deconstruction helped encourage debates across historical and generic lines and helped to frame literary topics in ways that often had significance for a wide range of professionals. One negative consequence of the common reading list in critical theory was the often mechanical application of these theoretical texts to specific literary works without much consideration for the historical differences between theory and literary practice. Derridean and Lacanian readings of Chaucer, Shakespeare, and Milton are by now as common as those of Joyce, Beckett, and Pynchon. And in defending themselves against frequent criticism that such readings ignored historical differences, literary deconstructors tended to universalize the claims of their theoretical models, often on the apparent warrant of the chief poststructuralist theorists.

But even the common language of critical theory, riven as it was by internal debates and vigorous attacks from more traditional scholars threatened by its ostensible challenges to their customary practices and values, hardly echoed outside the academy. And because the real battle for academics, especially in the humanities, between 1965 and 1985 involved the challenge posed by the mass media, the internal upheavals in the U.S. university, insofar as they concerned educational and research issues, resulted in only modest adjustments to the modern division between intellectual and public debate, between education as professional training and education as equipment for living. Since the 1930s and through many different dominant schools and movements, American Studies had preserved its purpose of social critique and intellectual activism, conveying this message quite effectively to several generations of students. One reason for the reluctance of many American Studies scholars of this period to embrace the "politics of critical theory" may well have been their sense that theory's overt political goals were too modest, its social critique too restricted to academic politics, and its popularity in higher education decidedly too literary.

I have written thus far primarily in the past tense to suggest that both "postmodern literature" and "poststructuralism," especially in its literary versions, are part of our recent history. I now consciously shift to the present, in which other feminist and minority studies, especially because they are generally described as "postmodern," suggest more significant changes in the traditional practices and study of U.S. literature and culture. I have already mentioned the suspicion of poststructuralist theories shared by feminists and scholars of ethnicity and minority cultures from the 1970s to the early 1980s.[14] This distrust was compounded, I think, by the treatment of gender and race in postmodern experimental literature between 1965 and 1975. Not only were the experimentalists primarily white men, but their works were profoundly patriarchal and often racist. William Gass's *Willie Master's Lonesome Wife* (1971) is a startling example, which metaphorizes the narrative itself as "Willie Master's lonesome wife," inviting the reader to "play" with her body, which at one point constitutes the centerfold of the text. Gass was not alone in the flagrant sexism of postmodern literary experimentation. Barth's *Chimera* appears to address positively the demands of feminists by casting Scheherazade and her sister, Dunyazade, in roles as brilliant storytellers and by causing the heroic Perseus to learn the meaning of his life from the stories woven by his savior, the Egyptian priestess Calyxa, who tells the majority of the *Perseid.*

In fact, these feminine characters are versions of the modernists' feminized muse, alter egos for the masculine imaginary. In the novels of John Hawkes, liberated sexuality generally has fearful consequences, and women are represented quite conventionally as helpless victims or demonic seducers. African Americans are treated in similarly problematic ways in postmodern literature. Pynchon's version of the systematic extinction of the Herero tribe under German colonialism in Southwest Africa acknowledges how integral genocide was to colonial ideology, but then he transforms the Hereros in both *V.* and *Gravity's Rainbow* into virtual embodiments of Western cultural entropy. Their "blackness" becomes a sign of their nihilistic "choice" to refuse to propagate and thus die out in pyrrhic defiance of their European colonizers. Barth's *Chimera* more liberally argues for the shared, albeit repressed, origins of Egyptian, Graeco-Roman, Islamic, and Christian myths, but his comparative mythology effectively legitimates a white, middle-class synthesis of cultural heritages with very different historical, racial, and political dimensions. Like Willie Master's "lonesome wife," the cultural body of the Moslem may be "played with" in Barth's version of the *1001 Nights, Dunyazadiade,* which is itself a comic version of the bourgeois sentimental romance.

The ends of deconstruction have often been declared to be the beginnings of cultural criticism, but once again we must avoid repeating the mistakes of a liberal evolutionary model of historical change. Contemporary cultural criticism in the United States has strong roots in the theories of the Frankfurt School for Social Research of the 1920s and 1930s, the social critiques and material analyses of the Birmingham School in England, the New Left political coalitions of the 1960s, and the political work of feminist and black activists. Many of these influences are evident in American Studies as well, with the possible exception of the Frankfurt School's work. As I have argued, the New Left acknowledged the postmodern "critique of representation" as fundamental to its methods and aims, but such a critique subordinated critical writing to political action. For all its idealism and naïveté, the New Left recognized that the struggle for power over the means of representation was not an internal academic debate but a public struggle among the mass media, governmental institutions, and various political interests. In these respects, the New Left followed the political leads of the Frankfurt School's critique of the rise of European fascism and of postwar consumer capitalism and the Birmingham School's commitment to working-class organization in political and cultural terms.

By the same token, the New Left acknowledged the subtle and pervasive power of popular mythologies, and it produced its own "postmodern writing" in the form of works intended to foster political activism. *The Autobiography of Malcolm X* (1965), Eldridge Cleaver's *Soul on Ice* (1968), Frances FitzGerald's *Fire in the Lake* (1973), and Kate Millett's *Sexual*

Politics (1971) are only a few examples of this "other" postmodern-ism. Each work addresses in its own way the social construction of race, class, gender, or cultural identity in and through a wide range of texts that are doing the work of cultural mythology. The ideological artistry of the texts explored by these writers—ranging from casual speech to foreign policy reports and including established literary classics—is what requires a critique of representation. Political empowerment for the antiwar movement, the Black Muslims and Black Panthers, and the National Organization of Women is complemented by efforts to read critically the ways we internalize and personalize—*domesticate*—racism, sexism, and nationalism. By the same token, the very terms "postmodern" and "poststructuralist," especially as scholars have tended to interchange them, may exclude certain works and authors crucial to the politics of the New Left.

Many works of the Black Arts movement of the late 1960s and 1970s are by no means formally "postmodern." As I have already noted, many African American artists of that period understood the white, bourgeois, masculine assumptions of postmodern fiction. Ishmael Reed may engage the issues of that fictional experimentalism, but *Mumbo Jumbo* is a sus-tained critique of the aesthetic ideals of modernism that survives in post-modern fiction. The political and historical commitments of black women writers of the 1970s are obvious; the writings of Alice Walker, Toni Morrison, and Toni Cade Bambara, for example, explicitly address the ideological assumption that "black" means "black male," even that "black woman" means "heterosexual black woman." As innovative and different as their writings are, however, they do not fit conventional aca-demic definitions of postmodern experimentalism, even though these authors align themselves with other social critics who understand how powerful cultural representations can be.

It is worth recalling that the term "cultural critic" was used frequently in the 1960s and early 1970s to designate the writer as activist, especially as he or she departed from the proprieties of scholarship and the narcis-sism of the literary avant-garde. In his introduction to Cleaver's *Soul on Ice,* Maxwell Geismar wrote in 1967: "Cleaver is simply one of the best cultural critics now writing, and I include in this statement both the for-mal sociologists and those contemporary fictionists who have mainly abandoned this province of literature for the cultivation of the cult of sensibility."[15] Residual elements of the New Left's postmodern politics still have a significant influence on contemporary cultural criticism. Yet it is fair to say that the writings of the New Left and the Black Arts movement, radical as they were in terms of both politics and literary form, have received far less scholarly attention than postmodern experimentalism and poststructuralism. However, American Studies can be credited, along with U.S. feminism and African American studies, for its attention to these neglected areas, but not as alternative versions of postmodernism. Most American Studies scholars considered the New Left important in relation to the heritage of the 1930s Left and studied the black arts movement for what it told them about the historical continuity of the African American protest from the days of abolition to those of the civil rights movement. Of course, American Studies scholars are right to situate such recent activisms in their historical contexts, but there are also considerable advantages in understanding the New Left, second-wave feminism, black arts, and black nationalism movements and a host of related political and cultural rights movements of the 1970s as alternative versions of postmodernism and as responses to the limitations of political and cultural modernism.

In the 1980s and 1990s, feminist and postcolonial scholars appropriated and in many cases refashioned poststructuralist theories to criticize hierarchies maintained by race, class, gender, and sexuality, as well as neocolonial practices in the United States and around the world. Admittedly, these influences have not always worked together happily, and much pioneering work in feminism and cultural criticism has ignored poststructuralism or vigorously criticized its ethnocentrism and abstraction. But in other instances, there has been a productive, albeit uneasy, hybridization of postmodern politics, theory, and cultural expression. I think that the most successful efforts to relate postmodern politics and poststructuralism can be traced to the influence of Continental feminism on U.S. feminism. In particular, the writings of Continental feminists like Luce Irigaray, Julia Kristeva, and Hélène Cixous have used the conventional criticism of poststructuralist theory and its neglect of gender and race to revise the basic assumptions of poststructuralism to include gender and race as central issues.

The Continental feminist challenge to poststructuralism depends upon an elaboration of one of deconstruction's principal claims: that the apparently undeniable materiality of experience is in fact constructed of verbal *materia*. The body itself, its biology, and nature are always already representational effects, so issues of gender, rather than sexuality, have to be reinterpreted in terms of their specific historical and cultural conditions of production. The often oblique and playful equation of verbal production with more material modes of production has had an important political consequence for poststructuralist feminists. If all human production is to be understood in terms of representation—that is, as already shaped and informed by certain hermeneutic assumptions and values—the economy of so-called natural production and reproduction has to be considered central not only to any simple economic system but also to the more sophisticated "economy" of cultural production. The political, economic, psychological, and legal rights of a woman to the productivity of her own body are thus inextricably related to the woman's rights to the representation of that body. Production, reproduction, and representation occupy the same body, at once a physically discrete and a textual body.

Insofar as the construction of feminine identity in patriarchal societies relies upon a complex intertextuality of economics, biology, law, psychology, sociology, and the various arts, it appears to be an appropriate site for comprehending yet other practices of social marginalization according to race, sexuality, religion, and class. And because postmodern feminism insists both upon the exploitative power of language and upon its emancipatory potential, it proposes to build a coalition politics for marginal social groups on the basis of their access to and employment of cultural representation. In this regard, the abstract "logical necessity" of deconstruction to find in the discourse of the Other a common cause against the formalized, referential, centered discourse of the real works itself out in more politically specific ways. Constituted by various forms of social and psychological repression, women and minorities must speak the Otherness that so threatens the patriarchal, Eurocentric voice and consciousness.

In this respect, postmodern feminism has unrecognized affinities with the anti-imperialist critiques of classic American Studies scholarship by Richard Slotkin and Richard Drinnon, but now they have been expanded to encompass the colonization of the body by way of such conceptual weapons as conventions regarding gender and sexuality. The very marginalization of women from the national interests and cultural traditions of modern Western nations has encouraged a certain strategic transnationalism and the identification of women with other peoples oppressed by various forms of colonial domination. A woman's body has often enough been treated as a "territory" to be "conquered" or as a fearful "dark continent" in need of enlightenment. Here the materiality of metaphor, itself a key concept in deconstruction, becomes understandable, because the metaphorization of a woman's body has had material consequences throughout history. It would be naïve, of course, to claim that postmodern feminism is unique for its identification with other marginalized groups; after all, nineteenth-century women's rights activists worked vigorously for the abolition of slavery, and turn-of-the-twentieth-century suffragists forged coalitions with working-class activists and the underclass in general.[16]

This historical tradition of feminist activism is one of the advantages that postmodern feminism has over less explicitly political versions of poststructuralism. Too often, the tradition or counter-tradition in which deconstruction claimed to work remained a version of *Geistesgeschichte*, even though deconstruction worked to reveal the ideology of such intellectual history. Yet even such a critical reading of the political implications of idealist history tended to stress deconstruction's historically privileged position as an avant-garde movement.

Like postmodern feminism, recent approaches to African American culture come out of a tradition of political critique and activism that rejects U.S. nationalism and often seeks coalitions with transnational and postcolonial movements. The postmodern dimension of African American scholarship and theory has openly acknowledged its debts to the civil rights movement and the New Left, as well as the long tradition of African American activism and cultural self-definition, which included links to the postcolonial and pan-African movements. In the 1980s, African American cultural theorists added to the work of feminists in developing a diverse, yet coherent, theory and politics of cultural difference, establishing foundations for critical race theory and for critical accounts of internal colonialism in the United States. In 1984, Henry Louis Gates Jr. edited *Black Literature and Literary Theory*, and in 1985 he edited a special issue of *Critical Inquiry* entitled *"Race," Writing, and Difference*. Both collections include essays that explicitly relate structuralist and poststructuralist theory to the study of African and African American literatures and cultures. Gates's *The Signifying Monkey* (1988) and an issue of *PMLA* that he edited (in January 1990) on the special topic of African and African American literature also refashioned poststructuralist theories, grafting them with African American and West African cultural practices, both to carry these theories beyond their own European horizons and to make African American scholarship more conversant with the prevailing theoretical paradigms. For Gates, the study of internal colonialism (slavery and socioeconomic racism in the United States), external colonialism, and postcolonial constructions of the "Third World" by the United States and Europe are coordinated issues.[17]

One of the crucial theoretical links in this work is the critical reading of anthropology as a Western discipline whose professional practices have helped legitimate various modes of colonial and postcolonial domination. This critical anthropology draws upon the theoretical work of postmodern anthropologists like Paul Rabinow, James Clifford, and George Marcus, among others, and it complements postmodern African American theories.[18] The African American appropriation of postmodern literary and anthropological theories has found deconstruction a useful method for exposing the racial unconscious of U.S. society and its more profound complicities with Eurocolonialism. This critique of colonial discourse attempts to interpret the ways explicit political forms of domination are internalized and lived—that is, psychologized. Literature, the arts, academic disciplines, and cultural practices often play crucial roles in this work, so the critique of ideology depends upon a deconstruction of the discrete boundaries separating the various disciplines through which racism, sexism, and colonialism are perpetuated.

Much as this critical theory of colonial discourse draws upon deconstruction's critique of aesthetic ideology, it aligns itself with traditional modes of African American scholarship and political activism in ways that give it special authority. These new theorists continue to work in the scholarly traditions of African American cultural definition. This is evident not only in the collaborative work of such theoretical collections as *Black Literature and Literary Theory* and *"Race," Writing, and Difference,* but in such influential anthologies as the *Norton Anthology of African American Literature* and archives such as *Black Literature, 1827–1940.*[19]

Of course, African American history and culture have long been part of the American Studies discipline, but more often than not as part of liberal pluralist accounts of the different ethnic cultures of the United States. The limitations of certain multicultural theories today can be traced to courses in American Studies that attempted to compare and contrast different ethnic communities and identities by way of a few representative works. African American and women's studies developed institutionally in the 1970s and in second-generation theoretical reorientations in the 1980s as responses to established disciplines, including American Studies, which had failed to represent adequately questions of race, gender, and class. American Studies may have stressed multicultural aspects of U.S. society, but it often did so in ways that incorporated different histories, communities, and identities into an overarching American myth or symbology. One way that feminists and African American scholars of the later 1970s and 1980s rebelled against such incorporation was to adapt poststructuralist theories to the specific histories and areas central to women's and African American studies. Similar claims could be made for the development of Chicano (and later Chicana) and Asian American studies, academic programs that were galvanized in part by American Studies' efforts to include them in representative and often very false ways in curricula and research projects on the basis of democratic inclusion. Insofar as American Studies clung to the "nation" as the horizon of analysis, it overlooked the transnational connections and postnationalist aims of ethnic and women's cultures.

In and of itself, however, deconstruction cannot be credited with such dramatic changes as we associate today with the emergence of ethnic and women's studies programs, postcolonial theory, and cultural criticism. As an increasingly popular hermeneutic practice in the 1980s, deconstruction produced primarily the collaborations of an avant-garde movement: manifestoes, common issues, and a "reading list" that encouraged discussion across disciplines and subspecializations. Yet it did not fully escape the models of belletristic authorship and critical argument that belong to the limited history of liberal bourgeois culture. Insofar as teaching and pedagogy are shaped by our research habits, the structure of the curriculum in literature and the hierarchies of the college classroom were not fundamentally changed by deconstruction. Postmodern feminisms, critical race theory, postcolonial theory, and cultural criticism have challenged the authority of the scholarly author and the classroom teacher by producing collaborative scholarship and encouraging team-taught, multidisciplinary curricula. By acknowledging specific intellectual and political antecedents, these approaches have been able to balance the attractions of the avant-garde with the authority of tradition, especially when such traditions have generally entailed the counter-tradition of resistance and critique. The pedagogical and curricular consequences of new areas of research certainly should produce comparable changes in American Studies, which has a tradition of community activism and public service as part of its educational mission and many of its formal degree programs. But it is also fair to conclude that in the 1980s and 1990s American Studies did not move as quickly as women's and ethnic studies in the direction of alternative pedagogies, especially those designed specifically to question the educational goals of the liberal, modern university to produce discrete, coherent individuals (or "citizen subjects") and to do so in a studiously apolitical climate.

The consequences of this coalition of feminism, African American theory, other minority cultures, and the critical study of colonial discourse remain to be seen, but it is likely that they will have profound influences not only on what is taught and written about, but also on the very departmental structure of most U.S. universities. There has been considerable professional discussion of the restructuring of the humanistic disciplines and their institutional forms, in part because postmodern critical theory in its many versions has repeatedly challenged these discrete epistemic specializations and in part because overspecialization in higher education has provoked heated public debate regarding the desirability of scholars' conducting research in very narrowly defined fields. Thus far the official warnings about abandoning departmental structures have predicted dire consequences: economic disaster, vulnerability to administrative manipulation, irrational tenure decisions, and the destruction of affirmative action programs and programs dedicated to women's and minority studies. Although we must keep these warnings in mind, we must also listen to what postmodern feminism and cultural criticism are trying to tell us about our outdated divisions of the "human sciences," especially as these lessons apply to fields like American Studies that have made commitments to transdisciplinary and intersectional research and pedagogy.

With or without our professional decisions, however, the existing disciplines of the humanities are likely to change formally in significant, even drastic, ways in the next two decades. The reason I make such a confident prediction brings me to my final category of the postmodern, one that has haunted the more specific postmodernisms from the literary experimentalists of 1965–1975 to the still contemporary work of feminists, African Americanists, and scholars of other minority discourses and cultures. The essentially textual character of all social reality and the enormous power of signifying systems—that is, of representation—is not some literary discovery or humanistic insight, but is part of the very nature of postindustrial societies. The postmoderns of the early 1970s celebrated and even fetishized the irreducibly figurative qualities of what we now recognize as the "information age," in which information must be comprehended in terms utterly different from those used in industrial societies, in which the instrumentality of language to refer either to so-called natural or manufactured objects seemed unquestionable. In the service- and information-oriented economy of the United States after World War II, very few "commodities" are understandable outside the rhetoric of both their production and their consumption. I do not mean simply to say that advertising has become such big business that we can no longer see the true object behind the hype, the practical utility through the aura of fashion and status. Important as advertising has become not only to our economy but to our conception of culture, it is only a second-ary effect, a sort of inevitable by-product, of a far more profound mode of production.

Today the value of what is produced either in words or from presum-ably more material substances is measured by the extent of its circulation rather than its consumption. The infinitely productive text dreamt of as a sort of ideal by postmoderns and poststructuralists is now the utopian image of capitalism revived, healthy as never before and likely to achieve the sort of geopolitical dominance once nightmarishly projected into the subject of our ultimate paranoia, the Red Threat of the Cold War. All that the early postmoderns offered as forms of resistance to a bourgeois world of automated reflexes and dehumanization are now available in the shopping mall of the postmodern economy. Television offers us not stereotypes, not the idealized bourgeoisie of *Donna Reed* and *Leave It to Beaver,* but the polymorphous diversity of the new family shows, in which virtually every combination is spun off the empty concept of the vanishing family. Upper-middle-class minority families (*The Cosby Show*), white yuppies (*thirtysomething*), gender role–reversed families (*Who's the Boss?*), decidedly nuclear families (*My Two Dads* and *Full House*) are jostled by their parodies and send-ups, *Roseanne* and *Married with Chil-dren.* Big box office art films about the Vietnam War, such as *Apocalypse Now, Coming Home,* and *The Deer Hunter,* provoke their answers in Stallone's aggressive Rambo, which in turn is answered by the more liber-al, yet still militaristic and patriarchal *Platoon,* which can produce its own antiwar responses by the same director, Oliver Stone, *Born on the Fourth of July* and *Heaven and Earth.* Indeed, the popular genre of the high-technology action film of the 1980s and 1990s was strongly influ-enced by a "Vietnam effect" and what Susan Jeffords has interpreted as a postfeminist "remasculinization" of U.S. culture.[20] Television and film are, of course, established disciplines of study in most major U.S. univer-sities, but the influence of such scholarship on American Studies—its genres and canons—remains relatively small given the dramatic influ-ence these media have had on the popular conception of what constitutes cultural representation and national identity.

The endless conversation and debate often cited by postmodern liber-als as the ultimate morality of the textualist situation has been achieved in the mass media, both on the Business Channel and in the talk show. The crudity of Jerry Springer's aggressive staging of confrontations be-tween the most adversarial groups is more subtly managed with the tol-erance with which the media represent every position and permit any discussion. Herbert Marcuse called this liberal entertainment of any adversarial position, without substantially changing the system, the "repressive tolerance" of late capitalism. For better or for worse, we *are* this ceaseless "conversation," debate and rebuttal, from the commentaries on the evening news and Sunday's *Firing Line* to the next wave of television sitcoms, popular films addressing political positions, and reality television.

The literary postmoderns paid little attention to the mass media; they paid even less attention to the banal details of postmodern economics. The conversation among different positions that seems at once to simulate the polyglot conversation still held as a utopia by many of today's cultural critics is made possible only in accordance with certain basic economic facts. With few exceptions, the dizzying figurality of our postindustrial economies admits only those with the capital, only those with the financial power to play. The African American activists confronted by neo-Nazi fanatics on television talk shows are finally just bit players whose debates are nothing but theater and whose issues are tamed by the larger drama: the production of semiotic power by the new authors of our age. Neither Jerry Springer nor Jenny Jones is the name that matters here; the actual authors are the invisible, nameless, anonymous producers of their shows, who are today our best and most dangerous cultural critics. Analyzing as they must market shares and audience segments, mass media producers can lay claim to the concrete evidence of their accuracy in assessing cultural trends: the ratings.

How, then, has American Studies changed under the influence of the postmodern? In more traditional and scholarly terms, I have tried to explain the impact of a more restricted "postmodernism" on formal scholarship and its curriculum. Insofar as this postmodernism has failed to take account of the postmodern economy, it has missed the ways in which that economy has turned the world into theater, transformed life into art, all for the usual reasons: to gain power over and control of an audience. In order for that work to proceed within the U.S. university, American Studies scholars will have to take more seriously the influence and complexity of the mass media and elaborate the existing logics of poststructuralism to deal more concretely with the aesthetic ideology of postmodern societies. In that regard, American Studies must recognize the contributions of new approaches to gender, sexuality, and minority discourses, especially as they have linked their critiques of gender, sex, race, and class to an overarching analysis of U.S. nationalism's internal and external forms of domination: its colonialism and its imperial system. While respecting these different disciplines, several of which exceed the specific horizon of U.S. culture, the new American Studies can also offer ways of enhancing the intersectional study of these areas and encouraging the coalition politics on which they depend. Those of us in the field will also have to assess more accurately and less academically just who sets the stage for our public debates, however various and technologically accessible they appear to have become over the past two decades. Institutional histories not only of American Studies but also of the modern university will be needed to allow us to formulate how to transcend the limitations of both an older, interdisciplinary, nation-based field and an educational system intent on producing citizen subjects suited to the civic ideals of the late nineteenth-century European or U.S. metropolis.

3.
Postnationalism, Globalism, and the New American Studies

Curricula and scholarship in American Studies have changed significantly over the past decade, reflecting the important influences of women's studies, ethnic studies, and postmodern and postcolonial theories. Earlier approaches, such as those of the Puritan Origins and Myth-and-Symbol Schools, attempted to elaborate those features of American identity and social organization that are unique national characteristics. Often implicit in this nationalist approach to the study of U.S. culture was the assumption that the United States constitutes a model for democratic nationality that might be imitated or otherwise adapted by other nations in varying stages of their development.

The criticism of such American exceptionalism has focused on both its contributions to U.S. cultural imperialism and its exclusions of the many different cultures historically crucial to U.S. social, political, and economic development. In response to concepts of American identity shaped by Western patriarchy and Eurocentric models for social organization, more recent critical approaches have focused on the many cultures that have been marginalized by traditional American Studies or subordinated to an overarching nationalist mythology. In articulating the many different cultures and social identities of the United States, scholars have often focused on the cultural, political, and economic boundaries dividing these cultures both from the dominant social order and from each other.

Such "border studies" of the intersections and interactions of the different cultures of the United States must also include a reconsideration of national cultural boundaries. If a single nationalist mythology of the United States no longer prevails, our understanding of just what constitutes the cultural border of the United States is no longer clear. Immigration has always shaped the United States in ways that demonstrate the shifting nature of such cultural boundaries. More traditional American Studies relied on the model of a single dominant culture that had assimilated immigrant cultures in a gradual, evolutionary manner. More recent approaches have stressed the cultural hybridities that have historically occurred among the many different cultures constituting the United States. Attention to these hybridities requires scholars to look at the multiple cultural influences involved in important social formations; such cultural complexity is often invisible when historical changes are viewed primarily in terms of the assimilation of "minor" cultures into a "dominant" social system.

The borders of both division and contact are also linguistic, and we should not equate and thereby confuse linguistic, cultural, ethnic, and national categories, even though there are many ways in which they may overlap and complement each other. In his recent "For a Multilingual Turn in American Studies" and his long-term project to republish non–English language works of U.S. literature, Werner Sollors has argued persuasively for the study of U.S. culture as a polylingual as well as a multicultural discipline.[1] Despite the long history of an ideology of a monolingual United States, which has been revived quite hysterically in recent years by E. D. Hirsch Jr. and Arthur Schlesinger Jr. among others, the United States continues to be a multilingual society with large segments of its population working and living successfully in multilingual contexts.[2] Statistical studies do not support the fear prevalent among conservatives and many liberals that recent immigrants are failing to learn English or that polylingual communities, such as major metropolitan areas, are linguistically, culturally, and nationally fragmented. Recent studies have shown that populations who immigrated to the United States in the last half of the twentieth century have learned English, while often preserving their native languages, more rapidly and universally than those who immigrated at any other time in U.S. history.[3] Far more likely to divide recent immigrants from the U.S. "national culture," as it is sometimes called, are social disparities in educational and economic opportunities. Class hierarchies, in other words, were far more divisive of peoples in the United States in the late twentieth century than were language or culture. Of course, class as a category is often bound up in social practice with historically established hierarchies of race, ethnicity, gender, sexuality, and religion. As Sollors and many of the respondents to his essay have argued, the new American Studies must address the multilingual reality of the United States in the curricular and scholarly reforms now underway in the field.[4]

By the same token, the dominance of the United States according to the nationalist paradigm has often led to the neglect of other nations of the western hemisphere, each of which has its own complex multicultural and multilingual history, as well as its own interactions with the other nationalities of the region. The new American Studies tries to work as a genuinely comparatist discipline that will respect the many different social systems and cultural affiliations of the "Americas." Rather than treating such cultural differences as discrete entities, however, this new comparative approach stresses the ways different cultures are transformed by their contact and interaction with each other. If we are to preserve the name "American Studies," we must take into account, at the very least, the different nationalities, cultures, and languages of the western hemisphere, including Canada. If we find this field too large and challenging, we should consider the area studies model that would redefine the American Studies taught at most U.S. colleges and universities today as U.S. Studies or North American Studies. Such comparatist work thus focuses with special interest on just the points of historical, geographical, and linguistic contact where two or more communities must negotiate their respective identities. This new interest in border studies should include investigations of how the many different Americas have historically influenced and interpreted each other. With very different histories of responding to ethnic and racial minorities, as well as constructing gendered and sexual hierarchies, these different Americas also help foreground the multilingual and multicultural realities of social life and economic opportunity in any of the Americas.

Such fundamental reconsiderations of what constitutes American Studies as a field (or fields) of study should be accompanied by theoretical investigations of our methodologies for conducting research and interpreting data. The history of the impact of various critical theories and methodologies on American Studies is complex and often contradictory; it is a subject especially in need of scholarly attention at this crucial moment in the reconceptualization of the field. As an interdisciplinary field, American Studies declared its theoretical purposes from its beginnings in the 1930s, and yet American Studies has often been particularly intransigent with respect to new theoretical models, ranging from modernist theories like those of phenomenology, the Frankfurt School, structuralism, poststructuralism, and deconstruction to more contemporary approaches like those of critical race theory, feminism, queer theory, postcolonial theory, and cultural studies.

A certain antitheoretical bias lingers in American Studies, sometimes disguised by appeals to "native" methodologies or vaguely defined traditions of American pragmatism.[5] At other times, an antitheoretical air surrounds those who insist that American Studies has anticipated (and often does a better job of) knowledge production than do the new methods. Such has often been the case for defenders of the Myth-and-Symbol School and for specialists in popular culture, especially in their responses to ideological criticism, New Historicism, and cultural studies. I want simply to point out that the very claim of priority by some scholars in American Studies ought to make new critical theories and cultural studies particularly appealing to them because they share common interests.[6]

Indeed, many of the most compelling postnationalist challenges to the study of the Americas as primarily (if not exclusively) coherent nation-states are the consequences of the impact of cultural studies on American Studies and related area, ethnic, women's, and gender studies. Developing in part out of earlier "critical studies of colonial discourse" and "colonial studies," as well as the *Ideologie-kritik* of the Frankfurt School, the materialist criticism and attention to popular and mass media of the Birmingham School, and important traditions of Latin American, African, South Asian, and East Asian anticolonialist writings and political activism, cultural studies often investigates the relationship between the rise of the Western nation-state and the development of European imperial systems of economic, political, linguistic, and cultural domination.[7] Thus the relevance of a postnationalist perspective to the new American Studies is evident in the new work being done on U.S. national ideology and the concomitant imperialist ambitions of the United States in North America, Latin America, and outside the western hemisphere. The contemporary scholarly efforts to link the earlier "internal colonization" thesis of crucial American Studies scholars—such as Robert Berkhofer, Richard Drinnon, Reginald Horsman, Annette Kolodny, Richard Slotkin, Ronald Takaki, and Jane Tompkins—with the argument that the United States has traditionally defined itself as a global power have obvious connections with the intellectual and political purposes of cultural studies' general interest in the origins, legitimation, and perpetuation of Euro-American imperial and neoimperial forms of global domination.[8]

In its claims to encompass the many cultures and political organizations in the western hemisphere, the new American Studies threatens to impose its own kind of cultural imperialism, a tendency often overlooked even by the most ideologically attentive scholars. We are now familiar with the ways the American Studies of the post–World War II era "often was enlisted in the service of quasi-official governmental policies and institutions" and how its success as a field of study could sometimes be tied to the exportation of American cultural ideals based on extraordinarily limited models of American identity and experience.[9] There are commonly overlooked practical factors driving the popularity of American Studies outside the United States, such as "the growing number of American-educated Ph.D.s teaching in other countries, the lure of relatively high-paying research grants and temporary teaching positions in the U.S., and the prestige of publishing in the U.S."[10] In short, the border dividing "native" and "foreign" versions of American Studies is increasingly difficult to draw. We distinguish the new American Studies from older versions in that it is not only more inclusive and diverse but also more vigilant with respect to its possible uses in the cultural imperialist agendas central to U.S. foreign policies from the Marshall Plan in postwar Europe to the multinational alliance we assembled to fight (and legitimate) the Gulf War. Yet just what separates cultural understanding from cultural imperialism is increasingly difficult to articulate in an age of technologically accelerated human, economic, and cultural mobility.

Often what U.S. specialists in American Studies overlook is our tendency to universalize our own interests and to appeal, however unconsciously, to our own "nativist expertise" as implicated in a larger agenda of cultural imperialism that both includes and exceeds specific articulations of foreign policies. In a recent discussion on the American Crossroads Project electronic discussion group, Jim Zwick expressed his surprise at the equivocal response of non-U.S. scholars to his idea of a centennial conference on the Spanish-American and Philippine-American wars. Unaware that some non-U.S. scholars considered such a project yet another effort by U.S. specialists to control the intellectual reception of these colonial wars; to disregard once again work already done by scholars in the Philippines, Spain, Cuba, and Latin America and to publicize the latest U.S. theoretical approach (cultural studies, critical study of colonial discourse, and so on) as the most appropriate for specialists in other political and intellectual communities, Zwick found himself criticized for an intellectual provincialism he thought he was working to overcome.[11] Many scholars, like Paul Lauter, Emory Elliott, and Alice Kessler-Harris, have worked recently to increase the participation of non-U.S. American Studies specialists in the American Studies Association and the exchange of scholarly work at conferences (and now by way of the Internet) for the benefit of both U.S. and non-U.S. scholars and in recognition of the very different purposes, interests, and institutional configurations American Studies may have around the globe.[12] The new International American Studies Association, founded in 2000, should continue this work and ensure that the exchange among American Studies scholars and students is conducted in genuinely transnational and dialogical, even polylogical, ways.

New institutes and forums for international scholars in American Studies are doing important work at many different U.S. colleges and universities; such work is more important than ever now that the United States Information Agency has been significantly downsized and valuable programs it once sponsored lost to fiscal exigencies. As we contribute to this important work, however, we should remember the dialectical and dialogical purposes of such intellectual exchanges. An older international American Studies of the 1950s and 1960s often drew upon the cosmopolitanism of Euro-American modernism, together with its implicit cultural mission to "enlighten" the foreign cultures from which it drew many of its most avant-garde materials and ideas. The new American Studies requires a new internationalism that will take seriously the different social, political, and educational purposes American Studies serves in its different situations around the globe. In short, U.S. and other western hemispheric scholars have as much to learn from international colleagues as they have to learn from us.[13]

A common purpose linking these different versions of American Studies should be the critical study of the circulation of "America" as a commodity of the new cultural imperialism and the ways in which local knowledges and arts have responded to such cultural importations—the study of what some have termed "coca-colonization."[14] What some cultural critics have termed the capacity of local cultures to "write back" against cultural and even political and economic domination should be considered part of American Studies, even as we recognize the practical impossibility of expanding our scope to include all aspects of global experience simply because of the global pretensions of First World nations like the United States. Nevertheless, the study of U.S. imperialist policies toward Native Americans should not be conducted without consideration of how native peoples responded to the specific historical circumstances investigated, just as the Philippine-American War should not be studied exclusively from the perspective of the United States or the response to the Vietnam War studied solely through U.S. texts. The Native American, Philippine, and Vietnamese perspectives must be represented in such studies (whether published research or classroom instruction), once again in keeping with the comparatist aims of the new American Studies.

These are only some of the ways in which the new American Studies should begin to reconstitute its fields of study, especially as the United States (along with other First World nations) claims an ever greater responsibility for global economics, politics, language, and identity. In the introduction and chapter 1 I have discussed how we might adapt Mary Louise Pratt's theoretical model of the "contact zone" and Paul Jay's model of the "cultural zone" to articulate a comparative American Studies that would include as one of its areas of specialization "comparative U.S. cultures." Like the geopolitical, linguistic, cultural, ethnic, and economic borders I have said are crucial to the reformulation of American Studies, the contact zone is a semiotic site where exchanges may occur from both (or more) sides of an issue, even when the configurations of power are inequitable (as they usually are).

Intellectuals who work closely with peoples and issues relevant to the actual borders where immigration is controlled, economic destinies decided, and individual lives immediately and irrevocably affected often warn us not to generalize too casually or abstractly with regard to these border regions.[15] We should heed their warnings and learn from their experiences, but we should also recognize that however real the border between the United States and Mexico and those separating Southeast Asian, Haitian, or Cuban boat people from safety in the United States, they are also discursively constructed borders that are all too often made to have terrible physical consequences for those forbidden to cross them. In other words, we can begin to reconfigure such borders by establishing intellectual and cultural contact zones where a certain dialectics or dialogics of cultural exchange is understood to be a crucial aspect of how the field of American Studies is constituted and how the related territories of the Americas and the United States ought to be understood. In this respect, teaching and scholarship can become direct, albeit never exclusive, means of effecting necessary social changes.

How is it possible for us to accomplish work so vast in scope and involving so many different specializations? One of the most common reactions to the progressive aims of the new American Studies is to reassert the importance of studying a common and national culture for reasons both ideal and practical. We must have a common culture, Hirsch and others tell us, to avoid the intellectual anarchy into which we are already drifting. We must have a unified American Studies discipline, department, program, and professional organization—which usually means one devoted to some version of nationalist study or American exceptionalism—because we do not have the resources, the time, or the expertise to do more, Sean Wilentz and others warn us as ethnic, women's, gender and sexuality, and cultural studies proliferate as new programs on college campuses around the world.[16] What, then, are the practical implications of the preceding description of what it seems intellectually crucial for the new American Studies to pursue if it is to avoid the mistakes of the past and draw upon the best of its traditions?

Part of the problem facing those committed to this new vision of American Studies is related to the increasingly antiquated model of the university, its disciplinary division of knowledges, and its model of instruction as the transmission of knowledge as information from an authority to receptive students. The conflict of the modern Enlightenment model of the university and its liberal educational ideals with new conceptions of education, the character of knowledge, and the circulation of such knowledge is by no means unique to American Studies.[17] Those of us in the field may simply face it more directly and immediately because we are in the course of reconstituting our field, forced to do so by rapidly changing ideas of the Americas, and because we have a heritage of challenging established academic procedures. But to achieve any part of what I have described in the preceding paragraphs, we will have to bring about fundamental changes in the way most modern universities educate.

However sweeping such changes may seem when described in this general manner, they may be realized in many small steps. First, we should not rush to defend "American Studies" as a program or department, especially against emerging programs in ethnic, women's, gender, and sexuality studies that often devote much of their curricula to topics relevant to the study of the United States, the Americas, and the "borders" or "contact zones" I have described earlier. As part of the work of our research group at the University of California's Humanities Research Institute in the fall and winter quarters of 1996–97, we met with faculty in American Studies and related programs on the different campuses of the UC system. On every campus, important curricular changes were underway in the several fields relevant to American Studies, most of them reflecting various intellectual and educational responses to the issues discussed earlier. Each campus had very different ideas about the future of

American Studies as a formal program on that campus, and it was instructive to discover how important local institutional and political factors had been in shaping these attitudes. Whereas established American Studies programs at UC–Davis and UC–Santa Cruz are working to help focus and organize curricular changes in their own and collateral disciplines, there were no plans to revive UC–Riverside's program, which was discontinued in the late 1970s, or UC–Irvine's comparative cultures program, which was discontinued in 1993, or to expand a small, primarily instructional undergraduate American Studies program at UCLA to include a graduate (and thus more research-intensive) component.

Open forums held at the 1996 American Studies Association Convention in Kansas City and the 1997 California American Studies Association Convention in Berkeley confirmed our sense that there can be no general model for the institutional future of American Studies in U.S. universities, even when interested faculty generally agree with the aims of the new American Studies I have outlined in this chapter. Different local issues, specific to both the university and its surrounding community, affect institutional arrangements in ways that can be generalized only in terms of a "new intellectual regionalism" that must be taken into account as we discuss the multiple futures of American Studies and the established and emerging disciplines with which American Studies must collaborate in the coming decades. This intellectual regionalism is often inflected by the new regionalisms established by the different demographies, ethnicities, and global economic and cultural affiliations characterizing such important border or contact zones as Southern California's relation to Asia, Mexico, Central America, and the Caribbean; greater Houston's relation to Mexico and the Caribbean; Atlanta and the Southeast's relation to the black Atlantic; and Miami's relation to Cuba, Haiti, and Latin America.[18] Universities ought to mediate between local and international knowledges, and the new regionalisms—not to be confused with older, more discrete regional identities, even those shaped in the major period of European immigration—ought to be taken into account by academics reconstituting American Studies and related fields on their different campuses.

Our consideration of the academic implications of these new regionalisms should also inform the internationalizing of American Studies I discussed earlier—an internationalizing that should avoid the one-sided, often neoimperialist cosmopolitanism of an earlier American Studies and might complement established international relations (cultural, economic, and political) already shaping the college's or university's local community.[19] Because new sources of academic funding, especially in support of the sciences, are following the channels of this new regionalism, there will be growing pressure from academic administrators for us to follow such leads. Properly vigilant and often resistant as American Studies scholars have been to the ideological consequences of certain academic funding—a vigilance as important in today's private funding situation as when the Department of Defense was our secret source—we should make serious efforts to direct some of this funding to cultural understanding and criticism, as well as to the expansion of foreign language instruction. Regard for these new regionalisms should, of course, avoid provincialisms of their own; University of California–Irvine students need to know about the black Atlantic as well as the Pacific Rim, Mexico, and Latin America. In short, our consideration of these local conditions should be contextualized in a larger understanding of the United States in the comparative contexts of the western hemispheric and finally the global study I have described earlier.

Despite the booming U.S. economy, colleges and universities continue to operate in a state of fiscal crisis as a means of justifying the downsizing that includes drastic transformations of their research mission, especially in the humanities, and the "consolidation" of academic programs. Smaller, newer, underfunded programs are, of course, at greatest risk, even though the overall savings they offer most universities have little impact on the total budget pictures of the institutions with which they are affiliated. In this academic climate, established American Studies programs should work cooperatively with traditionally allied programs in ethnic, women's, gender, sexuality, and cultural studies and critical theory by spelling out protocols for sharing courses and existing faculty defining new faculty positions, and recruiting new faculty. Successful American Studies programs should be aware of inclinations by administrators to use them to "consolidate" different programs those administrators often view as "fragmented," "incoherent," or "needlessly proliferating," especially when those programs are leading the changes in our understanding of the limitations of traditional knowledge production and its established disciplines.

Much as those of us at colleges and universities without formal American Studies programs might wish to have the opportunity to realize some of the ambitions of the new American Studies in established curricula and degree requirements, we ought to work toward those ends in cooperation, rather than competition, with colleagues in African American, Asian American, Latino and Chicano, Native American, women's, gender, and sexuality studies and in critical theory and cultural studies.[20] Local, national, and international interests should be worked out in cooperation among such complementary fields. What eventually emerges from such collaborative work may well be different from any of the American Studies, women's studies, and ethnic studies programs we have known before, and this flexibility with respect to the emerging knowledges and institutional means of producing and sharing such knowledges should help us avoid the failed intellectual orthodoxies of the past and perhaps bring about unexpected changes in traditional departments, where many of us working for such ends hold our primary appointments. Just such an openness to emerging fields, whose methods and objects of study are still debated and contested, characterizes the attitudes of many scholars who are in no hurry to revive or inaugurate formal American Studies undergraduate or graduate programs at colleges and universities that presently lack them. The absence of formal programs, in other words, need not indicate a lack of vitality on the part of the new American Studies, especially when it anticipates its future strength as a consequence of educational coalitions with ethnic, women's, gender and sexuality, and cultural studies and critical theory.

Cooperative work of this sort should be based on our intellectual experience with the many different fields now involved in American Studies and with the challenging theoretical questions the coordination of these fields involves. No scholar can claim to "command" any part of American Studies. The field is not just multidisciplinary; it is also a cooperative intellectual venture. No matter how innovatively we design curricula, cross-list courses, and bring in visitors to our own classes, we can never approximate this collaborative and collective intellectual enterprise until we transform the classroom from the traditional "scene of instruction" (often a theater of cruel discipline or trivial imitation) into the site of a joint venture involving many scholars, including our students as active researchers. Team teaching, coordinated classes, and other traditional responses to the active-passive and master-servant models of teacher and student can today be considered crude versions of the sorts of alternative learning situations offered by the Internet, distance learning, and other electronic means of instruction. Electronic MUDs (multi-user dimensions) and MOOs (multi-object orientations), virtual conferences, and hypertext databases should be used as more than merely tools in traditional classroom education and conventional research; they should be used as means of changing ideas of what constitutes education and knowledge in the humanities and social sciences. In these ways, we might also balance our national and international aims with different local interests.

The American Studies Association's support of Randy Bass's and Jeff Finlay's American Crossroads Project and Teaching American Studies (T-Amstudy) at Georgetown University has led the way for many other academic professional organizations in experimenting with education that transcends specific university sites.[21] There are, of course, ideological consequences to the use of the Internet in education that must be recognized; as primarily an English-language medium and a technology often shaped by protocols of the U.S. information industry, the Internet is in its own right another topic worthy of consideration in the study of U.S. cultural imperialism. Yet as a medium that we can use to put faculty and students from around the world in regular and immediate contact with each other, increasingly in a variety of languages, the Internet can be used to criticize, resist, and perhaps transform such cultural imperialism. Many "virtual research centers" already link international faculty and students for a fraction of the cost of real-life conferences. Our work as scholars must be complemented by the work of academic publishers, who must now take the initiative in defining the directions for the future of the electronic dissemination of scholarly work and ensuring that appropriate standards of quality are met even as such publishers guarantee the variety of different approaches and subjects.[22]

Michael Clough, senior fellow at the Council on Foreign Relations, a research associate at the Institute of International Studies at UC–Berkeley, and cochair of the New American Global Dialogue, recently wrote in an op-ed piece in the *Los Angeles Times:* "For better and worse, it is less and less possible for nationally minded elites, sitting in Washington and New York, to construct policies that simultaneously protect and promote the interests of Los Angeles, San Francisco and other emerging regional metropoles. Instead, a new, much more decentralized model of governance, one capable of accommodating the growing diversity of the American politico-cultural economy, must be developed."[23] A specialist in international relations, Clough is not thinking about postnationalist American Studies, but the new American Studies has been developing in its own way in the direction of a more "decentralized model," one that is attentive to the different intellectual "regions," or "contact zones," that more adequately represent the domestic and foreign determinants of the United States and the Americas than did previous American Studies. Nationalisms and neonationalisms of all sorts are, of course, very much alive not only in the politically, culturally, and linguistically diverse United

States but around the globe. The persistence and even revival of nationalism need not prevent us from trying to think of social organizations in contexts other than national consensus and its stereotypes of national experience and character. Postnationalist thinking about what constitutes the United States and the Americas may well offer us our best chance of learning from, rather than repeating, the past.

4.

The Resistance to Cultural Studies in the United States

It is a recurrent strategy of any anxiety to defuse what it considers threatening by magnification or minimization, by attributing to it claims to power of which it is bound to fall short.

—Paul de Man, "The Resistance to Theory" (1986)

American Studies scholars have done a great deal over the past thirty years to establish the theoretical and practical contexts for exciting multi-disciplinary work in the humanities, arts, and social sciences, then often denounced these aims when they have been endorsed by scholars identified with cultural studies. Of course, some practitioners of American Studies have seen cultural studies as yet another competitor for extra-mural and local funding, publishers' attention, students' interest, and colleagues' enthusiasm. The various disciplines traditionally represented by American Studies seem incessantly subject to legitimation crises and conflicting claims to authority, so it is understandable when some complain about yet another multidisciplinary school that threatens to incorporate our field into its more encompassing framework. Yet such disciplinary competition cannot entirely account for the vehemence with which scholars criticize cultural studies, condemning its impossible scope, failure to define its key terms, lack of theoretical self-consciousness, historical ignorance, the "easiness" of its topics for teaching and research, its obsession with "relevance," its reflex treatment of "race, class, and gender," its refusal to read *carefully*, and its insistent politicization of everything it treats.

American Studies scholars should recognize in this list of supposed failings many of the criticisms traditionally directed at their field. Rather than viewing cultural studies as an enemy or a hostile competitor, we should consider this approach an intellectual and political ally. At its best, cultural studies provides a more inclusive category for the multidisciplinary work American Studies represents. Because cultural studies treats its subjects in global and transnational contexts, it offers American Studies ways to reimagine its own scholarly projects outside strictly nationalist models while respecting the historical influence of such nationalisms in the formation of many social, cultural, and other group identities. In this chapter, I want to answer the criticisms commonly directed at cultural studies for two reasons: to define cultural studies as an effective intellectual movement and to assess its points of intersection with American Studies. In my defense of cultural studies, I assume that any school or movement is capable of producing bad work. Rather than responding to specific examples of bad cultural studies, I refer to my own work and a utopian conception of cultural studies.[1]

It is true that cultural studies sets its practitioners the impossible task of articulating those conditions whereby cultural conventions and values are accepted. Freud used the term "reality-principle," Althusser "ideology," and Foucault "epistème" to refer to the complex processes and systems whereby people in a given time and place agree to certain demonstrably relative truths. What constituted culture or society for Freud, Althusser, and Foucault was never something that any of these theorists presumed to define but rather what manifested itself in the social practices of people who accepted the term: nineteenth-century U.S. culture, the Victorian Age, the Second Empire, le fin de siècle, and so forth.

For these theorists, culture or society was the horizon of interpretation. The "nation" was simply one historical manifestation of a self-consciously coherent culture or society, so the national organization of intellectual inquiry had to be understood as itself historically situated and limited. It was the ability of these theorists to go beyond specific disciplinary practices to understand the demonstrable, working cohesiveness of culture that has enabled them to continue to influence our work in the humanities and social sciences, and they were certainly important predecessors for many contemporary cultural critics. But it is also fair to say that Freud, Althusser, and Foucault were products of modern European cultural practices, which according to their respective analyses were often structured around bourgeois individualism. And although each contributed importantly to the critique of the coherent philosophical subject and attendant myths, each was celebrated, along with many other modern intellectual "geniuses," as a singular font of cultural knowledge. Cultural studies abandons the impossible notion that any single intellectual, however unusual and brilliant, can possibly command the many different knowledges necessary to analyze basic conditions for prevailing cultural phenomena. Cultural studies must be a collaborative scholarly project or suite of different projects. Such collaborative scholarly practices are still very difficult for many of us in the humanities and some of the social sciences to understand in practical terms, but cultural studies does not call for every one of its practitioners to comprehend culture in a comprehensive and transdisciplinary manner. But cultural studies does ask us to think of our different scholarly projects in relationship to each other by way of the larger horizon of the specific cultural reality it helps us understand.

The determination of cultural and social boundaries is thus a topic of abiding interest for cultural critics. Socially constructed boundaries that distinguish between native and stranger, citizen and barbarian, master and servant, and self and other—to list only a few possibilities—are best understood by studying those instances of boundary crossing, transgression, and disavowal that cause social institutions to defend such boundaries, change internally, or lose credibility. In the era of the nation-state, which still powerfully governs us, transnational phenomena are crucial areas of study for understanding what constitutes the nation. Diasporas and willful emigrations, foreign and civil wars, revolutions, colonial ventures and imperial systems, anti-immigration and exclusion laws, xenophobias of all sorts, and cross-cultural influences and resistances are just some of the ways in which national identity is consolidated and constantly adapted to new social conditions. Studies dedicated to specific national literatures, histories, and cultural traditions cannot understand such nations exclusively from within their ideologies but must consider the points of national intersection that constitute the various boundaries— geopolitical, legal, cultural, ethnic, class, religious, et al.—of discrete nations (and other social organizations). As I argued in chapter 1, such an approach is inherently comparative, however contestatory or conflicted the terms of comparison might be. At the most elementary level, then, cultural studies builds upon fundamental principles of social construction that situate nation-specific knowledge in historically and socially comparative contexts. This general approach has the advantage of allowing

American Studies scholars to study the United States as a nation without tacitly making exceptionalist assumptions or uncritically universalizing U.S. nationalism as the model for other nations and societies.

Another frequently heard complaint is that cultural critics fail to define their terms and therefore lack intellectual foundations. In recent years, I have attended several lectures in which those critical of cultural studies have offered their own, usually philologically oriented, accounts of the historical and social vagaries of the term "culture."[2] The point customarily made is that culture is so relative to its sociohistorical circumstances as to be impossible to define, which leads these critics to the conclusion that "cultural study" is thus impossible. The model for study is, of course, the analytical tradition of modernity, in which epistemic value depends upon transhistorical truth and universal validity. But cultural critics are not as interested in providing a categorical and totalized definition of culture as they are in understanding how this term can be used to designate certain practices and values for a specific society. In other words, the term "culture" may well have referred to a totality for those nineteenth-century British who accepted the designation "Victorian culture," but the cultural critic wants to look primarily at the social, human, and natural consequences of that assumption, avoiding totalizing assumptions in his or her own work. Defining the term "culture" is beside the point; culture is whatever people happen to take it to be at a particular time and in a particular place. What matters is how that term works to organize diverse experiences and information.

The complaint that cultural critics do not define their terms is linked with the charge that they lack theoretical self-consciousness, or a metatheory. After all, if cultural critics knew what they were studying, they would know it as a consequence of processes that are articulable as theory. Therefore, cultural studies should respect the "higher" authority of critical theory, whose transhistorical perspective enables it to be used to adjudicate historically and culturally disparate claims.[3] Some cultural critics have responded to this charge by claiming that cultural studies is an eclectic, hybrid, unsystematic approach; indeed, it must have this improvisational quality, because it claims to encompass such an enormous set of different subjects. Still others have argued that the "American case" demands "American theories" and have thus rejected the strong reliance on "European philosophy and theory over American philosophy and theory."[4] I think both defenses are mistaken, the first because it reinforces complaints that cultural studies lacks a proper object of study and is primarily responsible for the lack of a metatheory and the second because it integrates American exceptionalism into the methodological framework of the critical approach.

Jean-François Lyotard argued that one of the distinguishing character-istics of the "postmodern condition" is an "incredulity with respect to metanarratives." This is a corollary of his notion that postmodernity is marked by the breakdown of the "grand narratives" of enlightenment and emancipation that distinguished modernity.[5] Contemporary cultural studies, especially as it has been influenced by recent movements in the United States and Australia, differs from 1960s British cultural studies (of the sort done in Birmingham and Manchester, for example) by virtue of its incorporation of crucial concepts from poststructuralist theories. Cultural studies is not deconstruction, but it draws on such poststructuralist con-cepts as the social construction of reality, the discursive construction of society, the textualist position generally, and thus the irreducibility of the signifier. As de Man puts the matter, "The resistance to theory is a resis-tance to the use of language about language."[6] Another instance of de Man's famous *doubles entendres,* this aphorism does not mean that the re-sistance to theory is a resistance to metalanguages in general. De Man means the opposite: that the resistance to theory depends on the repres-sion of the full consequences of the linguistic condition—that the "use of language about language" means there can never be a proper "meta-language." It might be argued that these ideas constitute in their own right a "grand narrative" of postmodernity or poststructuralism.[7] Derrida's ef-fort to substitute strategic interpretive terms—trace, *différance,* supple-ment, *écriture,* spectre—for foundational concepts or Kantian a prioris convinces me that he is using "nonconcepts," as he terms them, despite claims by critics of deconstruction that such departures from Enlighten-ment rationality render such thought irrational or illogical.

Cultural studies also imagines its work taking place within a chain of signifiers whose interruption is itself part of the historical and social pro-cess.[8] Like defining terms, theoretical self-consciousness in the sense of stepping outside that historical and semiotic process is not possible in any complete sense, but not because cultural critics are un-self-conscious.[9] It is the postmodern condition, Lyotard argues, that is characterized by "little narratives," none of which can be made to stand convincingly as the governing narrative under which other little narratives might be ruled or generated. This is not the fault of cultural critics, who are themselves products of such postmodern conditions; it is a consequence of the pre-vailing historical conditions for representation and interpretation. Under such circumstances, any claims made by cultural critics must be justified by a certain pragmatics of effect: What will this interpretation do, rather than What does this interpretive schema explain? Whether this action takes place in an academic or a wider social context, it is always political, so there can be no theory or metanarrative apart from the action cultural critics take in conjunction with their ideas.[10]

In response to the criticism that the postmodern condition refers only to very restricted historical circumstances and thus does not apply to the Ming Dynasty in China, Milton's England, pre-Columbian North America, or German romanticism, for example, the cultural critic's appropriate response should be that any of these pre-postmodern eras or movements is interpretable only within our present hermeneutic conditions. By the same token, Lyotard's Eurocentric conception of the postmodern condition can be scrutinized by critics operating within the institutional contexts still very much governed by such Eurocentrism if they question the consequences of just such postmodernity in other societies. How, for example, have Second, Third, and Fourth World nations been affected by the postmodern condition? As service and information industries have come to dominate the economies of the First World nations in late or postindustrial periods, which societies have assumed responsibilities for agricultural and industrial production? How have these global distributions of economic responsibility resulted in new hierarchies, power structures, and degrees of relative importance and value? In such contexts, we must do comparative work even when our object of study is nominally contained completely within U.S. borders. By the same token, European theory, like Lyotard's approach to the postmodern condition, should not merely be replaced with "American theory," but must be challenged with theories relevant (not always native) to the various societies necessary to the comparative method of inquiry.

The irreducible historicity and comparatism of cultural studies are thus at considerable odds with what critics often term its supposed "historical ignorance." There are really two different issues that are addressed in this criticism. On the one hand, scholars call attention to cultural studies' emphasis on the contemporary flotsam and jetsam of a thoroughly superficial (and very postmodern) world: comic books, women's fashion, grade-B movies, pornography, sports, Harlequin romances, and so on. On the other hand, these critics attack what Lauren Berlant terms the "tinny archive," by which phrase she refers to a prevailing sense that cultural studies is not "serious" about its scholarship or about the history behind its interpretive objects.[11] American Studies scholars traditionally have faced such criticism, because the field has always treated high, middle, and low cultural texts and artifacts as equally important in the formation of U.S. society. We should know better than scholars in most other fields that the "tinny archive" may well include the most important evidence of how prevailing cultural and social attitudes are formed, adapted, and maintained.

Ranging from Jameson's characterization of postmodernity's retro-effects, faux history, and irreducible "superficiality" to Neil Postman's complaint that we have lost a coherent public sphere and civic virtue, criticism of postmodernity's or cultural studies' "historical ignorance" often depends on nostalgia for Enlightenment rationality and its conception of history as a grand narrative.[12] Sometimes the archive the scholar must draw upon is tinny because other well-trained scholars have visited that library not very often, if ever. When I started writing in the 1970s on the U.S. cultural responses to the Vietnam War, there was virtually no serious scholarship on the topic. Today there is substantial work, but in those days I relied on popular journalism, bizarre historical and first-person accounts, gossip, and archives ranging from the Borgesian—taped testimonies of demobilized veterans stored alphabetically in a navy yard archive that measured the collection in miles—to the classified.

Fashion- and fad-driven as their phenomena often are, popular and mass culture may be even more crucially historical than other cultural products. Interestingly, it is often those scholars who elsewhere defend the universal values of canonical texts, ideas, or events who also criticize the ahistorical qualities of cultural studies. The literary history I was taught as an undergraduate and graduate student was primarily that of literary influences, literary movements, and the intellectual history that linked literature with other philosophical and aesthetic activities. My complaint about that education is that it was not sufficiently historical, in large part because it failed to take into account the larger political, social, and economic forces involved in such cultural production.[13]

One motive for criticizing cultural studies' lack of historical consciousness is to distinguish between important and fashionable historical phenomena. In "The Resistance to Theory," de Man clearly valorizes literature as a linguistic modality that foregrounds the "rhetorical or tropological dimension of language," but he hedges his bets by claiming that this "literature (broadly conceived)" may only make more manifest linguistic functions "which can be revealed in any verbal event when it is read textually."[14] At the very moment de Man deconstructs the hierarchies of linguistic representation that the poststructuralist theory of signification topples, he reinstates new hierarchies, perhaps because of his own (proleptic) resistance to cultural studies. Many scholars justifiably fear the ever-widening scope of the humanities and social sciences; the absence of criteria for selecting literary texts, historical events, philosophical problems, and sociological data is cause for alarm. But are we talking about an absence of such criteria or about a change in the criteria themselves? As I suggested earlier, cultural critics must sometimes rely on archives drastically different from those consulted by scholars studying nominally the same "periods" or "disciplines." In other cases, traditional prejudices against popular or mass cultural evidence prevent some scholars from recognizing its historicality.

In work I recently completed on John Rollin Ridge's (Yellow Bird's) 1854 popular novel about the legendary California bandit Joaquín Murieta, I found myself swamped with historical legends, texts, and data from several different historical registers: the history of the Cherokee tribe, its relations with the U.S. government, California in transition from Mexican to U.S. rule, the Gold Rush, Spanish and Latin American recyclings of the Murieta legend, and so forth.[15] For these very reasons, my principles of historical and literary selection were crucial to me, uppermost in my mind from the moment I selected Ridge's text as a means to better understand the cultural reception of the Mexican-American War. By contrast, the selection for interpretation of an indisputable literary classic—Henry James's *Portrait of a Lady* or *The Wings of the Dove,* for example—raises far fewer problems of basic selection, no matter what I am planning to do with the classic text. In writing about Ridge's *Life and Adventures of Joaquín Murieta* I have to be constantly attentive to the larger historical and cultural purposes served by what I might term this cultural synecdoche than I would be in treating one of those novels by James, because I know that my readers are likely to be complaining: "What's the point of reading about this old potboiler?" In short, choosing a noncanonical text often places greater demands on the scholar to justify his or her treatment of it. And because that justification rarely can be made in terms of the "universal value" of noncanonical or of popular or mass-market texts, the argument must be profoundly, irreducibly historical.

The preceding remarks about the historicality of cultural studies allow me to treat quickly but effectively two other common objections: that the topics chosen by cultural critics for research and teaching are easy and only superficially relevant. There is nothing easy in trying to explain how and why Ridge's story of the Sonoran bandit Joaquín Murieta appealed both to Latin American miners who were persecuted in and driven from the California goldfields and to U.S. citizens who were eager to impose their cultural values on the new state of California. Although Ridge's text is lexically easier to understand than a novel by Henry James, its cultural and political contexts are at least as difficult to interpret—and those of many popular and mass-audience texts are considerably more difficult to comprehend—than those of canonical texts or events. In contemporary literary criticism, we often write about the intentional fallacy and about a textual unconscious that cannot be commanded by any author or even described in the most comprehensive account of the text's author function, but we nevertheless have some confidence that a writer working in an established literary tradition possesses a high degree of self-consciousness regarding his or her sense of that tradition and how his or her work should ideally be situated in it. Such a general description applies as well to avant-garde, politically radical, and socially marginalized writers who wish to fundamentally challenge the terms of such a literary tradition.

Such "literary history" as Paul de Man once viewed as constituted by the dialectics of "literary history and literary modernity" seems quite restricted (and restrictive) when measured against the theoretical and practical problems facing the cultural interpreter interested in explaining how and why *Titanic* was the highest-grossing film of all time or Sylvester Stallone's Rambo character so captivated global audiences in the aftermath of the Vietnam War or in examining the social, ideological, and economic work done by the Book-of-the-Month Club or Harlequin romances.[16] Indeed, one reason that few American Studies scholars took very seriously de Man's poststructuralist approaches to literary study as foundational to social semiotics is that in the 1960s and 1970s they already practiced a multidisciplinary methodology that encouraged them to address the more complex and unpredictable relations among mass, popular, and high media for cultural representation.

The difficulties of interpreting and understanding these interrelations are compounded when we try to *teach* such materials to students who have been accustomed since grade school to distinguish between high and low cultural materials in terms of their relative seriousness and value. Students are often horrified, embarrassed, or downright angry about studying texts that they consume happily and willingly outside the classroom, but feel should not be part of the university's curriculum. Yet once they accept the immodest proposal that they should interpret seriously what they watch, read, and listen to, not necessarily for its intrinsic or enduring value but for what it tells them about their culture and themselves, these students are excited, energized by literary, historical, philosophical, or social studies, often for the very first time.[17]

To be sure, this sounds much like the arguments made for teaching "relevant" materials that we used to challenge the curricula defended by our teachers in undergraduate and graduate programs around the country in the late 1960s. Another criticism cultural studies shares with American Studies is, We tried that in the sixties, and it didn't work. Despite a handful of courses, often taught by graduate teaching assistants, that experimented with new texts and topics, most humanities curricula in U.S. colleges and universities from 1965 to 1975 focused on traditional topics and texts. The exceptions were courses in emerging feminist, ethnic, and some American Studies programs, almost all of which were institutionally marginalized and underfunded (which may be the same thing) and whose curricular and scholarly work we ought to recognize today as foundational for contemporary cultural studies.[18] Intellectual and pedagogical alliances among ethnic studies, women's studies, cultural studies, and American Studies may well enable scholars in these fields to bring courses and curricula long marginal to the Enlightenment university into the center of the postmodern university.

A broadly multicultural, multimedia, multidisciplinary curriculum in the humanities was not attempted until many associated with cultural studies (and other intellectual disciplines as well) proposed major redefinitions of Western civilization introductions and other influential undergraduate and graduate courses in the humanities. Often those changes were linked, for better or worse, with new requirements in "American cultures," prompted in part by the academic and popular sense that what constituted American identity, even in its exceptionalist configuration, could no longer be represented by a single archetype. Such new graduation requirements as those for the American cultures curriculum at the University of California–Berkeley were adopted in the 1980s to address just such needs.[19] To be sure, the identification of multicultural education with American culture ended up reinforcing American exceptionalism and the mistaken idea that U.S. multicultural society is a model for the world.

What is often behind the claim, It's been done, and doesn't work is profound anxiety regarding changes in familiar curricula, methods of teaching, and texts. "Relevance" is a code word, as it was in the 1960s, for "what the students want," and for that very reason it is somehow suspect or corrupt. Actually, undergraduate students are not the primary voices urging faculty to teach popular and mass-cultural materials, to broaden the humanities and social sciences to include non-European cultures and histories, to respect the many different and often competing traditions within any national culture. Fortunately, there is probably no generalization that can be used today to describe what students want or do not want. Students are too politically, culturally, sexually, ethnically, regionally, and class diverse.

It is just this extraordinary diversity of students that argues in favor of the topics, interdisciplinary methods, and collaborative intellectual spirit of cultural studies, and it is this very diversity of the student population that troubles many of the critics of cultural studies. The disappearance of the homogeneity of student bodies should be a matter of pride to those of us who believe that much of the promise of the postwar United States depended on extending opportunities for higher education to a much wider and thus a more diverse segment of the population. In other words, cultural studies is relevant to today's students, and thus interests them, because it addresses questions of self-evident importance to those students' daily lives and experiences. It is just this argument of everyday importance that American Studies in all its different methods and schools has consistently made from its beginnings. Rather than competitor or antagonist, cultural studies is American Studies' proper ally and complement.

The same sorts of arguments may be made in response to complaints that cultural studies relies on formulaic or predictable considerations of race, class, gender, and sexual orientation, categories of obvious importance in American Studies. These considerations are important precisely because they help map so many social fields and because so many people have something to say about them. They thus have the advantage of providing us with very useful points of reference for comparative interpretations and understandings. Race, class, gender, and sexual orientation also have the advantage of bringing together economic status and social affiliations, potentially avoiding the Marxist overdetermination of economic factors and the exclusive focus on identity politics that has sometimes limited approaches to feminist, gay, and ethnic studies. The ideology behind the criticism of "race-gender-class critics," as John Ellis reductively terms many cultural critics, is an older assimilationist ideal that was founded on Enlightenment models of a single type of "rational human being."[20] What such critics cannot understand is that many scholars committed to cultural studies do not share these modernist notions and are committed instead to articulating a spectrum of identities, beings, subjectivities, and community affiliations that are more appropriate to the different peoples and cultures studied today by the humanities and social sciences. In this case, many of the humanist critics of cultural studies are right to be nervous; cultural studies calls for reconceptualizations of the singular models for humanity, reason, civic virtue, and domestic responsibility outlined in the synthetic modern theories of Kant, Hegel, Marx, Engels, and Freud.

The complaint that cultural studies fails to "read closely" is another significant, potentially disabling complaint, because it is often made by deconstructive critics with whom many cultural critics share the poststructuralist model for language and cultural semiotics. Jacques Derrida's work has enormously complicated the task of cultural interpretation, because it requires us to recognize the always arbitrary boundaries of any specific act of interpretation. Taking into account the full range of retentions and protentions involved in any utterance, however trivial, theoretically involves the interpreter in a recapitulation of a history and potential reception that exceeds the hermeneutic command of any particular interpreter, or even any team of interpreters. Given this textualist situation, which cultural studies generally accepts, "close reading" in the formalist sense of a thorough *explication de texte* is impossible and every textual occasion demands scrupulous attention to the complex intertextuality it involves, whether that occasion is nominally an effect of popular, mass, or high culture. Another way to put this would be to write that cultural critics are always faced with the problem of reading, knowing that any particular act of interpretation depends upon exclusions, omissions, and even politically significant repressions that may have serious consequences. Once again, these are issues American Studies traditionally recognizes as part of its multidisciplinary project and believes must be addressed in its scholarship—How are "objects of study" constituted?—and pedagogy—What is a proper "field" of instruction?

Yet virtually all the complaints regarding cultural studies' lack of attention to textual complexity come from scholars interested in canonized texts and authors. If Kant is criticized for contributing to an Enlightenment model of humanity, Kantian defenders complain that these critics have not "read closely enough" to discover just how postmodern Kant is. Ditto for Hegel, the "New" Nietzsche; Marx and Engels in the wake of Baudrillard; Freud in the wake of Lacan; Lacan in the wake of Žižek; Derrida in the wake of Cixous and Irigaray; and so on. I have no objection to historically revisionist interpretations of major figures and texts, as long as the interpreter makes clear why he or she is recontextualizing that figure. All acts of reading are limited and limiting; every interpretation establishes an arbitrary hermeneutic frame. Every reading is also a misreading—of original intentions, of cultural norms, and of implied reading dynamics. Behind the demand for close and careful reading there is a profoundly conservative impulse to keep us focused on familiar texts that are recognized as difficult and serious. But too often the criteria for retaining these serious texts are left unarticulated or defended. How important is it to study William Shakespeare, John Keats, Karl Marx, Henry James, or Sigmund Freud today? Some will insist that studying these great Western intellectuals hardly needs to be justified. Others will more carefully explain, defend, locate, justify, and argue about the contemporary relevance of these figures, thereby participating in just the sort of intellectual debate that makes for valuable teaching, useful scholarship, and historically vital intellectual exchanges.

In the course of these arguments about canonical figures, there will inevitably be efforts to situate them with respect to claims made for Mary Wollstonecraft, Mary Shelley, Margaret Fuller, Frederick Douglass, Lydia Maria Child, Harriet Jacobs, Harriet Beecher Stowe, Nick Black Elk, Frantz Fanon, Alejo Carpentier, Ngũgĩ wa Thiong'o, Salman Rushdie, and Toni Morrison. That sort of comparative reading strikes me as closer to the poststructuralist model of intertextuality and unlimited interpretive horizons than the ideal of "close" and intricate reading of discrete texts often advocated by those complaining of cultural studies' failure to "read," such as Richard Rorty's passionate appeal for "the necessity of inspired reading."[21] The textualist position teaches us that everything is reading and interpretation, that students are always, already surrounded by a massive onslaught of signs demanding their attention. They must read on the run, make new loops and connections, all without hope of reaching an end or a proper conclusion.

I do not mean to argue that we represent only this sort of postmodern echolalia in our classrooms and formal interpretive acts. Training in close reading of texts can be valuable as long as we teach our students that it can be learned by reading any text. Are some texts more important than others? Why? How? When? Our students should learn how to ask such questions, and we must provide them with the means to formulate their own answers. Shakespeare and Henry James will not survive in the twenty-first century simply because of their self-evident and undeniable literary virtues. They will be read by successive generations of students because they will be interpreted in ways relevant to the historical and social contexts in which they are received.

Finally, I wish to address the most common criticism of cultural studies: that it politicizes knowledge, which should remain neutral and value free in our contemporary political debates. American Studies scholars will recognize this criticism as one frequently directed at their own field. Indeed, our tradition of political and social critique has often caused American Studies to be academically marginalized, despite the popularity and importance of its subjects. My reason for not treating this objection until the very end of this chapter is that we cannot comprehend the irreducibly political character of cultural studies without first investigating its defining predicates: its commitment to understand the non-totalizable relations of different cultural forces in the determination of human meanings and values; the relativity of these forces to their specific historical and social circumstances of usage and acceptance; the impossibility of understanding such circumstances in the terms of any universal or exceptionalist theory or model; and the need for helpful terms of comparison, such as race, class, gender, and sexual orientation, by means of which to pursue comparative interpretations of different historical and cultural situations while avoiding the temptation to essentialize such terms. Reviewing these parts of the definition of cultural studies, we should conclude that cultural critics cannot imagine knowledge that is separable from its political and social functions, even when such knowledge is presented as politically neutral, value free, or scientifically universal (or essential). Even if we should wish to stand outside the framework of cultural studies by insisting upon the possibility of knowledge that is free of its political and social significances, the cultural critic would reply that his or her interest centers on how such apolitical knowledge functions within specific social, political, and historical circumstances. To the challenge of its critics, Why must all knowledge be political? cultural studies replies, If knowledge is not political, then what social function does it perform? Phrasing the criticisms in this way, we may begin to recognize that the heated debates regarding the politicization of the academy may hinge upon different interpretations of what we mean by politics. For the cultural critic, the term refers generally to social governance and the intellectual abilities of subjects and groups within democratic societies to assume their responsibilities for such governance. Everything is political in liberal education, because liberal education prepares students to become thinking, critical, good citizens.

I have tried to analyze some of the ideological reasons behind the contemporary resistance to cultural studies, arguing along the way that this criticism involves more embedded resistance than the demands for better scholarship, theoretical self-consciousness, and careful reading suggest. Paul de Man concluded "The Resistance to Theory" by dramatizing the rhetorical deconstruction he had advocated in the essay, cleverly arguing: "Nothing can overcome the resistance to theory since theory *is* itself this resistance."[22] Cultural studies may also be said to offer a critical resistance that negates and demystifies the arguments of its critics. But cultural studies or cultural criticism must accomplish this work in a variety of "linguistic moments," including those institutional, curricular, pedagogical, and public situations in which rhetoric involves more than a simple change of name or witty turn of phrase. The resistance to cultural studies masks a more profound conservatism in the academy that clings to canonical texts and figures, established curricula, and disciplinary divisions in a historical period and institutional circumstances in which intellectual, pedagogical, and scholarly changes are inevitable. American Studies scholars should recognize in cultural studies a complementary intellectual enterprise whose global scope encourages the sort of comparative cultural work that American Studies needs to do in order to overcome a narrowly nationalist or exceptionalist model.

Part II.
Textual Examples

5.

Hawthorne's Ghost in Henry James's Italy

Sculptural Form, Romantic Narrative, and the
Function of Sexuality in the Nineteenth Century

Miss Hosmer is also, to say the word, very willful, and too independent by half, and is mixed up with a set whom I do not like, and I can therefore do very little for her. . . . She may or may not have inventive powers as an artist, but if she have will not she be the first woman?

—William Wetmore Story to James Russell Lowell, February 11, 1853

Story's "Hatty" is of course Miss Harriet Hosmer, the most eminent member of that strange sisterhood of American "lady sculptors" who at one time settled upon the seven hills in a white, marmorean flock. . . . [T]heir rise, their prosperity, their subsidence, are, in presence of some of the widely scattered monuments of their reign, things likely to lead us into bypaths queer and crooked.

—Henry James, *William Wetmore Story and His Friends* (1903)

In "Swept Away: Henry James, Margaret Fuller, and 'The Last of the Valerii,'" I argued that Henry James began his literary career by repeating and in some cases extending the antifeminist views of his most important New England predecessors, notably Emerson, Henry James Sr., and Hawthorne.[1] I based my argument primarily on the paternalism and defensiveness seen in these male transcendentalists' accounts of their friend and literary colleague, Margaret Fuller, and on the younger Henry James's subsequent references to Fuller in his reconstruction of that interesting colony of American artists and socialites in Rome from the

83

1840s to the 1870s in *William Wetmore Story and His Friends,* in which he claims to represent the "old relation, social, personal, aesthetic, of the American world to the European" and ends up revealing his own psycho-poetic and cultural roots.[2] In particular, I examined James's motives in *William Wetmore Story* for representing Fuller as what he terms the "Margaret-ghost," a specter of the past that he links with that other hauntingly tragic figure for the Victorian imagination, Beatrice Cenci, whose portrait by Guido Reni hung even then in the Palazzo Barberini, where the Storys took up residence on the third floor in 1856 (*William Wetmore Story,* I, 337).[3]

Both Fuller and the nineteenth-century popularity of Beatrice Cenci explicitly link James's reflections in *William Wetmore Story* with Hawthorne's fiction, notably *The Blithedale Romance* (1852) and *The Marble Faun* (1859), as well as with Hawthorne's accounts of his own Italian experiences in his *French and Italian Notebooks.* Long considered the origin of Hawthorne's Zenobia in *The Blithedale Romance,* Fuller was one of several possible models for the mysterious and tragic Miriam in *The Marble Faun.* Indeed, Fuller's involvement in the Italian republican revolution of the 1840s and her marriage to another follower of Mazzini, Marquis Angelo Ossoli, gives added credibility to the seemingly playful suggestion in Hawthorne's 1860 "Postscript" to *The Marble Faun* that Miriam's "secret" past somehow involves the turbulent politics of post-1848 Italy and the struggle between republican forces and Pope Pius IX, whose claims to political power in the Papal States were defended by Napoleon III's French army of occupation from 1849 to 1870.[4] Although Hawthorne's "Postscript" is often rightly considered his effort to tease readers intent upon "solving" a romantic mystery designed to invoke our postlapsarian history and allegorize original sin and *felix culpa* in a modern drama, his *jeu d'esprit* may also refer to the "family connections" Fuller made by marrying Marquis Ossoli, whose father was an officer in the Papal Guards and a staunch antirepublican.[5]

For the younger Henry James, Margaret Fuller, with her public commitments to women's rights and abolition, condensed many of his literary fathers' anxieties about the attention women intellectuals and artists were attracting for their cultural work. Yet my exclusive focus in that essay on Margaret Fuller, however motivated it was by Hawthorne's and Henry James's obsessive fascination with a woman both overtly trivialized, caused me to neglect the diverse group of women writers, artists, and sculptors Hawthorne met during his two years in Italy (1858 and 1859), who are recorded in his *Italian Notebooks* and are recalled, often quite curiously, by Henry James in *William Wetmore Story and His Friends*. In the latter work, James not only evokes the era of his literary fathers but entangles it with his own memories of his visits to Italy in 1869, 1872–73, and 1873–74, when he met some of the survivors of the cultural scene Hawthorne had enjoyed in Italy two decades earlier. These Italian visits gave Henry James much material for his short fiction of the early 1870s, in which he both worked through the influences of his New England precursors and developed his own post-Romantic themes and styles. Derived from all of these complex Italian influences, certain nineteenth-century masculine anxieties regarding feminine personal independence and self-assertiveness, political challenges to patriarchy, and growing public acclaim for women's artistic and intellectual achievements continued to play through James's writings as they did through Hawthorne's. In what follows, I shall notice both similarities and differences in Hawthorne's and James's efforts to defend masculine authority, both sexual and literary, against imagined feminist challenges and to negotiate the homosocial, homoerotic, and homosexual desires encountered in the changing sexual politics of nineteenth-century America.[6]

In "Swept Away," I interpreted the excavation and subsequent reburial of a classical sculpture of Juno in "The Last of the Valerii" (1874) as emblematic of James's efforts to engage and then repress the threatening power of the New Woman—a feminine authority for whom Fuller had found historical precedent in the heroic women of Greek myth and tragedy.[7] James's references to the "recovery" of classical sculpture include far more than just Fuller's transcendentalism; nineteenth-century archaeology and sculpture played complementary roles in promoting the romantic classicism in sculpture, architecture, and painting that extended from the 1820s to the 1870s.[8] Although they commented on its artists and works in somewhat different periods, Hawthorne and James were fascinated and at times troubled by paintings and sculptures in this mode. Millicent Bell and, more recently, Rita Gollin and John Idol have eloquently explained how Hawthorne used the pictorial and plastic arts in his fiction.[9] Elaborating on their work and the many James scholars, like Viola Winner and Adeline Tintner, who have worked to uncover James's debts to the pictorial arts, I want to interpret Hawthorne's and James's defensive responses to these sister arts. In one sense, each author incorporated sculptural and pictorial representations in his fiction in order to relate his work to more venerable artistic media; in another sense, each author was actually competing for the publicity and celebrity enjoyed by many of these nineteenth-century sculptors and painters.

Nowhere was this anxiety more evident than when the artists were also women. In the epigraphs to this chapter, I offer two masculine responses to Harriet Hosmer, one of the most important American sculptors in the romantic classical mode. William Story's patronizing judgment of Hosmer betrays his own fears that Hosmer's artistic achievement and talent might be superior to his own, as most modern art historians agree they were. In his preface to *The Marble Faun*, Hawthorne diplomatically claims, "Were [the author] capable of stealing from a lady, he would certainly have made free with Miss Hosmer's admirable statue of Zenobia," thereby including Hosmer's heroic sculpture *Zenobia in Chains*, to which Hawthorne refers, as one of the several allusions of the romance, albeit segregated from the sculptures by male sculptors that are allowed to figure in the romance's dramatic action. In fact, Hawthorne includes at least two explicit allusions to Hosmer's work in the dramatic action of *The Marble Faun*. Kenyon's sculpture of a marble hand, modeled on Hilda's, that he shows Miriam in "A Sculptor's Studio" (chapter 13), recalls *The Clasped Hands*, which Hosmer cast from the Brownings' hands—a now famous Victorian sculpture of romantic love (*The Marble Faun*, 120). Hawthorne's frequent references to Beatrice Cenci, albeit made primarily in reference to Guido Reni's portrait, also refer to Hosmer's sculpture *Beatrice Cenci* (1856), which shows Beatrice reclining on "a raised block that serves as couch in her prison cell," her "deep sleep" and "natural" pose striking a sharp contrast with her reputation in the Victorian imaginary as a monstrous hybrid of abused innocence and vengeful parricide.[10] James's identification of Hosmer with the "white marmorean flock" of that "strange sisterhood of American 'lady sculptors'" in Rome seems to be the most mocking and patronizing of the three (*William Wetmore Story*, I, 257), recalling Hawthorne's own desperate complaint against the "d[amne]d mob of scribbling women," who had "occupied" the "public taste . . . with their trash."[11]

Harriet, or "Hattie," Hosmer (1830–1908) traveled from America to Italy in 1852 and to Rome in 1855 to study with John Gibson, the English sculptor working in Rome, who was "heir to the neoclassical tradition of Flaxman" and was himself a student of "Canova and Thorwaldsen."[12] During her many productive years as a sculptor in Rome, Hosmer achieved prominence as one of the most important American neoclassical sculptors and as one of the central women artists in a group that included Margaret Foley, Maria Louisa Lander, Emma Stebbins, and Edmonia Lewis.[13] James mentions none of these other women sculptors by name in *William Wetmore Story*, although he does refer identifiably and in a

Harriet Hosmer, *Beatrice Cenci,* 1856

racist manner to Edmonia Lewis (1845–?), who was the "daughter of an Indian [Chippewa] mother and a Negro father, both of whom died when she was three years old."[14] Well known for her sculptures of historical and ideal subjects "drawn from the struggles of the Negro cause or from the life and legends of the Indians," Lewis is trivialized and racially marginalized by James: "One of the sisterhood, if I am not mistaken, was a negress, whose colour, picturesquely contrasting with that of her plastic material, was the pleading agent of her fame" (*William Wetmore Story,* I, 258).[15] In James's account of these "American 'lady sculptors,'" Hattie Hosmer represents them all, as if the "odd phenomenon of their practically simultaneous appearance" in Rome and "their rise, their prosperity, their subsidence" can be accounted for in some manner typical of their "sisterhood" (*William Wetmore Story,* I, 257–58). "Miss Hosmer had talent," James admits, almost begrudgingly, but thereby implies that the other "lady sculptors" did not (*William Wetmore Story,* I, 258).

Hawthorne scholars know that many nineteenth-century readers of *The Marble Faun* considered Hattie Hosmer a possible model for Hilda. Many also thought that Louisa Lander, who had done a bust of Hawthorne and knew the Hawthornes socially, was a model for Miriam.[16] Lander (1826–1923) had gone to Rome in 1855 and had worked as a student assistant in Thomas Crawford's studio. Lander had experienced an uncommonly free lifestyle even for an emancipated woman of the mid–nineteenth century, and her "indiscretions" in Rome had caused "fellow artists" to form a "committee," led by William Wetmore Story, "to reprimand her" for living out of wedlock with "'some man'" and for having "'exposed herself as a model'" in what must have been the nude.[17] On behalf of this self-appointed committee of morality, Story asked Lander to "go before the American minister and swear that the rumors were untrue," which Lander had the good sense and effrontery to refuse to do.[18] Lander had completed the bust of Hawthorne in 1858, before the scandal about her conduct had become a public issue among the colony of American artists in Rome. After her refusal to obey Story's command, she was socially snubbed by that community, including the Hawthornes, who paid for the portrait bust but never picked it up.[19] Gossip transformed her into a figure for all that was scandalous in the new and artistic women in Rome, and even Hosmer distanced herself from her colleague.[20]

T. Walter Herbert has suggested that the Hawthornes' efforts to "disown" Lander's portrait bust of Nathaniel were entangled with their defensive reactions to rumors of Lander's sexual misconduct; the fact that Nathaniel had "posed" for her, perhaps in some state of undress (his bust conventionally represents a portion of his bare upper torso); and the psychic tangle of such libidinal associations in the weirdly repressive atmosphere of nineteenth-century U.S. morality.[21] Lora Romero points out that Hawthorne often responded to the success of popular women writers by criticizing them for offering "an unmediated transcription of their private lives"; in one notable passage, Hawthorne describes Fanny Fern throwing "off the restraints of decency" to "come before the public stark naked."[22] Literal and figurative public "nudity" variously registered nineteenth-century American anxieties regarding sexuality, and these cultural tensions typically reflected contemporary political issues, such as women's rights and abolition.[23]

The accomplished sculptors in Rome were only some of the many nineteenth-century American sculptors, painters, and writers composing the group that the art historian Wayne Craven terms the "second generation" of Americans in Italy, following such neoclassical pioneers as Horatio Greenough, Hiram Powers, and Thomas Crawford.[24] Many of these nineteenth-century expatriates used their neoclassical artistic styles to address the political topics of abolition and women's rights. Hiram Powers's celebrated sculpture *The Greek Slave* (1843), which helped make the nudity of subsequent neoclassical sculptures acceptable to prudish American audiences, contributed to abolitionist politics in antebellum

America, even though Powers's sculpture was actually an allegory of "the heroic struggle of the Greek people to free themselves from their tyrannical masters, the Turks."[25] William Wetmore Story's *Cleopatra* (1858), which "brought Story the greatest international fame in his own time" and which Hawthorne places in Kenyon's studio in *The Marble Faun,* and his *Libyan Sibyl* (1861) both substitute African models and features for the "pure classicism" of Greek feminine figures. In part, Story was simply contributing to the romantic escapism of his age, which drew upon the archaeology done in the "valleys of the Nile, the Tigris and Euphrates, and into the deserts of the Holy Land" to explore civilizations that antedated the Greeks.[26] In part, Story was protesting in his own remote and often misunderstood way the persistence of Southern slavery by mythologizing the roots of nineteenth-century African Americans in his heroic sculptures of legendary African women.[27]

Harriet Hosmer's *African Sibyl* (1868?) is far more politically explicit than either Story's *Cleopatra* or his *Libyan Sibyl.* As Hosmer's biographer, Dolly Sherwood, notes, Hosmer's sculpture "had its genesis in the sixties, with emancipation as its theme." The "black female figure" has a "small Negro boy at her feet," to whom she is "said to be foretelling the freedom of her race."[28] Although Hosmer had been an antiabolitionist as a young woman in the late 1840s and early 1850s, probably influenced by the "moderate Whig philosophy" of the Crows, the family with which she had lived while studying in Saint Louis, Hosmer became a vigorous critic of slavery in the years leading up to the Civil War.[29] James praises Story's sculptures for turning their dynamic qualities into virtual "narratives," in which each sculpture tells a complete story by way of both the figure's pose and its various adornments. In most cases, however, Story's sculptural narratives are judged by James to be conventional evocations of "subjects . . . already consecrated to the imagination—by history, poetry, legend—and . . . offered . . . with all their signs and tokens, their features and enhancements" (*William Wetmore Story,* II, 77). But the stories James reads in Story's mythic and ideal subjects are "frankly and forcibly romantic," concerned with dramatizing and thus realizing ancient legends that "previous generations" of sculptors had treated less successfully as "dim Academic shades" (*William Wetmore Story,* II, 77, 78).

Hosmer's sculptures are often just as narrative in their dynamic qualities, their stories told in ways that are obviously relevant to nineteenth-century political issues. Her *Zenobia in Chains* (1859) is nominally based on the third-century Queen of Palmyra's rebellion against Rome, her capture by Aurelian, and her symbolic humiliation in Rome. In her regal,

Hiram Powers, *The Greek Slave*, 1843

William Wetmore Story, *Libyan Sibyl*, 1861

dignified deportment and the Greek classical lines of her shoulder-to-floor costume, Hosmer's Zenobia is as much a nineteenth-century idealization of mythic woman as Fuller's Juno, Iphigenia, and Antigone in *Woman in the Nineteenth Century*.[30] When on March 15, 1859, Hawthorne visited Hosmer's studio and viewed the clay model for the final sculpture of *Zenobia in Chains*, he was powerfully impressed by Hosmer's "high, heroic ode," especially its ability to represent Zenobia's dignified march through the streets of third-century Rome: "[T]here is something in Zenobia's air that conveys the idea of music, uproar, and a great throng all about her; whilst she walks in the midst of it, self-sustained, and kept in a sort of sanctity by her native pride. The idea of motion is attained with great success; you not only perceive that she is walking, but know at just what tranquil pace she steps, amid the music of the triumph. The drapery is very fine and full; she is decked with ornaments; but the chains of her captivity hang from wrist to wrist; and her deportment—indicating a soul so much above her misfortune, yet not insensible to the weight of it—makes these chains a richer decoration than all her other jewels. . . . [C]ertainly I have seldom been more impressed by a piece of modern sculpture."[31] Although Hawthorne insists in his Preface to *The Marble Faun* that he has not stolen *Zenobia in Chains* from Hosmer, this passage suggests that he has indeed borrowed heavily from the sculpture he so admired not only in his representation of Miriam's independence, mystery, and dignity, but also in the more general ambience of the Roman carnival that becomes the virtual psychic landscape for the moral anarchy Miriam and Donatello's acts have unleashed.

Despite his morally problematic translation of Hosmer's Zenobia into characters and moral issues in *The Marble Faun*, Hawthorne understood quite well the transfiguration Hosmer had intended to express in the defeated and chained Queen of Palmyra, forcibly marched through Rome, who had become Hosmer's occasion to dramatize the nineteenth-century oppression of women. In this sense, her "chains," which loop from wrist to wrist across the graceful drapery of her form and thus add to the dynamism of the sculpture (that is, its representation of Zenobia in motion), had become for Hawthorne "richer decoration than all her other jewels." Interestingly, Hawthorne later returns to just this detail of Hosmer's sculpture in an entry made in a notebook recording his travels, but only after he records his chance meeting with "General Pierce" while walking up the "Via Babuino," recalling both Pierce's patronage of Hawthorne and their old friendship, a strong homosocial bond Hawthorne seems to offer almost as a kind of defense against the undeniable feminine power of Hosmer's Zenobia (*French and Italian Notebooks*, 494). At the very end of the entry for March 15, Hawthorne concludes: "Zenobia's manacles serve as bracelets; a very ingenious and suggestive idea" (*French and Italian Notebooks*, 495).

Harriet Hosmer, *Zenobia in Chains*, 1859

In this afterthought, Hawthorne seems to allude to the "bridal gift" that Miriam leaves on Hilda's table in the final chapter of his romance: "It was a bracelet, evidently of great cost, being composed of seven ancient Etruscan gems, dug out of seven sepulchres, and each one of them the signet of some princely personage. . . . Hilda remembered this precious ornament. It had been Miriam's; and once, with the exuberance of fancy that distinguished her, she had amused herself with telling a mythical and magic legend for each gem, comprising the imaginary adventures and catastrophe of its former wearer. Thus, the Etruscan bracelet became the connecting bond of a series of seven wondrous tales, all of which, as they were dug out of seven sepulchres, were characterized by a sevenfold sepulchral gloom " (*The Marble Faun*, 462). As Arlin Turner points out, "Hawthorne had seen the original of this bracelet worn by Mrs. Story and had described it in his notebook as having the same components and the same history as Miriam's bracelet."[32] In the long history of feminine ornament, jewelry often serves as a valuable fetish for the woman, who herself testifies in her beauty, wealth, or lineage to the husband's authority. Although Miriam's magical bracelet, woven as it is of Christian sevens, ostensibly serves the conventional purpose of the bridal dowry, its subtler function in the symbolic landscape of *The Marble Faun* is the transmission of Miriam's mysterious feminine power to the otherwise "pure" and "innocent" Hilda. That feminine power has been entangled throughout the narrative with a certain pre-Christian, pagan, and even atavistic force that frightens characters like Kenyon and Hilda, as well as their author, Hawthorne. What fascinated Hawthorne in Hosmer's *Zenobia in Chains* is just what casts such a tragic aura over the dramatic action of *The Marble Faun*: it is the threat of the rebellious woman, linked for Hawthorne with the uncontrolled Dionysian power of a pagan world never adequately controlled by early Christianity.

Although James pretends that these faded, old "ghosts" are merely quaint reminders of a vanished age, the erotic terror Hawthorne feared in self-reliant women, especially that "scribbling mob" and those women sculptors in Rome, surfaces in James's recollection of how Story's sculpture of *Cleopatra* is incorporated into Hawthorne's *The Marble Faun*. Noting how "the mysterious Miriam . . . comes, in her sad unrest, to the studio of Kenyon, and makes acquaintance there with the image of a grand seated woman, . . . who is none other than a fine prose transcript of Story's Cleopatra," James quotes Kenyon's recollection of the "source of his vision" in that passage in which Hawthorne wonderfully captures the erotic power of artistic creation: "'I kindled a great fire in my mind and threw in the material . . . and in the midmost heat uprose Cleopatra as you see her'" (*William Wetmore Story*, II, 85–86). James subordinates the sexual, pagan, and decisively African power of Cleopatra to Kenyon's artistic process, terming this "the phenomenon of a recognition, an assimilation," by which the book takes the place of the sculpture and thus Hawthorne's narrative displaces the threatening femininity of the legendary queen. James reads the fictional scene in which Miriam and Kenyon sexually desire each other through the medium of the sculpture as an erotic sublimation, which he interestingly figures as the casting of drapery over a presumably nude sculptural figure: "She saw her, Miriam, as romantically as the artist could have wished, weaving fine fancies about her in the gentle Hawthornesque way; as a result of which, and of the talk, of the scene, of the whole charming context and confusion, the beautiful light mantle of the book, all loose and soft and ample, is thrown over the statue" (*William Wetmore Story*, II, 86).

James's graceful metaphor for Hawthorne's *The Marble Faun* as classical drapery thrown over the nudity of the sculptural form of Story's *Cleopatra*, who in fact reveals only one breast in symbolic anticipation of the asp, suggests that literary narrative sublimates the eroticism more flagrantly displayed in the neoclassical sculpture of the period. Story's poem "Cleopatra" concludes with lines that expose Story's own interpretation of Cleopatra as a link to the primitive sexuality more clearly delineated in ancient rituals and myths than in our sophisticated modern arts. Calling for Antony to return, she appeals to their common animal passions:

> Come, as you came in the desert,
>   Ere we were women and men,
>   When the tiger passions were in us,
>   And love as you loved me then![33]

Stilted as Story's poetic sentiments are, they nonetheless evoke the undifferentiated animal sexuality that James seems intent on controlling with the form of the romance, whether Hawthorne's or his own.

In the main, James is following Hawthorne's lead; Hawthorne praises Story, referring to his *Cleopatra* in particular, for his sensibility to "something deeper . . . than merely to make beautiful nudities and baptize them by classical names" (*French and Italian Notebooks*, 71). Rita Gollin and John Idol conclude that Hawthorne's "offhand remark about 'beautiful nudities' conveys contemptuous disapproval of the commonplace neoclassical works of most of the other expatriate sculptors."[34] Despite his admiration for Hiram Powers as "a great man," Hawthorne nonetheless judges the *Venus de Medici* so superior to the modern Venuses, including "Greek Slaves" and "Eves" by "Gibson or Powers, or a hundred other men who people the world with nudities," as to condemn these poor imitations to be "burnt into quicklime, leaving us only this statue as our image of the beautiful" (*French and Italian Notebooks*, 302).[35]

Of course, James's views at the turn of the century should not be equated with Hawthorne's in the 1850s, even when James appears in *William Wetmore Story* to be repeating and even underscoring Hawthorne's reactions to artworks and artists in Italy. As I argue later in this chapter, James's appropriation of Hawthorne's opinions represents more general changes toward gendered, racial, and sexual politics, including the greater visibility of women and the articulation of homosexuality in the public sphere in James's era.[36] The transformation of women's rights into such specific political movements as suffrage, and the contrary demonization of same-sex relationships in the medical and legal practices of the late nineteenth century, do not mean, however, that the cultural repression of such matters in the earlier part of the century had rendered such sexual politics invisible. Hawthorne's and James's attitudes were different, even when they employed some of the same artworks, artists, and historical locales, but in their mutual interpretations they effectively represented the defenses of middle-class, white males—in this case, two highly intellectual and imaginative ones—against changing social values with regard to race, sex, and gender.

Although James notes Story's love of the "nude, as the artist, in any field, essentially and logically must" and how Story "paid . . . such frank tribute" to it "in marble, in verse, in prose," he devotes particular attention to Story's use of sculptural drapery, connecting it less with the pure technique of the sculptor than with the more general "narrativity" by which Story told the "story" of his sculptural subject, whether nominally nude, partially nude, or fully clothed: "Drapery, that is, folds and dispositions of stuff and applications, intimations of ornament, became a positive and necessary part of his scheme from the moment that scheme was romantic; nothing being more curious than the truth that though the nude may have a dozen other convincing notes it is eminently destitute of *that* one—or possesses it only when conscious, contrasted or opposed" (*William Wetmore Story*, II, 82–83).[37] James's comment is understandable in the context of nineteenth-century views that nudity in sculpture, erotic passion in opera and music, and the representation of sexual themes in literature could be acceptable only when formally contextualized, aesthetically sublimated, and stylistically coded, or in James's term "draped."

In his account of his breakfast meeting with Harriet Hosmer and other artists at the Storys' on May 23, 1858, Hawthorne notes his suggestion to Hosmer "for the design of a fountain,—a lady bursting into tears, water gushing from a thousand pores, in literal translation of the phrase; and to call the statue Niobe, all Tears," in which the very "beautiful drapery about the figure" would be composed of her tears or, in strictly technical terms, the water of the fountain, at once suggestively revealing the feminine figure and yet hiding it with the very bodily fluids by which Niobe's loss of her children is eternally expressed (*French and Italian Notebooks*, 217–18). Hawthorne's weirdly defensive design anticipates James's concern that the sculptural narrative, either in Hawthorne's *The Marble Faun* or in Story's somewhat gimmicky allegorical sculptures, would "drape" the otherwise flagrant sexuality and erotic power manifest in neoclassical sculpture and more generally in the changing roles of women and racial minorities in the latter half of the nineteenth century.

In his interpretation of Hawthorne's *The Marble Faun* in *William Wetmore Story*, James understands Hawthorne's attempt to sublimate and control the libidinal energy represented by Miriam, because James shares Hawthorne's anxieties about the new feminine authority in culture and politics. Hawthorne's romance is, among many other marvelous and interesting effects, a cathartic narrative, in which all that Donatello and Miriam represent may be entertained imaginatively for the sake of a ritual literary purgation that allows Hawthorne and the ideal reader to affirm the conventional division of gender represented by Kenyon and Hilda, as well as to assign each of these happy, Protestant characters the domestic duties of love and reproduction and the public responsibilities of cultural representation. In Kenyon's *Cleopatra* and Hilda's copy of Guido Reni's *Beatrice Cenci*, the dangerous eroticism, revolutionary politics, and pre-Christian atavism of Donatello and Miriam may be expressed and controlled, much in the manner in which Nietzsche understood the Apollinian powers of Platonic philosophy to have rationalized the Dionysian energies of pre-Attic Greek ritual and the subsequent Greek tragedy in which such religion assumed social forms.[38]

The curiously triangulated relationship in *The Marble Faun* among Donatello, Miriam, and the mysterious Capuchin emissary or stalker, whom Donatello will hurl from the Tarpeian Rock in nearly mystic accord with Miriam's suggestive glance, purports that these fears encompass far more than instabilities in conventional nineteenth-century relations of masculinity and femininity.[39] Donatello and the Model are more like *Doppelgänger* for Miriam than sexual partners or antagonists; much as Hawthorne tries to convince the naïve reader to believe that Donatello and Miriam are merely conventional lovers, their relationship suggests a deeper compatibility or spiritual complementarity. The unnaturalness of each character seems to be that he or she is androgynous: Donatello is too "faunlike" to be only a man, and Miriam is too mysteriously powerful to be merely a woman. The unstable gender roles of Donatello and Miriam, as well as the intriguing ambiguity of their romantic relationship, are part of the supernatural aura of *The Marble Faun*. It is an atmosphere that reflects nineteenth-century anxieties about sexuality that were prompted in part by destabilizations of conventional gender hierarchies.

Scott Derrick has argued that in *The Scarlet Letter* "Dimmesdale's dislocation from a conventional relation to a stabilizing and idealized femininity produces a mobility of desire in his relations to other men," notably to Roger Chillingworth.[40] In an analogous sense, Miriam's mysterious triangular relationship with the Model and Donatello represents Hawthorne's sense that emancipated women have disrupted, if not disfigured, the conventional gender relations socially authorized in marriage and the family. The consequences of such gender destabilizations include the surfacing of a threatening homoeroticism that conventional modes of homosociality cannot control. In this latter regard, Kenyon's and Donatello's incomplete friendship, qualified as it is by their sometimes conflicting sexual desires for Miriam and even at times for each other, is a good example from Hawthorne's romance. Hawthorne feminized a threatening homoeroticism, in ways compatible with the antebellum U.S. repression of homosexuality that resurfaced in disguised ways in the public conflicts regarding women's rights. As I argue later, James relied on gender differences as occasions for entertaining same-sex desires and struggles. James was no less defensive about gender and sexual questions than Hawthorne, but James's attitudes were more typical of late nineteenth-century cultural attitudes.

That Hawthorne should have imagined *The Marble Faun* in its title, Roman settings, and major themes according to metaphors of sculpture should not surprise us when we consider that nineteenth-century neoclassical sculpture achieved notoriety for its sculptures not only of nude women but also of men. What historians of American sculpture consider the "breakthrough" of Hiram Powers's *Greek Slave* in terms of using female nudity to express a serious theme, such as slavery, in a classical style led to a wide range of nude or partially draped male and female figures that are profoundly erotic, even while legitimated for public viewing by their allusions to classical forms and their treatment of serious topics. For many nineteenth-century sculptors, like Powers, the justification for their technically brilliant celebrations of the nude body included their religious convictions that "they were in a position to improve upon the art of the ancient Greeks because their contemporary art was not an art of heathen idolatry but one imbued with Christian virtues and morality."[41]

The celebration of the nude classical figure led to a host of nineteenth-century sculptures of fauns, satyrs, shepherds, and young rustics, some based on classical myths and others generalized according to classical originals viewed in Rome, Florence, and Athens. Among the sculptures Hawthorne mentions in his preface and transports in the romance to Kenyon's studio is Benjamin Paul Akers's (1825–61) *The Dead Pearl Diver* (1858), which depicts a nude young man, draped only about his loins with his pearl-divers' net, arched on his back upon a rock, his head tilted backward, eyes closed, his arms beneath his head and thighs apart, with feet crossed. Art historians attribute the great celebrity of this sculpture to the way it gives the viewer "that strange pleasure of indulging in a languishing contemplation of death."[42] This is just how Miriam views Akers's sculpture in "A Sculptor's Studio" (chapter 13 of the romance), where it has become Kenyon's work.[43] Obviously foreshadowing the fates of Miriam and Donatello, allegorizing their doom rather than the death of the Model, the statue of the pearl diver represents a body that even outside Hawthorne's romance is distinctly androgynous. Miriam complains to Kenyon that "'physically, the form has not settled itself into sufficient repose,'" and this criticism represents the discomfort, albeit a titillating one, of viewing a nude male form whose sculptural dynamism combines the death throe and sexual desire, the troubling conjunction of thanatos and eros (*The Marble Faun,* 117).

I commented earlier on Henry James's admiration of William Wetmore Story's use of both sculptural drapery and narrativity to cover the nudity that otherwise disturbed him in neoclassical sculptures. Hawthorne used a similar technique in *The Marble Faun,* introducing a celebrated neoclassical sculpture into his narrative in order to control the vagrant sexuality represented by Miriam and Donatello. The "death" of Akers's pearl diver and the tragic death of the Model in the romance are displacements of the sexual ambiguities these figures represented in nineteenth-century culture. There is something false, after all, in James's appeal to Story's use of sculptural *parerga* to tell his romantic story, because a nude form, like that of Powers's *Greek Slave,* whose chains do not hide the beauty of her body, readily communicates a story of abjection and servitude.

On several levels, James's admiration for Story's sculptures seems

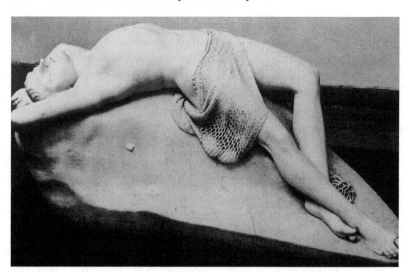

Benjamin Paul Akers, *The Dead Pearl Diver,* 1858

forced. He lacks enthusiasm for Story as a biographical subject, whose career as a dabbler in several arts typified all that James struggled in his own work to avoid.[44] James claims in *William Wetmore Story and His Friends* that Story was simply "non-narratable," a subject whose story cannot be successfully told, but then leaves the reader in some doubt about what this means. At times, James suggests hopefully that Story was a "renaissance" man, whose many talents were beyond the biographer's limited talents. More often, James hints at Story's inadequacies, as when he concludes that Story's "preference" for "the figure for which accessories were of the essence" was "doubtless a proof . . . that he was not with the last intensity a sculptor" (*William Wetmore Story,* II, 83). James probably has in mind here sculptures like Story's *Medea* (1864), whose thoughtful pose is balanced by the dagger she grips in her right hand as a somewhat gimmicky comment on just what she is planning. Yet the moment James has passed this negative judgment, he hastens to claim that Story's literary interests were "active diversions" that prove not so much that "he failed to grasp the plastic, but much rather that he saw it everywhere" (*William Wetmore Story,* II, 84). In his ambivalent account of Story and his reputation as a sculptor, James ends up using Story to pursue his own aesthetic interest in the ways prose fiction should employ narrative to "drape" its subjects. By identifying Story's limitations as a storyteller in stone, James can then offer to supplement Story's deficiencies with his own writing.[45]

William Wetmore Story, *Medea*, 1864

What Story had accomplished unevenly or diffidently, James claims in 1903 to have achieved with the highest rhetorical skill. Thus even as James gently satirizes Story for his sculptural "accessories" and "drapery," he translates the narrative devices of sculpture into the finer narrative means of prose fiction. And what James claims in *William Wetmore Story* to prize in the subtler qualities of literary narrative is its ability to disguise, transform, and complicate what otherwise is the merely exposed, "nude" subject. This may appear merely to be James's graceful way of talking about the subtleties of his version of literary realism, in which the mere crudity of the actual literary subject—naïve realism—is replaced by that embroidered tapestry of social relations, in which a more complex reality is represented. Nevertheless, it is remarkable how often the nominal topic of James's fiction revolves around specific issues of sexuality, ranging from the courtship, marriage, and adultery plots of so many of his novels to the narratives of psychological development from child to adult, in which the former issues of explicit sexuality are also involved. In his early short fiction, strongly influenced by Hawthorne's romantic themes, James's narrativization of sexual themes is particularly evident, perhaps because he had not yet mastered the rhetorical means of disguising these underlying concerns. The early stories of the late 1860s and early 1870s are also notable for their explicit treatments of homoerotic and heterosexual themes and plots, reflecting his own unstable sexuality in his early adulthood. In "Swept Away," I concluded my historical recovery of James's efforts to control the threatening feminine identity of Margaret Fuller by interpreting "The Last of the Valerii" as a story in which the power of the New Woman, rhetorically connected with heroic Greek women, virtually "feminizes" Count Valerio, the protagonist, who must surrender to his wife's command that they rebury the unearthed sculpture of Juno if he is to preserve his masculinity and save his marriage.

In "The Last of the Valerii," homoeroticism is suggested in the switching of gender roles between Count Valerio and his stony Juno, who assumes a phallic authority over him, even down to the fetish of her hand that he will secretly preserve after the statue is safely reburied.[46] In "Adina," published in *Scribner's Monthly* in 1874, only a few months after "The Last of the Valerii," homoerotic imagery and intersubjective relations structure the plot and dramatic action. In this respect, "Adina" far more closely resembles the homoerotic focus of "A Light Man" (1869) than "The Last of the Valerii," although the latter story more obviously shares the Italian setting and religious theme of Catholicism versus Protestantism found in "Adina." Set in Rome, the surrounding *campagna*, and the Alban Hills,

"Adina" tells the story of how the cynical and very modern Sam Scrope tricks a young Italian peasant, Angelo Beati, out of a priceless Roman intaglio Angelo has unearthed in the countryside. Out of revenge, Angelo woos and marries Scrope's fiancée, the innocent Adina Waddington, and the defeated and disgusted Scrope tosses the intaglio into the Tiber.[47] Narrated by Scrope's unnamed friend, the story follows a familiar romantic triangle with certain vaguely Gothic effects that James borrows from Hawthorne.

The triangular relationship in the story operates primarily among the three male characters, Sam Scrope, the narrator, and Angelo Beati. Adina Waddington is a mere plot device, hardly a character: "She was short and slight and blonde, and her black dress gave a sort of infantine bloom to her fairness. She wore her auburn hair twisted into a thousand fantastic braids, like a coiffure in a Renaissance drawing, and she looked out at you from grave blue eyes, in which, behind a cold shyness, there seemed to lurk a tremulous promise to be franker when she knew you better."[48] The narrator notes that "her pretty name of Adina seemed to me to have somehow a mystic fitness to her personality" ("Adina," 359), but he never glosses the meaning of the name. A variant of Edna, "Adina" derives from a Hebrew word meaning "full of menstrual fluid," and more generally "rejuvenation." It is the answer God gives Sarah, Abraham's wife, when she asks how she can still be fertile at more than one hundred years old, when she learns that she is pregnant with Isaac.[49]

Another more contemporary allusion found in the name "Adina" is to the heroine of Gaetano Donizetti's *L'Elisir d'Amore*, the romantic opera in which Adina (the soprano) is the wealthy owner of a country estate, where she falls in love with the young peasant Nemorino (the tenor). The "elixir of love" is the cheap Bordeaux wine sold to Nemorino by the quack doctor Dulcamara (the bass), but this is a mere operatic device to work out themes of conflict between country and city, peasantry and gentry, man and woman.[50] Both the Old Testament's Sarah and Donizetti's and Romani's Adina suggest far more feminine power than James's Adina Waddington initially displays, although they identify her with a noble cultural genealogy. In James's narrative, the erotic power this typically Victorian woman-child will display later in the narrative is the result of the phallic sexuality unleashed in the text by the conflict between Sam Scrope and Angelo Beati for the priceless intaglio.

The Roman topaz intaglio is a fetish representing the psychosexual authority over which Sam and Angelo fight and whose struggle the narrator tries precariously and unsuccessfully to mediate. Angelo accidentally

unearths this ancient intaglio in a scene so charged with erotic significance as hardly to require interpretation:

> He had observed in a solitary ilex-tree, of great age, the traces of a recent
> lightning strike. . . . The tree had been shivered and killed, and the earth
> turned up at its foot. The bolt, burying itself, had dug a deep, straight
> hole, in which one might have planted a stake. "I don't know why," said
> our friend, "but as I stood looking at it, I thrust the muzzle of my old gun
> into the aperture. It descended for some distance and stopped with a
> strange noise, as if it were striking a metallic surface. I rammed it up and
> down and heard the same noise. . . . I . . . dug, and scraped and scratched;
> and, in twenty minutes, fished up a little, rotten, iron box. It was so rotten
> that the lid and sides were as thin as letter-paper. When I gave them a
> knock, they crumbled. . . . In the middle lay this stone, embedded in earth
> and mould. There was nothing else. I broke the box to pieces and kept the
> stone. *Ecco!*" ("Adina," 353)

This scene of excavation, like the unearthing of the figure of Juno in "The
Last of the Valerii," is full of references to Hawthorne; perhaps none of
the possible allusions is more important than the episode in chapter 46,
"A Walk on the Campagna," in *The Marble Faun*, where Kenyon, waiting
to meet Miriam and Donatello at the ruins of a suburban Roman villa,
casually uncovers a Greek sculpture of Venus that Hawthorne declares
superior to the Venus de Medici or the Venus de Milo, a "sculpture in
which we recognize Womanhood, and that, moreover, without prejudice
to its divinity" (*The Marble Faun*, 424).[51]

It is not ideal Womanhood, however, that is excavated in James's story,
but instead masculine sexuality and power. Although the intaglio remains encrusted with earth and mold, in ways evocative of the scatologi-
cal motifs of its discovery, Angelo declares that it is the priceless gem
"Julius Caesar had worn . . . in his crown" ("Adina," 353).[52] Trivializing
Angelo's claims, Scrope tosses ten *scudi* on the ground and canters away
with the intaglio in hand before Angelo can accept or reject the offer.
Back in Rome, Sam takes the stone to his chamber and employs "the best
methods of cleansing, polishing, and restoring" it while keeping its existence a secret and swearing the narrator to secrecy. The language James
uses in this episode is also profoundly erotic: Scrope goes about "whis-
tling and humming odd scraps of song, like a lover freshly accepted," and
the narrator imagines himself and Scrope riding away from Angelo "like
a pair of ravishers in a German ballad" ("Adina," 356).[53]

Angelo's Christian name appears to be used as merely an obvious way to underscore the religious subplot of the story, in which modern New England Protestant values struggle with Italian Catholic values in James's youthfully schematic treatment of two religions that we know are far more complex and historically intertwined. Angelo was also one of the given names of Giovanni Angelo Ossoli, Margaret Fuller's husband, the object of both Hawthorne's and Henry James's criticism of Fuller for falling "victim to lust." The Marquis Ossoli was hardly a rustic Italian peasant, but Hawthorne took note of "Ossoli's extraordinary good looks and his lack of intellect," both of which are crucial to the characterization of Angelo Beati in James's "Adina."[54] James's Angelo seeks revenge on Scrope, going to Rome dressed in an urban suit that crudely but effectively helps sophisticate him and enables him to challenge the American. Indeed, by the end of the narrative, Angelo and Adina have moved to a Roman apartment, completing the Hawthornelike emplotment of action from the country to the city.

James introduces Angelo in the pose of one of the many fauns, satyrs, and classical shepherds that had provided such erotically charged subjects for nineteenth-century neoclassical sculptors: "We came upon a figure asleep on the grass. A young man lay there, all unconscious, with his head upon a pile of weed-smothered stones. A rusty gun lay on the ground beside him, and an empty game-bag, lying near it. . . . One of his legs was flung over the other; one of his arms was thrust back under his head, and the other resting loosely on the grass; his head drooped backward, and exposed a strong, young throat; his hat was pulled over his eyes, so that we could see nothing but his mouth and chin" ("Adina," 350). James had seen his own version of this Hawthornesque pastoral figure on one of the many horseback rides he had taken on the Roman *campagna* in the spring of 1873, usually in the company of American women such as Sarah Wister, Mrs. Charles Sumner, and Lizzie Boott.[55] In his 1873 essay "Roman Rides," later collected in *Italian Hours* (1909), James describes his chance view of "a shepherd" who "had thrown himself down under one of the trees in the very attitude of Meliboeus," the shepherd who had found and raised the abandoned baby Oedipus and who typifies the rustic displaced from his pastoral home. "He had been washing his feet . . . and had found it pleasant afterwards to roll his short breeches well up on his thighs. Lying thus in the shade, on his elbow, with his naked legs stretched out on the turf and his soft peaked hat over his long hair crushed back like the veritable bonnet of Arcady, he . . . little fancied that he was a symbol of old-world meanings to new-world eyes."[56] Both of James's Italian rustics suggest an easy, familiar, and innocent sexuality that James would associate throughout his career with the charm and appeal of Italy.

But it is hardly this sort of innocent sensuality that Sam Scrope reveals at long last as a consequence of his secret rubbing and polishing of the topaz intaglio he has stolen from Angelo Beati. The narrator tells us that in his enthusiasm, Scrope "made his way into" the narrator's "room," long "after I had gone to bed," and "shook me out of my slumbers as if the house were on fire" to reveal the secret of the intaglio:

> In the centre was a full-length naked figure, which I supposed at first to be a pagan deity. Then I saw the orb of sovereignty in one outstretched hand, the chiselled imperial sceptre in the other, and the laurel-crown on the low-browed head. All round the face of the stone, near the edges, ran a chain of carven figures—warriors, and horses, and chariots, and young men and women interlaced in elaborate confusion. Over the head of the image, within this concave frieze, stood the inscription:
> DIVUS TIBERIUS CÆSAR TOTIUS ORBIS IMPERATOR.
> . . . It was in every way a gem among gems, a priceless treasure. ("Adina," 356–57)

At first glance, Scrope's "discovery" of a large topaz intaglio of "superb" ancient workmanship and representing the Emperor Tiberius, or Tiberius Claudius Nero Caesar (born 42 BCE, died 37 CE, reigned 14–37 CE), appears to be merely a romantic device in James's story to mark the boundary between the pagan and Christian eras, because Tiberius was the reigning Roman emperor when Christ was crucified in Judaea (29 CE). Like Shelley's fictional Ozymandias (1818), Tiberius testifies to the vanity of man's imperial and divine aspirations. Viewed from the Christian era, from which vantage point it is clear that the muck of history must be scraped from his image, Tiberius's deification ("divus") by the Romans and his claim to be "Emperor of the entire earth" ("totius orbis imperator") are mocked by the scattered ruins of ancient Rome visited by nineteenth-century American tourists. Like "The Last of the Valerii" and "At Isella," "Adina" criticizes the Americans who invaded Italy in the last half of the nineteenth century and commodified classical civilization. In *William Wetmore Story and His Friends*, James recalls that he was one of the select company in Rome "during the winter of 1873–1874," listening to Story read "so richly and forcibly" his tragedy *Nero*, but it is clear that James considers Story's experiment in neoclassical drama even more forced and artificial than some of his sculptures (*William Wetmore Story*, II, 254).[57]

The details James adds to the "splendid golden topaz," such as Tiberius's "naked figure" and "young men and women interlaced in elaborate confusion" seem at first merely to reflect conventions of nineteenth-century neoclassical sculpture. For example, in fulfilling his congressional commission to do a colossal state sculpture of George Washington (1841), Horatio Greenough delivered a marble sculpture of Washington that was 11.33 feet (3.45 meters) high and was seated, seminude, in the pose of the Greek god Zeus, holding his right hand up, with the index finger pointing heavenward, as he extends a sheathed sword with his left hand, as if to suggest the swift punishment that violation of his divine authority will bring. Contemporary with Powers's *Greek Slave*, Greenough's *George Washington* was roundly ridiculed for its reference to despotic and pagan authority. Draped from the waist down, part of his royal toga tossed over his upraised right arm, Washington appears especially absurd because his nude upper torso is so obviously intended to evoke the classical convention of physical power as a symbol of divine authority.

James's narrator is careful to point out, however, that the intaglio represents Tiberius as "a full-length naked figure," which leads him to mistake the figure at first for "a pagan deity" ("Adina," 356). Swerving from neoclassical artistic conventions to psychosexual commentary, James develops Sam Scrope's interpretation of the gem and its symbolic figure: "'I've annulled the centuries—I've resuscitated a *totius orbis imperator.* Do you conceive, do you apprehend, does your heart thump against your ribs? . . . This is where Caesar wore it, dull modern—here, on his breast, near the shoulder, framed in chiselled gold, circled about with pearls as big as plums, clasping together the two sides of his gold-stiffened mantle. It was the agraffe of the imperial purple.' . . . and he took up the splendid jewel, and held it against my breast" ("Adina," 357). Mock heroic and ironic as the modern Scrope is in this histrionic scene, James nonetheless condenses in it a number of more serious moments from Hawthorne's fiction, including the secret homoerotic scenes between Dimmesdale and Chillingworth in *The Scarlet Letter* and the numerous hypotyposes of sculpture in *The Marble Faun,* including such central events as Kenyon's display of the marble hand of Hilda to Miriam and his excavation of the suburban Venus in the ruins of the Roman villa.

The intaglio also departs significantly from, almost reverses, the hieratic marble forms of neoclassical sculpture. The design of an intaglio is cut into the stone, produced by concave surfaces rather than by the convexity of the sculptural shape. And the intaglio is small, necessitating the close examination that differs so markedly from the distant view required to

Horatio Greenough, *George Washington*, 1841

take in a large sculpture to full effect. In his *Italian Notebooks,* Hawthorne comments on the different perspective required to examine gems; the contrast he makes is between his viewing of the Venus de Medici in the Uffizi and a visit to the "gem-room" in the Florentine gallery: "I next went . . . to the Uffizi, . . . where the Venus di Medici [sic] deigned to reveal herself rather more satisfactorily than at my last visit. . . . The contents of the gem-room especially require to be looked at separately in order to convince one's self of their minute magnificences. . . . Greater [larger] things can be reasonably well appreciated with a less scrupulous though broader attention; but in order to estimate the brilliancy of the diamond eyes of a little agate bust, for instance, you have to screw your mind down to them and nothing else. . . . You must sharpen your faculties of observation to a point, and touch the object exactly on the right spot, or you do not appreciate it at all" (*French and Italian Notebooks,* 404). James suggests a similar phenomenology in the intricate and microcosmic design of the intaglio in "Adina," even at the risk of his reader's recognizing the technical absurdity of his claim that Tiberius's nudity might be represented in an intaglio's engraved surface in any way in which we might perceive it. The intaglio represents, then, the reverse of sculptural form, yet it incorporates precisely the "nudity" to which James would object thirty years later in his discussion of "the draped and the nude" in neoclassical sculptures (*William Wetmore Story,* II, 83).

In part II of "Adina," James develops Scrope's engagement to Adina Waddington, Angelo's vengeance against Scrope in wooing and marrying her, and his apparent conversion of her to Roman Catholicism, in a Gothic gesture that must have made many of James's New England readers shudder in horror.[58] James does not directly represent Angelo's efforts to change Adina's affections, leaving such scenes to the imagination of the reader in a manner reminiscent of Hawthorne's and thereby reinforcing the secrecy through which Angelo counters the trick Scrope has played upon him.[59] It helps, of course, that Angelo is physically beautiful, whereas Scrope is said to be "very ugly the poor fellow" ("Adina," 349). Yet what really appears to drive Adina into Angelo's arms is Scrope's proposal that his fiancée accept the intaglio as a wedding present and then "'wear it one of these days as a medallion,'" which she finds impossible, given her religious convictions: "'The stone is beautiful, but I should feel most uncomfortable in carrying the Emperor Tiberius so near my heart. Wasn't he one of the bad Emperors—one of the worst? It is almost a pollution to have a thing that *he* looked at and touched coming to one in such direct descent'" ("Adina," 367).

Modern historians have largely discounted legends of Tiberius's cruelty, blaming his ill-chosen praetorian prefects, Sejanus and Macro, for despotism, while the legends of his licentious lifestyle have been totally discredited. In the Victorian imagination, however, the emperor who ruled when Christ was crucified typified the social and personal decadence identifiable with the "decline" of the Roman Empire. Where an innocent young woman should wear some Christian emblem, such as a cross, Scrope cynically proposes to pin this sign not only of pagan despotism but also of his ownership of this "blonde angel of New England origin" ("Adina," 367). The narrator tries to dissuade Scrope from his plan by arguing that such a "massive medallion" might be worn as "a necklace," but only by "a splendid, dusky beauty, with the brow of a Roman Empress, and *the shoulders of an antique statue*" ("Adina," 361, emphasis mine). "A fair, slender girl," like Adina, would "feel as if it were pulling her down to the ground, and giving her a mysterious pain" (361). Hawthorne's themes of sin, a fall, and redemption are here charged with the erotic conflict of Adina's being subjected to a fetish of phallic power that will cause her "mysterious pain."

Unquestionably, the topaz intaglio is a fetish representing Adina, another instance of the familiar commodification of nineteenth-century women whereby masculine desire takes the place of the woman herself. The conventional fetishism supporting patriarchal hierarchy in this period is further complicated by the narrator's sense that this priceless gem is "appropriate" only for a pagan "lady," whose "dusky beauty" recalls Miriam's mystery and the curious entanglement of threatening femininity with racial otherness in the nineteenth century, insofar as the intaglio also incorporates the homoerotic bond between Scrope and the narrator: "'Down on your knees, barbarian, we're in a tremendous presence! Haven't I worked all these days and nights, with my little rags and files, to some purpose? I've annulled the centuries—I've resuscitated a *totis orbis imperator*. . . . [D]oes your heart thump against your ribs?'" ("Adina," 357).

Adina abandons her stepmother and affianced, Sam Scrope. Angelo whisks her away to an apartment in Rome, where the narrator visits the couple to determine if they are truly happy, only to learn the customary Jamesian lesson that there is little way to distinguish between Angelo's love for Adina and his love for his triumph over Scrope. Meeting Scrope in Rome, the narrator accompanies him onto the "bridge of St. Angelo," leading in one direction to the Castel Sant'Angelo, the gloomy prison of Beatrice Cenci. There, midway across the bridge, in a symbolic action too neat and conventional for the art James would later achieve, Scrope tosses the "curse," that "golden gem, with its cruel emblems," into the Tiber, from whence so many ancient treasures were excavated from the Renaissance to our own century ("Adina," 382). Standing together in ritual secrecy, Sam Scrope and the narrator achieve a bond that entangles homosocial authority with homoerotic desire: "Then he drew a small velvet case from his pocket, opened it, and let something shine in the moonlight. It was the beautiful, the imperial, the baleful topaz. He looked at me and I knew what his look meant. It made my heart beat, but I did not say—no!" ("Adina," 382). Of course, the antecedence is strategically ambiguous, anticipating more important and complex moments of moral and erotic undecidability in James's fiction, such as the moment when the reader wonders just what Miles sees in his final moments in the arms and over the shoulder of his governess in *The Turn of the Screw*. Whether it is the aesthetic beauty of that intaglio, the phallic power of its naked central figure, Tiberius, or Scrope's significant "look," what makes the narrator's "heart beat" and what he does not refuse is also a splendid amalgam of a passion affirmed and repressed: "I did not say—no!"

James's responses to Story's sculptural works and Hawthorne's Italian fiction reveal his cultural forebears' anxieties about the instabilities of sexuality and gender occasioned by the nineteenth-century women's rights movement and the achievements of independent women such as Hosmer, Lander, and Hawthorne's Miriam. Aligning himself in 1903 with the defensive and culturally conservative postures of Hawthorne and Story, even as he tries to push both of these predecessors into a distant past for the sake of his own cultural identity, James nevertheless affirms those values in ways that manifest their arbitrariness and historical specificity to the patriarchal traditions from which he himself attempted to depart in his literary career. In the course of registering his own defensiveness regarding "the white marmorean flock" of women sculptors in Rome, the titillating nudity of neoclassical sculptural figures, and the libidinal threats of androgynous characters like Hawthorne's Donatello and Miriam, James reveals his homoerotic desires and lack of interest in merely "decorative" or "conventional" feminine characters like Adina Waddington or Martha Valerio—those "angels in the house" produced by the Protestant American imaginary. In response to this frightening but exciting homoerotic passion, James would learn to project his literary identity in a variety of ways, notably into strong feminine characters that shared his own literary and imaginative powers. Ironically, such feminine characters, like Isabel Archer, Olive Chancellor, Miriam Rooth, Maisie Farange, Kate Croy, Milly Theale, and Charlotte Stant, would display many of the best qualities of Hawthorne's Miriam and of her historical models, Hattie Hosmer and Louisa Lander. Nonetheless, James's imaginary women would also require his literary forms for their completion, thereby constituting an aesthetic identification of author and character that would enable James to sublimate a forbidden homoeroticism.

Whether or not James was a product, perhaps the inevitable issue, of the sexual repressions resulting from the strict gender divisions of his forebears' New England culture, as Scott Derrick argues, or whether he merely tapped into homosexual passions that were an untraceable part of his sexual identity as a writer and a man, I shall not attempt to decide.[60] Even when Hawthorne and James were discussing the same artists and artworks, the differences of their cultural eras are eminently clear despite James's indebtedness to his real and cultural fathers. The anxiety of Hawthorne was clearly fixed on the feminine and on the dislocations of bourgeois masculinity it threatened. For James the conflict among homosocial, homosexual, and heterosexual relations was far more evident in early fiction like "Adina" and was aestheticized and thereby psychosexually defended in later work, like *William Wetmore Story and His Friends.* There are several conclusions to be drawn from these interesting observations about the always fascinating, ever surprising influence of Hawthorne on Henry James. The first conclusion is that this specific influence, itself so powerfully inscribed in the subsequent American literary imaginary, has much to tell us about changing sexual, gender, and racial relations in nineteenth- and early twentieth-century U.S. culture. Second, we need more sophisticated theories and practical interpretations of how the arts contribute to cultural repression and such related effects as commodification and fetishism. Finally, the extent to which Henry James's sexual desires—homoerotic, homosexual, ascetic, homosocial, onanistic, and heterosexual—contributed to the productive tensions that shaped his literary, autobiographical, critical, and historical narratives is worthy of study for what it teaches us about changing cultural values. Our scholarly interest in James's sexuality is not, as some have recently argued, merely a projection of the tendencies of our hypersexualized era—a "sexualization of everything," as one critic wearily complains—onto James's early twentieth century, but instead an effort to comprehend the sexual behaviors and values so crucial to modernity.[61]

6.

Modern Art and the Invention of Postmodern Capital

The contact and habit of Tlön have disintegrated this world. Enchanted by its rigor, humanity forgets over and again that it is a rigor of chess masters, not of angels. Already the schools have been invaded by the (conjectural) "primitive language" of Tlön; already the teaching of its harmonious history (filled with moving episodes) has wiped out the one which governed in my childhood; already a fictitious past occupies in our memories the place of another, a past of which we know nothing with certainty—not even that it is false.

—Jorge Luis Borges, "Tlön, Uqbar, Orbis Tertius," trans. James E. Irby

Modernism can no longer be discussed apart from postmodernism. The perplexing relations between the two terms have occupied a central place in critical and theoretical discussions of the humanities for the past three decades. Until recently, however, the majority of the literary discussions centered on the experimental writers of the 1960s and early 1970s in North America, Latin America, and western Europe and the degree to which they derived from or superseded their modernist heritages. The French sociologist Jean Baudrillard and philosopher Jean-François Lyotard have posed the question What Is Postmodernism? in socioeconomic terms, in which literary experimentalism is simply one form of production among others. Baudrillard's early works, such as *The Mirror of Production* and *For a Critique of the Political Economy of the Sign,* and Lyotard's *The Postmodern Condition* focus on an economy based on sign systems—information, fashion, service, advertising, entertainment—that govern material forms of production.[1] Just how art and literature function in a postindustrial economy centrally dedicated to the production and reproduction of signs remains an important and unresolved question for both Baudrillard and Lyotard. It is quite certain in the writings of both theorists, however, that aesthetic function can no longer be understood apart from production and marketing unless that very difference—between "high art" and mass culture, for example—is part of ideological work. Baudrillard's and Lyotard's discussions of a postmodern economy merely focus a certain tendency that has been seen in what has been loosely termed "poststructuralist" theory in the humanities and social sciences. The relation between relatively technical literary and philosophical issues and socioeconomics has been accomplished in large part thanks to Althusser, Foucault, and Derrida, each of whom has attempted to rethink the relation between abstract and material productions according to the controlling grammar of a particular cultural situation. Although poststructuralists have been criticized for essentializing certain characteristics of the sign—Derrida's *différance*, Lyotard's *differend*, and Foucault's archive, for example—poststructuralism has remained profoundly historical in its efforts to understand the peculiar rhetoric of contemporary Western cultures. Even as their historical subjects vary widely—Derrida's ontotheological tradition of Western philosophy, Althusser's Marx, and Foucault's Enlightenment reason—these poststructuralists are always writing about the history that informs our postmodern society. It is within this historical matrix of poststructuralist theory, then, that I will interpret the troubled relation of modern art to the emergence of a postmodern economy.

I will attempt to describe the current situation by way of an exaggerated structural formulation of the relation of modernism to postmodernism. In the late industrial and late colonial cultures of the West that we have come to call "modern," literary and artistic movements have been characterized by their postmodern desires: quite simply, the guiding motivation for the artist is to exceed the boundaries and limitations of modern society and its discursive conventions. The modern artist stakes his or her claim by insisting upon the figural and connotative variety of literary style. By contrast, the "language of the marketplace" is simply denotative and suppresses figural play for the sake of useful, literal meanings whose references to things and concepts are established by consensus.

In a postmodern culture, the discursive relation of art to culture is significantly different; for the purposes of my rather schematic model, I shall contend that it perfectly inverts the modern situation. Postmodern, postindustrial societies in the West are characterized by an economy concerned with the production of representations. We commonly speak of the new "information" and "service" economies, but these two terms come from the rhetoric of an older industrial economy that insists upon defining products as things. When we speak of representations as products, we are referring more obviously to the effects of certain processes, in the same way that we understand a representation (re-presentation) as always already the figuration of something that existed prior to it or outside its discursive field. In a postmodern culture, the representation is always already a representation of a representation, like the light on this computer screen that represents the hermeneutic and linguistic representations that belong to scholarly discourse. A postmodern economy accepts this condition for production—that which is produced reveals its derivation from some accepted pretext—and makes no effort to disguise or to naturalize the artificial qualities and conditions of its product. Whereas industrial capitalism struggled to give some natural credibility to its products and the conditions of their manufacture, a postmodern economy accepts the utterly fictive origins of human information. Under these conditions, then, everything that belongs to social reality is always already understood to be highly figurative, both charged with its local significance and informed by its more general derivations.

Thus we should not be surprised that contemporary television advertising is extremely self-conscious about its own medium. A 1986 advertisement for an Isuzu automobile stresses the simplicity of its product, in explicit contrast with the conventionally exaggerated claims of television ads for automobiles. A 1980s advertisement for Coors Beer starring Mark Harmon, former quarterback for UCLA and star of a contemporary prime-time soap opera, *Saint Elsewhere,* was organized in several related narrative parts, in the manner of a soap opera, while openly playing on the convention of the football star as a natural, "no-frills" human being. Both ads are fundamentally intertextual; both are extremely self-conscious about their forms and media. Neither advertisement expresses any anxiety or even irony regarding this situation, even though irony may be used as a technical device, as it is in the Isuzu commercial. The intertextuality of language and the highly figurative scene of representation are accepted as conditions of postmodern life, of an economy in which representation is the proper product. In this cultural situation, the claim that there is some sharp distinction between literary and ordinary language—such as that made by the high moderns—seems simply old-fashioned, anachronistic.

The easy and rapid adaptation of mass culture to the conditions of this postmodern economy has not always been matched by high-cultural artists, especially the heirs of the modernist tradition. From the late 1970s through the middle of the 1980s, there was an identifiable reactionary turn to the views of some nominally postmodern artists and many critics who were alarmed by the postmodern cultural inclination I have described. The anxious reaction to which I refer antedates and is in no obvious way identifiable with the right-wing politics of such culture war veterans as William Bennett, Lynne Cheney, and Dinesh D'Souza. In fact, virtually all of the artists and critics I have in mind staunchly distanced themselves from conservative politics and elsewhere attacked the policies of the Reagan and (George H.) Bush administrations. John Gardner's *On Moral Fiction* (1978) was first greeted as an attack directed primarily at the "surfictionists" of the 1960s and 1970s, among whom he himself had at one time been counted. Gerald Graff's *Literature against Itself* (1979), John Aldridge's *The American Novel and the Way We Live Now* (1983), and Charles Newman's *The Postmodern Aura: The Act of Fiction in an Age of Inflation* (1985) are similarly directed at the bankruptcy of countercultural artistic experiments and the superficiality of a postmodern literary aesthetic.[2] Each of these critics, despite radically different theoretical and political postures (from Aldridge's liberal humanism to Newman's Marxism), suspects that the decline of distinct literary values may be the result of a postmodern economy whose dizzying rhetorical performances outstrip the most energetic efforts of conventional literary representation or criticism. In sum, each of these critics of postmodern experimentalism confirms Philip Roth's famous contention in 1961 that "the American writer in the middle of the twentieth century has his hands full in trying to understand, and then describe, and then make *credible* much of the American reality. . . . The actuality is continually outdoing our talents, and the culture tosses up figures almost daily that are the envy of any novelist."[3] Graff and Newman in particular attack the superficiality of the experimentalists' claims regarding the essential fictionality of reality, in part because what had been a bold claim on the part of moderns as diverse as Kafka and Henry James, Proust and Gertrude Stein, Pound and Stevens had become the condition for a postmodern economy and its social reality.

These critics were not just isolated or idiosyncratic reactionaries; their respective cries for a literature that would revive the critical edge and subversive claims of great literature from the past were often joined in this period by artists, like John Gardner, whose works had often been identified with the postmodern avant-garde. What was celebrated by many in the 1970s as "metafiction" swerved for some scholars and writers from the modernists' celebration of literature's fictionality and figurality to a certain self-consciousness regarding the culture's artistic capabilities. Thus the "neorealism" of Raymond Carver could be considered metafictional, in the sense that it offers its own minimal realism as an alternative to a social reality that Geoffrey Hartman some time ago characterized as a world of "superfetated [sic] meanings," of "excess signification," a world in which the dizzying vertigo of the postmodern novel has become the condition of everyday reality.[4] In Gabriel García Márquez's *Autumn of the Patriarch,* the arts by which a brutal dictator maintains his precarious rule and those by which the narrative voice operates are nearly impossible to distinguish. By the same token, the psychic fabulation of the woman in D. M. Thomas's *The White Hotel* is disentangled by a psychotherapeutic narrative that finally reveals the origin of her neurotic fantasy in one episode of the Holocaust at Babi Yar. More obviously, John Irving's *The World according to Garp* incorporates Garp's metafictional stories within another metafictional frame—Irving's own narrative—that seems intent upon exposing the dangers of such fabulation and returning Garp to everything that his act of fiction making had helped endanger: bourgeois individualism, the family, interpersonal relations, an apolitical realism.[5] The novels, stories, and theoretical writings of William Gass, often celebrated in the 1970s in conjunction with the surfictionists, achieved new fashion in the 1980s because their claims regarding a discrete and coherent fictional world—a world realized in the precise and formal language games of the author—are properly understood as alternatives to the groundless and irrational textuality of postmodern reality.[6]

From neorealism to self-conscious metafiction, nominally postmodern literature often claimed to be a curious alternative to postmodern reality. Of course, the cultural anxiety regarding the postmodern condition I have described in the previous paragraphs is by no means the only or even the prevailing response to that condition. Yet this particular reaction is interestingly symptomatic of a more widespread literary and artistic return to modernist cultural and aesthetic values, often under the banner of postmodern avant-gardism, in which literal and stable meaning is given particular centrality. Viewed in this way, certain aspects of aesthetic postmodernism may be understood as the lingering effects of high modernism, now pushed into a cultural situation in which the utopian project of modern art has been perversely realized. As a consequence of this changed and constantly changing cultural situation (an economy of ceaseless change, in Marx's worst nightmare of capitalism run wild), the literary experimentalists seem to have been unexpectedly caught by an "imitative fallacy" occasioned by a new historical situation.

I have somewhat reductively described the relations of art to modern and postmodern societies in terms of a rhetorical chiasmus, which I offer in the place of any more decisive demarcation of the boundary separating modern and postmodern aesthetics:

> The modern age's literature and art are postmodern;
> The postmodern age's literature and art are modern.

Such a model suggests, of course, that the changed relations of literature to the dominant culture are primarily the effects of historical transformations occasioned by changes in the economic conditions. In what follows, I will argue that such transformations are indeed dialectical and that the artist's avant-garde and utopian claims for creative work produced in the modern age helped effect the transformation of an industrial economy into a postmodern, postindustrial economy of representation. The same reading experience that gives us the uncanny sense that literary experimentalists of the 1960s and early 1970s merely imitated postmodern reality—an experience that has prompted some to react against such postmodern "realism"—applies as well to the polemical utopianism of the high moderns.

I cannot hope to offer in this chapter some far-ranging analysis of the ways that the high modernists tangibly contributed to the realization of a culture in which the figural qualities of experience, the play of competing subjectivities, the necessary stylization of art and fashion have become the common assumptions. So I shall simply speculate about the ways in which certain utopian impulses in Henry James and Ezra Pound helped give credibility to discursive strategies initially intended to question only the apparent "naturalness" of modern social reality. Yet what made possible even the literary claim for such avant-garde discourse was a particular desire for transformation that informed the late age of industrialism and colonialism that we call modern culture. In short, the modern literary avant-garde, so well represented in its beginnings by Henry James and in its heyday by Ezra Pound, was one manifestation of the ideological transformation from a modern material economy to a postmodern economy of immaterial representations. My argument fundamentally depends on Fredric Jameson's theory of modernism, which served as the prelude to his subsequent analysis of postmodernism in *Postmodernism, or The*

Cultural Logic of Late Capitalism (1991) and in his earlier *Fables of Aggression: Wyndham Lewis, The Modernist as Fascist* (1979) and *The Political Unconscious: Narrative as a Socially Symbolic Act* (1981).[7]

For Jameson, Henry James quite clearly figures the swerve into aestheticism occasioned by the exhaustion of nineteenth-century realism, which was produced by ideological contradictions that were so evident by the end of the nineteenth century as to frustrate the traditional legitimating functions of the realistic novelist. We should note here that James and Ezra Pound serve not only Jameson's general conception of modernism, but that each also represents a particular theoretical discourse that finds at least one of its respective origins in modernism. Pound, together with Joyce, represents for Jameson the aesthetic "mythography" that we associate with the archetypal criticism of Northrop Frye. Henry James quite explicitly serves in Jameson's narrative as the prototype for the literary formalism drafted by T. S. Eliot and codified by the Anglo-American New Critics.

Jameson believes that Henry James typifies the literary response to the crisis of the philosophical subject occasioned by the history of capitalism's alienation of the individual. Capitalism lays special claim to the individual subject as the figure capable of affirming, expressing, and reproducing itself in and through a capitalist economy. This may well be the fundamental irony of capitalism and is in fact the great artistic achievement of capitalism; capitalism turns into a philosophical origin and end the very individual that capitalist economic practices seem intent upon destroying. By now, the solution to this apparent paradox is familiar enough. Alienating workers from the coherent processes and products of their own labor power, capitalism invents a philosophical and idealist category of the subject that defines itself just insofar as it can distinguish itself from its material circumstances. This idealist subject, ceaselessly struggling to liberate itself from the wear and tear of time and the servitude of labor, finds its proper expression in the abstract discourse of philosophy. A bourgeois transcoding of the aristocrat's "natural rights" to property and rule, the subject has its own history of idealist legitimation, whereby certain disciplines and processes are necessarily separated from the conditions of everyday labor.

In Jameson's view, Henry James valorizes point of view as a technical device, precisely because he imagines the form of the novel to be not only homologous with but constitutive of an aesthetic consciousness, the very center of fictional relations, that would be the best alternative to the alienating forces of modern industrial societies. The "central consciousness" in

James is at once the protagonist (around whom the "ado" of consciousness is organized), the dispersed author (always effaced in order to achieve metonymic realization through character and reader), and the implied reader: "In James, . . . the reader (or Implied Author) is in a position to hold private or monadic experience together with an external moral perspective in the unity of a single act of consciousness. Jamesian irony, therefore, unlike the judgments [Wyndham] Lewis' narratives sometimes seem to project, unites point of view with ethical evaluation in an immanent way."[8] Within nineteenth-century bourgeois culture, self-consciousness and the capability of representing that self became indispensable tokens of literary authority and its rights to rule.

The Jamesian drama of consciousness is for Jameson a key to the ideological function of the metaliterary themes that are so dominant in James's fiction, especially in his later, modernist works. What Jameson terms "the ideal of theatrical representation" is James's valorization of the constitutive activity of consciousness once it has been freed from some illusion of empiricism—from the "reality-principle" that haunts James's characters, especially in their efforts to enter the ruling social order and to understand its codes. James's "scenic art" then effectively transforms the narrativity of the novel, with its traditional emphasis on history and temporality, into the theatricality made available to the spectatorial consciousness, which receives literary representation as if from the privileged vantage of the theatergoer—at once inside and outside the dramatic action. Jameson is thinking here of the essentially theatrical quality of nineteenth-century English and U.S. societies, in which the class contradictions were made to *appear* coherent and structurally unified by way of those social arts that would assign individuals their proper roles within the drama.

In this view, then, the battle of the Jamesian "fine conscience" with the illegitimate authorities of the bourgeoisie became James's own means of compensating for a vanished aristocracy with a new, artistic aristocracy. By the same token, the hereditary, even genetically encoded, right to rule claimed by the landed aristocracy was then claimed by those initiates into the "religion" of consciousness, whose inheritance was the literary and intellectual tradition so relentlessly erased in the gray wash of the modern and the dehumanizing experiences of the masses. In exposing "false consciousness," generally that of the bourgeoisie (Maud Manningham in *The Wings of the Dove*, for example), or the impotence of a deposed aristocracy (Lord Mark in *Wings of the Dove* or Prince Casamassima in *The Princess*

Casamassima), James emphasized the imitative and derivative qualities of his bourgeois characters.

By failing to express themselves, by imitating the practices of a bankrupt aristocracy, James's bourgeois characters show themselves to be slavish followers, bad artists, and inadvertent reactionaries. Rather than representing their age in some exemplary way, they refuse to aggressively assert their own unique power. Thus Adam Verver in *The Golden Bowl* appears to us not as the aggressive industrialist who acquired such a fortune, but as an aesthete striving to build in American City some simulacrum of that monument to aristocratic patronage: the European museum. By the same token, Christopher Newman in *The American,* for all his deliberate Americanisms, uses all his democratic charms in the interests of social climbing. Always trivializing his actual accomplishments as a capitalist, Newman typifies nothing so much as the cynical shape shifting of the bourgeois entrepreneur; his innocence is a deliberate strategy of protean adaptation. For similar reasons, the vulgar product manufactured by the Newsomes in *The Ambassadors* is never mentioned, not so much because James considers it crassly material but because the Newsomes do. Thus Mrs. Newsome's patronage of Strether's literary journal, her desire for Chad to be "cultivated" and well married are the signs of a bourgeois leadership that refuses its own authority for the sake of some imitation of aristocratic pretensions. In his own reading, of course, James identifies just these contradictions as central to bourgeois ideology, thus offering some of the most cogent and sophisticated criticism of capitalism that we have had in modern literature.

The ideological subtext that governed James's formal and technical practices is thus clear enough. Capitalist alienation caused the self-conscious writer to imagine an alternative space, wherein he staged precisely those forces that had driven him out of the world, into fiction. Rather than seeing this corner as a space of merely powerless stylization, the "impressionistic" novelist reified his own technical strategies, such that they themselves became the fetishes of an artistic identity that compensates for the social corruptions revealed in the narrative. The entire act of the Jamesian novel, then, is quite traditionally a coming to self-consciousness, but only of the means and techniques by which such self-consciousness has been thematized.

What such aestheticism accomplishes, against its own better judgment, of course, is the reinstatement of that individualism dreamt of by bourgeois ideology. And the Jamesian novel does this work precisely by distinguishing between masters and servants, between those capable of equating being with doing and those who merely labor for others—for some alien, external social authority. In his novels James mercilessly attacks the provincialism of closed societies, made up of those who substitute their understanding of social conventions for true knowledge, but Jameson argues that James's own aesthetic morality substitutes such ideals as intersubjectivity and observational knowledge for subjective agency in social, economic, and political domains. Together with the New Critics spawned by this Jamesian formalism, Jameson includes other psychological realists, such as the neo-Freudians, who would offer their own psychic equivalents to the literary self-consciousness of the Jamesian novel: "Jamesian point of view, which comes into being as a protest and a defense against reification, ends up furnishing a powerful ideological instrument in the perpetuation of an increasingly subjectivized and psychologized world, a world whose social vision is one of a thoroughgoing relativity of monads in coexistence and whose *ethos* is irony and neo-Freudian projection theory and adaptation-to-reality therapy. This is the context in which the remarkable transformation of Henry James from a minor nineteenth-century man of letters into the greatest American novelist of the 1950s may best be appreciated."[9]

What distinguishes James's artistic consciousness, the authorial self, from the bourgeoisie's slavish imitation of aristocratic identity is the artist's acceptance of the utterly fictive bases for any such authority. Unlike English law and capitalist economics, the Jamesian novel never naturalizes the process of human consciousness. Henry James is extraordinarily consistent in his dissociation of artistic form from anything faintly resembling nature. Even in his most realist pronouncements, James insists only upon the relation of art to experience, life, or reality: "Humanity is immense and reality has myriad forms; the most one can affirm is that some of the flowers of fiction have the odour of it, and others have not; as for telling you in advance how your nosegay should be composed, that is another affair."[10] Even the "flowers of fiction" mock any naïve correspondence of art to nature; already "composed" in a "nosegay," they have grown out of the "myriad forms" of humanity and its different realities. The complexity of social reality and its history for James reminds us of the compositional forms that expose both as elaborate contrivances, fictions of human construction, albeit with very tangible consequences.

The artist's appeal for the reader to recognize the fictive origins of social reality is a common motive and aesthetic rationale for many moderns. Insofar as industrial capitalism repeated the efforts of the landed

aristocracy to naturalize social reality, it not only mystified the real relation of men and women to their social conditions of existence; it also
undermined its own legitimacy by imitating the rhetoric of an older
order—one that it had attempted to supersede. Artistic identity and authority, then, offered an alternative to this social repetition compulsion,
and throughout modern literature and thought we find a persistent distinction between good fictions and bad fictions: the former reveal their
own terms of representation and most often expose the disguises by
which the latter assume some natural or conventional status. The modern writer thus established a kind of literary world between the real and
the fictive, the natural and the artificial, in which fiction could claim its
own formal reality.

This modernist "antiterra" offers some very tangible utopian prospects,
most of them written into the aesthetic imperatives of reading and writing
the modernist text. The implied reader of a James novel is thus committed to recognize the fictive bases of social reality, at least as such society is
represented in the James novel. Such a recognition—recognition scenes of
this sort are common structural moments in James's fiction—promises a
certain liberation from the constraints of ordinary experience.[11] In the
first place, this recognition (or self-consciousness) encourages character
and reader to question the self-sufficiency of the present and to explore
the historical (social and personal) forces conditioning any apparently
current event or action. That such a history is, in fact, a history of representations, of fictions, is in no way surprising, given the terms by which
such a consciousness of history is made available. It is no step at all to the
common modernist conclusion that history itself is nothing but a series
of complexly interrelated texts that are individually and collectively calling for their interpretation. As I suggested in chapter 5, such a fictional
history is by no means superficial but is often thickly rendered both to respond to complex historical circumstances and to emphasize how the aesthetic function also has historical agency.

Thus the literary author's capability to work with texts and to write
and know by way of the wayward rhetoric of this textual situation gives
such an author a special credibility in the modern age—a credibility that
this same author often claims has political relevance. The historical self-
consciousness offered by literature exposes the fictions of discrete historical periods, nationalities, and canonical traditions (in the arts and
other disciplines), as well as social conventions of gender, class, and working relations. The modernist's will to expose such fictionality involves an

appeal to counter-traditions, "foreign" cultures, and transnational issues. James's "international theme," for example, is not just an occasion for literary drama; it typifies the modernist's general effort to unveil the fiction of nationality by way of a strategic, literary cosmopolitanism.

The high moderns sought a particular kind of aesthetic internationalism, which was prompted in part by their various quests for literary traditions other than those that often had helped shape the nationalism of their countries of origin. The rallying cry "Make it new" had a repeated undertone: "Look elsewhere." A "world elsewhere" is the figure by which the aestheticism and formalism of the moderns has been variously celebrated and condemned, but this repudiation of American and European nationalism often worked perversely to recover its most contradictory political values.[12]

In the writing of Ezra Pound, such internationalism is carried to an extreme unmatched by any other modern, insofar as it is offered both as a political utopia and as a poetic theory. The historical and cultural hubris of Pound's poetry exceeds the most sublime madness of any previous epic poet, because Pound's poetic promises to be the mythic foundation for a new culture that will encompass all the different cultures and periods in recorded human history. The utopian culture of the *Cantos* is global and multicultural only according to the first recognition of modernism: the fictionality and thus textuality of history. James worked to achieve this recognition for his characters and his implied readers; in fact, James's art is often nothing but this recognition. Pound, however, began with this modernist assumption, elaborating in complex ways the kind of postmodern utopia implied by such knowledge.

Even in his early poetry, Pound interprets nature in terms that are always informed by poetic or social conventions. Nature may be the place of seasonal change and renewal employed in the haiku and tanka, the referent for the Chinese ideogram, the mythic space of Greek classicism, the ordered cosmos of Western medievalism, the resources misused by capitalist usury, and the like. Students of Pound are often confused by his apparent appeal to some "natural ground," especially in his adaptation of Fenollosa's theory of the Chinese written character or his earlier theory of the poetic Image, because Pound seems to vacillate between a naïve poetic realism and the symbolists' conception of an artificial nature, a contrived, fabricated space constituted by poetic discourse. From the early poems of *Personae* to the final *Cantos*, however, Pound remains true to the idea that nature is the effect of a certain textuality. In "'Blandula, Tenulla, Vagula,'" he writes:

> Will not our cult be founded on the waves,
> Clear sapphire, cobalt, cyanine,
> On triune azures, the impalpable
> Mirrors unstill of the eternal change?[13]

And he virtually answers this question in Canto CXVI:

> But the record
>   the palimpsest—
> a little light
>   in great darkness—
> cuniculi—
> An old "crank" dead in Virginia.[14]

The "palimpsest" of history as textuality produces its own internal "light"; its own natural "illumination" shines only through the "underground passages" or "mine shafts" *(cuniculi)* cut through history by Pound's poetic practice, his strategic intertextuality. History itself is always already the natural ground, but it appears chaotic without the organization or illumination of poetic form. As it cuts passages, finds resemblances, and contrives certain influences, poetry claims to make history visible. Pound repeatedly metaphorizes his poetry as a form of energy that regathers actions scattered through history into the energetic nodes or clusters of the image, ideogram, or strong personality. Pound poetically gathers the limbs of Osiris or, as in the preceding passage from the *Cantos,* revives the political authority of Thomas Jefferson, who otherwise is simply "an old 'crank' dead in Virginia."

The modern author is thus not simply an anatomist of social fictionality but a masterful manipulator of such textuality. The very fact that Pound can and does move the texts of history into new and unexpected contexts, thereby violating conventional boundaries, testifies to their figural and fictional qualities. At some level, intolerant readers of Pound are quite right: there is a sense of purely virtuoso performance in the *Cantos.* But beyond that sheer performance, that shameless display of learning, Pound builds a monument of his own to those authors who engage history by learning to read and use the figurative, connotative potential of otherwise denotative texts and historical records. The hero of the *Cantos* is an amalgamated character who draws upon the virtues of Homer, Confucius, Malatesta, Dante, Adams, Jefferson, Mussolini, and Pound himself, among many other so-called thrones, to claim some sociopolitical authority for poetry and art.

Pound's thrones serve as vortices that draw together into characters (or ideograms) the force of transnational, transindividual, and ultimately transhistorical ideals of literature.[15] Pound's throne is similar to the "strong personality" Jameson interprets as central to Wyndham Lewis's writings: "The ideal of the 'strong personality'—too complex to be resumed under the current term of 'elitism'—is in fact the central organizational category of Lewis' mature ideology, and the primary 'value' from which are generated all those more provocative, yet structurally derivative ideological motifs and obsessions of racism and sexism, the attack on the Youth Cult, the disgust with parliamentary democracy, the satiric aesthetic of Otherness, the violent polemic and moral stance of the didactic works, the momentary infatuation with Nazism as well as the implacable repudiation of Marxism."[16] Insofar as this "negative" determination of the strong personality or the throne is self-conscious, as I think it must be understood to be when applied to the Pound of the *Cantos,* it is conceived as the "negation of negation," the effective cancellation of an ideological ressentiment that has marginalized artistic representation. In this regard, the archetype of Pound's throne is the satirist.

But as Jameson makes clear in his treatment of Nietzschean ressentiment in Lewis, the identification of such ressentiment as the "weakness" of contemporary culture is possible only by virtue of the artist's own ressentiment—his own reaction to the time, change, and becoming that have resulted in his contradictory situation. Pound's thrones, which have for so many critics the virtue of providing some means of understanding the productive logic of the language machine of the *Cantos,* end up miming the very will to authorial power they were designed to supplant. *Thrones de los cantares* (1959), specifically 96–109, focus on *philology,* as Hugh Kenner argues in *The Pound Era.*[17] The cast of characters gathered under the category of thrones constitutes Pound's peculiar etymology of the qualities of the effective leader; each is explicitly a product of a certain textual history, even Pound's contemporaries, such as Douglas and Mussolini. And each of Pound's figures metaphorized as a throne may be said to incorporate the diversity, divergence, and contradictoriness of human language and its history in an intertextuality that represents the higher reality of Pound's poetic epic and its utopian social aims.

The throne or strong personality derives his (he is decidedly a patriarchal figure for Pound) authority from his recognition of a world of dizzying textuality and his willingness to accept his social responsibility to find some channel or passage to action amid these prior interpretations. Whatever limited freedom he may claim comes from just this knowledge that the essential figurality of language makes any social representation manipulable, adaptable to some new purpose. Unlike the antihero of modern fiction or Pound's own poetic double, Hugh Selwyn Mauberley, the throne claims his right to rule on the basis of his awareness that the textual condition demands decisive action:

> JEFFERSON was guyed as a doctrinaire. It is difficult to see what doctrine covers his "Embargo" unless it be the doctrine that when an unforeseen emergency arises one should try to understand it and meet it.
>
> The truth is that Jefferson used verbal formulations as tools. He was not afflicted by fixations. Neither he nor Mussolini has been really interested in governmental machinery. That is not paradox, they have both invented it and used it, but they have both been more deeply interested in something else.[18]

In the *Cantos*, Jefferson is frequently characterized as a master of language, a *bricoleur* capable of patching together a solution to a present problem from the rhetoric of the past. What distinguishes such leadership—what Pound elsewhere terms the "right reason" of Mussolini—from mad obsession and tyranny is its reliance on a certain critical function that carves a passage or channel for action within the welter of different interpretations: "The DUCE sits in Rome calling five hundred bluffs (or thereabouts) every morning. Some bright lad might present him to our glorious fatherland under the title of MUSSOLINI DEBUNKER" (*Jefferson and/or Mussolini*, 35). In the immediately following paragraphs, Pound answers the criticism that his poetry is derivative: "An acute critic tells me I shall never learn to write for the public because I insist on citing other books. How the deuce is one to avoid it? Several ideas occurred to humanity before I bought a portable typewriter. De Gourmont wrote a good deal about breaking up clichés, both verbal and rhythmic. There is possibly some trick of handing out Confucius, Frobenius, Fenollosa, Gourmont, Dante, etc., as if the bright lad on the platform had done all of their jobs for himself, with the express aim of delighting his public" (*Jefferson and/or Mussolini*, 35). This is not just free association; Pound links Mussolini as debunker with his own poetic practice and with the shortlist of literary and scholarly thrones to whom he here pays allegiance.

What justifies this manipulation of history's language is, of course, the use to which such rhetoric is put, and poetic use is always contrasted with the "usury" and ownership of capital:

> Ownership? Use? there is a difference.
> The temple is not for sale.
>
> (Canto XCVII, 678)

The only "currency" that promises use rather than a system of exchange that encourages accumulation is language. The "temple" in whatever cultural figuration—from the Greek temple to Malatesta's *tempio* to the Confucian body—is always already a poetic temple, an altar to language. The "throne" in the "temple" is thus the figure legitimating the proper use of language, and this throne figures proper use as both critical and decisive in the same gesture that allows the strong personality to make laws—that is, to respond to local circumstances by adapting the language of history. The linguistic constructs of Pound's thrones hold out the promise of some poetic economy and discipline that might avoid the sheer usury of historical drift and waste: the mere accumulation of historical surpluses. Thus the energetics or synergy of Pound's poetry in the *Cantos* is offered quite literally as an alternative to the waste, dispersion, and fragmentation of the various material economies that culminated in Western industrialism and its "monetary system." The poetry claims to produce what more material manufacture has failed to yield: culture and its principles of order.

With extraordinary prescience, it would appear, Pound anticipates the postmodern economy by way of the textual cosmos of the *Cantos*. It is remarkable how often Pound identifies his thrones with a coming age whose economy will be based on the production of culture and its representation, thereby superseding the material economies of industrial capitalism. His criticism of Marx, when it is not just crankily directed at what Pound judges to be Marx's economic naïveté, concerns Marx's fixation on purely industrial economies:

> The fascist revolution was FOR the preservation of certain liberties and FOR the maintenance of a certain level of culture, certain standards of living, it was NOT a refusal to come down to a level of riches or poverty, but a refusal to surrender certain immaterial prerogatives, a refusal to surrender a great slice of the cultural heritage.
>
> The "cultural heritage" as fountain of value in Douglas' economics is in process of superseding labour as the fountain of values, which it WAS in the time of Marx, or at any rate was in overwhelming proportion. (*Jefferson and/or Mussolini*, 127)

For Pound, Mussolini's Italian fascism "is the first revolution occurring simultaneously with the change in material bases of life" (*Jefferson and/or Mussolini*, 127). The "immaterial prerogatives" of the "cultural heritage" are quite obviously what Pound's critical reading of history offers us in the *Cantos*. His identification with thrones whose authority is at once poetic and political, rhetorical and legal, prefigures more than just his desperate desire to claim some power for the artist in an age that increasingly has little use for artistic and mythic wisdom. Pound's poetic throne fabricates a certain identity and authority that will become well suited to lead the postmodern age and its economies. Power is for such a figure an effect of rhetoric, but not simply an act of rhetorical performance. It includes the critical capacity to turn the language of the past, the language of history, to certain contemporary purposes, and for that work the postmodern leader must operate critically, creating "passages" in such history that will lead, however tortuously, to his situation. In this way, the author, understanding himself to be nothing but a potential effect of language, positions himself so that such language will speak him into being.

In a purely reflectionist theory, Pound's *Cantos* express well the historical disorder, the "sea-wrack," generated by the fragmenting and alienating forces of modern European industrial society. From the standpoint of Jameson's "ideology of form," Pound's *Cantos*, like Lewis's futurist experiments in the novel and prose satire, deconstruct the traditionally legitimating functions of the aristocratic epic or the realistic novel.[19] Yet what this modern epic has deconstructed is not ideology, but merely literature's presumed independence from ideology, thus revealing the secret reason for art's secondary, derivative status. Under the circumstances, Pound vainly struggles to invent his own ideology—a precarious balance of political, historical, artistic, psychological, and hermeneutical forces. As sublimely absurd as it is for me to claim that an author invents his own ideology, it is nonetheless a vainglory characteristic of modernism at its limit: that point at which it recognizes that its own experimentation is already anticipated by, even necessitated by, historical currents.

Pound's cosmopolitanism, unlike Henry James's or Wyndham Lewis's, already carries within its cultivated voice the echo of its daemonic double: the communication of the Western tradition to every corner of the globe by force of words or arms; the insistence that its chaos might be redeemed by "two gross of broken statues, / For a few thousand battered books," as Pound himself parodies this cultural colonialism in *Hugh Selwyn Mauberley*.[20] With the breakup of the European colonial empires, nation-states faced a legitimation crisis that required something like a paradigm shift from the material rhetoric of industrialism and colonialism to the immaterial rhetoric of postmodernism. As Jean-François Lyotard has argued, postmodernism involves the delegitimation of those grand narratives of emancipation and education that had propped up the modernization process, including industrialism and the Enlightenment rationality behind its technological innovations (*The Postmodern Condition*, 37–38). The very different uses to which Pound puts the traditional epics, ranging from the *Odyssey* and Greek mythology to Jeffersonian republicanism, in the *Cantos* help delegitimize them. By taking cultural expressions out of their material, historical contexts, the moderns transformed such narratives into abstract, ahistorical verbal assemblages that could be used to create a poetic space, a world elsewhere, for poetic authority with no necessary obligation to the historical networks from which these stories had been borrowed. Even those most critical of modernist literary theory and practice have found the self-conscious allusions of the modern poet harmless enough, mere signs of the poet's defensive bid for power in an increasingly scientific age. Therefore, modern literature could be condemned for its vainglory, for its actual impotence, for its nostalgia, and for its sad withdrawal from the exigencies of a changing world. The utopian dream of Pound's *Cantos* was decidedly not realized by Mussolini's fascism; instead, it was paradoxically achieved by precisely those "sensitive kindly professors who have never affirmed anything in their lives, who are possibly too cultured to make an affirmation, or too polite to risk stating an opinion that might jostle their colloquitor" (*Jefferson and/or Mussolini*, 59). Indeed, with a certain self-contempt, we might recognize the cosmopolitan dream of Pound's poetics not in some social utopia but in the academic reality of the international conference, the exchange of scholarly papers, and the community of scholars sustained by such difficult modernist writings as the *Cantos*.

However, there is another side to this story, which unfortunately does not redeem the scholarship in part spawned by the herculean and protean literature of high moderns like Henry James and Ezra Pound. The apparent anarchy of competing discourses, none of which makes any pretense of representing a material reality, has become one of the distinguishing characteristics of postmodern culture. The shift from industrial to postindustrial society is being accomplished by the change from material to immaterial products. Such a basic economic change offers a perverse solution to what classical Marxists judged the ineluctable problem of capitalism: the alienation of labor power from itself, the consequent commodity fetishism, and the ultimate class struggle that it was thought such internal divisions would occasion. Once the object of labor shifts from a concrete product to an immaterial one, such as information or service, alienation must be redefined. In industrial economies, capitalist rhetoric may be designed primarily to mask the real sources of alienation, thus generating competing discourses, such as philosophy and psychoanalysis, which stake their respective claims to understanding the causes of individual alienation—causes that are always figured as prior to or beyond the actual economic conditions. Nevertheless, such mystification not only can be exposed but will inevitably reveal itself as such as the worker continues to work at his problem. In postindustrial economies, however, there is no conflict between referent and representation, precisely because social value is governed by representation. The product is the process, and every worker apparently has access to what is produced according to his or her level of competency in the technologies involved. The machine is neither glorified nor anthropomorphized; it is nothing but an instrument that serves the operator according to his relative mastery of its rules. James's valorization of "experience" as "the very atmosphere of the mind"—that is, as a purely mental category that depends upon intellectual capabilities—is effectively realized in postmodern culture. Postindustrial societies thus can relegitimate class distinctions by elaborating the elementary distinction between those who can *use* the information produced and those who cannot. The myth of the information revolution is that such information becomes potentially accessible to everyone and that the privatization of life occasioned by and historically intensified by nineteenth-century capitalism may well vanish as the media for multiple forms of communication (from the telephone to the computer modem and the Internet) become affordable enough to be integral parts of individuals' domestic as well as commercial economies. By the same token, the very division between domestic and public spaces, between the family and job, promises to disappear as the same technology that makes it possible for individuals to work at home is employed to perform basic domestic chores.

I need hardly argue how insidious are these claims to informational egalitarianism; each of us knows in his or her own way that this apparent and promising unification of all those social practices that were alienated from each other under industrial capitalism—domestic from commercial life, labor power from its product, the individual from social governance and authority, and so on—are merely redistributed in some new myth of information that promises democracy while maintaining the old class distinctions or recasting class (and other social) divisions in even more invidious ways. As Lyotard cogently argues, the apparent egalitarianism of the new information age merely disguises the hierarchical relations best served by the new technologies: "No money, no proof— and that means no verification of statements and no truth. The games of scientific language become the games of the rich, in which whoever is wealthiest has the best chance of being right. An equation between wealth, efficiency, and truth is thus established" (*The Postmodern Condition*, 45).

Lyotard offers *paralogy* as an alternative to the efficiency criteria currently employed to judge scientific knowledge: "It is necessary to posit the existence of a power that destabilizes the capacity for explanation, manifested in the promulgation of new norms for understanding or, if one prefers, in a proposal to establish new rules circumscribing a new field of research for the language of science" (*The Postmodern Condition*, 61). Lyotard's solution is, in fact, a reversion from within postmodern culture to modernist literary values. His new science might resist the equation of truth, efficiency, and capital (or rather their synonymity) by approximating the alternative rhetoric of artistic, figurative expression. Indeed, in keeping with his fundamental Kantianism, Lyotard relates *paralogy*, the *differend*, and other strategies for what poststructuralists have termed heterogeneity and dissemination to "the quintessential form of imaginative invention" and that which characteristically deconstructs consensus as a criterion for knowledge (*The Postmodern Condition*, 60). His utopian alternative would rely on something like a strategic "dissensus," which itself would be the standard for measuring the *use* of knowledge. Every claim for knowledge would be tested by the competing claims it provoked and by the previously "unthought" that it would help bring into the culture's cognitive field. This paralogical method of thinking accords well, of course, with Lyotard's well-known definition of the postmodern as "the presentation of the unpresentable," and it resembles nothing so well as modern art's effort to maximize its signifying potential (*The Postmodern Condition*, 78). Thus the claims for "connotative richness," "plurisignification," "infinite interpretation," and "dissemination" that are so often made for the works of high modern art have been translated into the predicates of Lyotard's oppositional postmodernity.

What Lyotard ignores is the degree to which modern art and aesthetics paved the way for the postmodern cultural situation of our current information age. James's self-conscious author/reader and Pound's throne prefigured more than just the competent scholar; they prefigured the promoter, advertising executive, television or film producer, software engineer, web designer, and dot-com entrepreneur, each of whom must assess the marketability of his or her product in terms of its ability to situate itself in relation to competitive products. When those products are understood to be representations, the task of marketing becomes equivalent to the avant-garde artist's problem of discovering some voice or style. The normal function of this immaterial economy, in short, is the production of that which will appear to be new, even as postmodern culture acknowledges that pure novelty, utter originality, is impossible. What is marketable as new is some recontextualized version of the old, achieved by means of a critical reading of what has lost its figurative freshness. In brief, the "retro" phenomenon of postmodernity is not simply a passing fashion, but integral to the mode of production. In modernist culture, the artist distinguished his work from that of mass culture by insisting that the latter was composed of nothing but clichés, mere conventions that had become unreflective or purely instrumental. In postmodern culture, desirability depends upon endless novelty, the repeated critique of clichés, and the recycling of old stories in new contexts. The boundary between the domains of high and mass culture is constantly transgressed.

For Lyotard, the solution to what he terms "technocratic terrorism," by which he means the reinstatement of the old industrial class system according to the new criterion of performative efficiency, is "differential or imaginative or paralogical activity" that would measure efficiency and performance according to the production of new "ideas, in other words, new statements" (*The Postmodern Condition*, 65). As Jameson points out in his foreword to Lyotard's *The Postmodern Condition*, this appeal to a poststructuralist mode of disseminative knowledge merely reproduces one of the guiding assumptions of industrial capitalism: "The dynamic of perpetual change is, as Marx showed in the *Manifesto*, not some alien rhythm within capital—a rhythm specific to those noninstrumental activities that are art and science—but rather is the very 'permanent revolution' of capitalist production itself: at which point the exhilaration with such revolutionary dynamism is a feature of the bonus of pleasure and the reward of the social reproduction of the system itself" (*The Postmodern Condition*, xx). Jameson's argument seems confirmed by the fact that our postmodern economies have merely intensified and renewed the basic philosophical aims of capitalism. Whereas James and Pound might have envisaged something beyond industrial capitalism, such as James's utopia of artistic sensibility or Pound's dystopia of fascism, the West's postindustrial economies of information, service, and representation have enabled capitalism to transform itself from a system of material production to one of immaterial development and distribution. By refiguring the authority of such production from the natural (or divine) rights of the aristocrat and the rational ingenuity of the capitalist to the rhetorical competency (literacy) of the modern artist, modern writers like James and Pound helped transform the contradictions of modern culture (late industrialism and colonialism) into the productive resources of a postmodern economy. The "death of the novel," the withdrawal of poetry behind academic walls, and the gradual disappearance of "high" literary forms ironically may signal not the triumph of science over art, but simply the perverse realization of the modern artist's dream. The old forms of modernist art—novel, poem, and play—have helped dream the postmodern world into existence and are reproduced in the lives we are compelled to lead.

7.

Another Modernism

Poetic Justice in Muriel Rukeyser's *The Book of the Dead*

Poetic justice: justice, as in some plays, stories, etc., in which good is properly rewarded and evil punished; justice as one might wish it to be.
—Webster's New World Dictionary of the American Language

The use of truth is its communication.
—Muriel Rukeyser, *The Life of Poetry* (1949)

In order to foreground the role of literary modernism in shaping concepts and behaviors appropriate to an emerging postmodern economy, I have used the modernist aesthetics of Henry James and Ezra Pound as representative of certain tendencies. It would be a mistake, of course, to allow these views to represent the diverse and complex artistic modernisms we now recognize to be critical of the modernization process. As Cary Nelson points out in *Repression and Recovery: Modern American Poetry and the Politics of Cultural Memory, 1910–1945*, "Literary history . . . is always written in the midst of—and constituted by—the multiple social determinations of literariness."[1] Thus such literary history must take into account the aesthetic varieties that such different social forces prompt, as well as recognize the equally diverse strategies these different literatures employ in response to these social determinants. Today most scholars recognize the important contributions of the Harlem renaissance and the 1930s Left to modernist aesthetics and social critique in the

135

United States, even if Asian American and Native American modernisms still receive too little attention. These "other" modernisms have significantly changed the way we understand the dialectical relationship between modernist aesthetics and ideology, so that we can no longer allow high modernism to "represent" the historically diverse responses of twentieth-century U.S. authors to modernization and even incipient postmodernization.

Writers interested in groups minoritized and marginalized by the modernization process often understood particularly well the rhetorical subtlety and discursive power of U.S. ideology well before it was commonplace for intellectuals to criticize such cultural colonialism. Nelson warns us not simply to add "neglected" writers and works to the established canon of U.S. literary modernism; we must instead reconceptualize modernist aesthetics as a variety of different interpretations of the relationship between art and ideology.[2] In so doing, we should be challenging the very restricted, albeit influential, model for U.S. literary modernism I outlined in the previous chapter. As I argued, this model helped accustom people to a "textualist" metaphysics that served well not only avant-garde literary interests but also emerging postindustrial economic practices.

By paying more attention to these other modernisms, we might recover not only interesting literature, as Nelson demonstrates, but alternative strategies for challenging both modernizing and postmodernizing socioeconomic processes. In doing this work, we might also be led to reconsider the so-called high modernists in terms of their possible associations with political, social, and aesthetic strategies suggested by these other traditions. Recent gay and queer approaches to Gertrude Stein and Hart Crane and critical race studies of Stein, Faulkner, and William Carlos Williams have revalued these modernists and, in some cases, found more productive affiliations for them with more politically committed or aesthetically different artists.[3] The work of recovering neglected, in some cases "lost," cultural traditions that has been done by feminists, ethnic scholars, and specialists in popular culture has in many cases produced new contexts for reading and interpretation. I have written elsewhere in this book that the new American Studies must be a thoroughly "comparatist" discipline, and we should remember that this comparatism must include cultural and literary traditions differently conceived and recognized, even when those traditions belong to the same national or group history. At the most elementary level, every course reading list should be understood as a comparative enterprise.

With these issues in mind, then, in this chapter I want to consider one example of the many other modernisms in order to avoid the impression of the previous chapter that all literary modernisms perform the sort of ideological work I identify with Henry James's and Ezra Pound's aesthetics. Muriel Rukeyser's long poem *The Book of the Dead* is a particularly good counter-narrative in this regard, because it is deeply committed to the politics of the U.S. Left of the 1930s and also employs avant-garde poetic devices and motifs obviously derived from such high modernists as T. S. Eliot, Ezra Pound, and Hart Crane. Criticized in its own time by both dogmatic leftists and the conservative Right, the poem does not so much chart out some "middle ground" as attempt to overcome the ideological limitations of both political perspectives. In so doing, Rukeyser manages to criticize the U.S. modernization process in very specific ways while calling for intellectual and social changes that often take into account an emerging postindustrial economy. Published in her collection of poetry *U.S. 1* in 1938, *The Book of the Dead* is composed of twenty shorter poems drawn from Rukeyser's interviews of family members of the victims and the workers who survived what Martin Cherniack terms "America's worst industrial accident": Union Carbide's exposure of its workers to dry silica and the resulting deaths of between 476 and 2,000 workers from pulmonary silicosis (fibroid phthisis), a disease in which the alveoli of the lungs harden or, in Rukeyser's terrifying words, the lungs "turn to glass."[4]

As Walter Kalaidjian tells the story, in 1929 Union Carbide "contracted through one of its subsidiaries, the New Kanawha Power Co., to divert river water through a three and three-quarter mile tunnel to be dug from Gauley Bridge to Hawk's Nest, West Virginia, for a new hydroelectric plant, which . . . would sell the power . . . to another Carbide subsidiary, the Electro-Metallurgical Company." While drilling this tunnel, Union Carbide discovered a huge deposit of pure silica—the raw material of glass, which also has many other industrial applications—and began to dry drill the silica as a by-product to be used at "Electro-Metallurgical's steel processing operation in Alloy, West Virginia."[5] In the 1930s, the accepted procedures for mining silica included the use of "hydraulic water drills, safety masks, and frequent relief teams" to protect workers from the toxic silica dust, but Union Carbide ignored these procedures and dry drilled the tunnel without "any prophylactic equipment" and without relieving workers.[6] Such cost-cutting measures were by no means unusual in the massive civil engineering projects of the 1930s; workers building Hoover Dam in Black Canyon, Nevada, also dry drilled spillway tunnels and suffered numerous respiratory diseases as a consequence.[7]

Union Carbide clearly planned to cover up what it expected would be an "acceptable" number of casualties, but the total number of deaths from silicosis (ranging from 476 to 2,000) and the efforts of the Communist Party of the United States of America (CPUSA) to publicize the industrial "accident" led to front-page stories in such major news magazines as *Time, Life, Newsweek,* and *The Nation.* Interviews with surviving workers and the families of victims were used as the bases for testimony in congressional hearings that revealed Union Carbide had attempted to cover up its misconduct by bribing company doctors to misdiagnose silicosis as pneumonia, pleurisy, or tuberculosis; hiring the local mortician to bury the dead quickly and cheaply out of public view in makeshift graves dug in a local cornfield; and ignoring personal protests and fighting lawsuits brought by the families of victims, most of whom were too poor to mount substantial cases against the company and its corporate legal team.

Just as Rukeyser had visited Decatur, Alabama, in 1933 as part of the CPUSA's team investigating judicial misconduct in the Scottsboro case, she and a friend, the photographer Nancy Naumberg, traveled to West Virginia to gather informants' testimony, gain firsthand experience of the region, and take photographs to strengthen the case against Union Carbide for the congressional hearings. Rukeyser also intended to write a long poem about the scandal.[8] Written using a combination of modernist poetic techniques, such as montage and mythic symbolism, and multiple poetic personae (including several borrowed from the people she interviewed) with documentary techniques, such as the use of interviews, letters, newspaper stories, and medical reports, Rukeyser's *Book of the Dead* is more than just another example of modernist "interdisciplinary" and "multimedia" poetry. Unlike such modernist tours de force as Eliot's *The Waste Land,* Hart Crane's *The Bridge,* and Faulkner's Yoknapatawpha fiction, *The Book of the Dead* does not claim to master its subject or substitute its poetic achievement (or form) for modern corruption. The subject position of the poetic author (or her delegate, the narratorial voice) is not offered as an "answer" to the social problems represented. Indeed, what is remarkable about Rukeyser's use of both documentary and avant-garde poetic techniques is how they tend to minimize the poetic author's own controlling presence. Like James and Pound, Rukeyser calls attention to the textualist conditions of everyday reality—Union Carbide's use of medical reports, the media, and "official letters" to cover up the scandal. But, unlike James and Pound, Rukeyser argues that such a discursive world requires multiple authors (readers and writers); the men and women she has interviewed, along with Rukeyser herself, become the proper agents of social change. The writing of Rukeyser's poem is itself simply one of the several different representational practices necessary to expose social problems, in this case a particular corporate scandal, and the poet claims that the coalition of these different representational practices with specific modes of social activism can turn social criticism into effective and lasting social reform. In *The Book of the Dead*, then, Rukeyser identifies the points of intersection where poetry, kinship, law, politics, and science can combine to produce reform and thus achieve greater social justice.

These intersections are identifiable in the poem's use of key myths that serve practically to identify the point at which one discourse requires another. Rukeyser's mythopoesis thus differs significantly from that of high moderns like Eliot, Pound, Hart Crane, and Joyce. The central mythic narrative of the poem is drawn from ancient Egyptian religion both in the titular reference to the Egyptian *Book of the Dead* and in Rukeyser's references to the Isis-Set(h)-Osiris narrative of seasonal and spiritual regeneration. In an early review of the poem, "The Osiris Way," Philip Blair Rice argued that the entire poem is organized around the Egyptian *Book of the Dead*, the collection of magic incantations, prayers, and exorcisms used as a guidebook for the dead on their journey through the underworld.[9] M. L. Rosenthal and Walter Kalaidjian both stress the fact that Rukeyser argues in the poem that the modern version of this negotiation of the underworld and thus her way of "resurrecting" Union Carbide's dead workers (or at least making them useful) will depend primarily on the mythic figure of Isis rather than on the Osiris stressed in Rice's review and in modernist treatments of ancient Egyptian religion.[10] Attentive as Rosenthal and Kalaidjian are to Rukeyser's use of this feminine mythic archetype, however, they treat it primarily in terms of its relevance to Rukeyser's 1930s leftist feminism, itself a criticism of the masculinist ideology of the CPUSA and its Popular Front.[11]

Interpreted in this way, Rukeyser's "mythic feminism" is a quaint reminder of an earlier feminism that pitted feminine maternity and ideals of nurture and domesticity against the ruthlessness of capitalist exploitation in the workplace and against authoritarian patriarchal structures in the public sphere. There is undoubtedly some truth to this historicized version of Rukeyser's mythic feminism, but I also find in the poem a more sophisticated understanding of how feminism calls for a wide-ranging revision of conventional ideas of work, worker, the family, domesticity, and feminine agency. Rukeyser was strongly influenced by romantic poetic traditions, in the manner of such contemporaries as Robert Frost and Hart Crane, whatever their political differences, and *The Book of the Dead* builds a romantic organicist argument and thus a romantic reader response, despite its recognizably modernist fragmentation, poetic montage, and admixture of documentary elements. Yet the uses to which Rukeyser puts the organic development of argument, poetic voice, and the implied reader are considerably different from the aims of most romantic and high modernist works.

Early in the poem, Rukeyser represents the history of the Union Carbide scandal by way of survivors who bear witness to the basic facts. A railroad engineer, Vivian Jones, "remembers how they enlarged / the tunnel and the crews, finding the silica," reminding the reader how Union Carbide expanded the tunnel and the workforce as soon as the company knew there was a profitable by-product of the hydroelectric project (*The Book of the Dead*, 14). Rukeyser quotes from a letter sent by a sick miner, Mearl Blankenship, to Union Carbide: "Dear Sir, my name is Mearl Blankenship. / I have Worked for the rhinehart and Dennis Co / Many days & many nights / & it was so dusty you couldn't hardly see the lights" (*The Book of the Dead*, 18). While telling the story of the scandal, Rukeyser also represents the workers' complaints as true, sad, and by themselves ineffective. The sick workers die, their complaints and lawsuits against Union Carbide are ignored, and fellow workers, like Vivian Jones, try to forget the futility and even the damage of their labor: "Never to be used, he thinks, never to spread its power, / jinx on the rock, curse on the power-plant, / hundreds breathed valued, filled their lungs full of glass / . . . he turns and stamps this off his mind again / and on the hour walks again through town" (*The Book of the Dead*, 15).

On the other hand, Rukeyser's women take action, in part because they survive and in part because they gradually recognize how the injury their husbands and sons have suffered is shared by nonfamily members. In "Absalom," the eighth poem of the twenty comprising *The Book of the Dead*, Mrs. Jones—namesake of the railroad engineer but unrelated to him—bears witness to the silicosis of her husband and three sons—Cecil, Owen, and Shirley—and then combines maternal nurture with political activism by begging money on the road for independent X rays, which she will use as evidence in lawsuits that will eventually succeed in closing the mining camps: "I went on the road and begged the X-ray money, / the Charleston hospital made the lung pictures, / he took the case after the pictures were made. / . . . The case of my son was the first of the line of lawsuits. / They sent the lawyers down and the doctors down; / they closed the electric sockets in the camps" (*The Book of the Dead*, 19–20).

What Mrs. Jones initiates for her own family soon influences the lives of other workers, suggesting a continuity between family and social relations violently denied by Union Carbide and also actively resisted by the 1930s leftists' understanding of what constitutes work, labor, and thus the proletariat.[12] Although the women in Rukeyser's poem are decidedly domestic—the poem antedates the significant increase of women in the U.S. workforce prompted by the war economy of the 1940s— the value of women's labor is emphasized: "They asked me how I keep the cow on $2. / I said one week, feed for the cow, one week, the children's flour" (*The Book of the Dead*, 20).

Through its title, "Absalom," Mrs. Jones's poem is the first poem of *The Book of the Dead* that centrally alludes to a biblical or mythic urtext. Published two years after Faulkner's *Absalom, Absalom!* Rukeyser's "Absalom" transforms Faulkner's somewhat conventional adaptation of King David's lament for his rebellious son, Absalom, into Mrs. Jones's commitment to turn the tragic deaths of her husband and sons into political protest. Whereas the reader of Faulkner's novel can hear the Biblical lament of King David, "Would God I had died for thee, O Absalom, my son, my son" (II Samuel 15:6), in the tangled family destinies that pit Henry Sutpen against Charles Bon and leave the reader only with a sense of futility and bittersweet elegy, Rukeyser rewrites the Bible with a powerful feminine affirmation: "He shall not be diminished, never; / I shall give a mouth to my son" (*The Book of the Dead*, 20).[13] From this point on, what Walter Kalaidjian astutely terms Rukeyser's "mythic feminism" structures both the poem and the political purposes of the several activist practices with which the poem identifies itself.

In my view, Rukeyser's mythic feminism anticipates more recent ecofeminisms, for which there are few precedents in the 1930s. Drawing on her own romantic, particularly American transcendentalist, precursors, Rukeyser contends that the political and legal reforms demanded by the exposure of Union Carbide's deliberate endangerment of its workers must be accompanied by a broadly based reconceptualization of our social relations to the natural world. As social protest and as an extension of the specific lawsuits and congressional hearings regarding Union Carbide's malfeasance, *The Book of the Dead* both mourns the dead and victimized workers and "resurrects" them in the social reform work to which the poem contributes. At times, this work is very concrete, as in the documentary portions used to establish Union Carbide's culpability. In the penultimate poem, "The Bill," Rukeyser virtually restates the congressional mining reform bill that was the result of the hearings. The congressional bill, however, merely "recommended" reforms, saying it "can do no more," even though it recognizes: "These citizens from many States / paying the price for electric power, / To Be Vindicated" (*The Book of the Dead*, 36). Rukeyser's poetic version goes beyond the bill to "vindicate" the dead miners both by publicizing Union Carbide's crime and by reminding us of the legal, political, and moral power that remains in the miners' surviving wives and mothers. Like the Egyptian *Book of the Dead*, the poem "guides" the dead through the underworld and gives them new life. At one level, of course, this play upon the allusion of the title does little more than Hart Crane's "descent" in his "The Tunnel" section of *The Bridge*, which formally prepares us for the purely metaphoric resurrection of the poet in the ecstatic "Atlantis" that concludes the poem.[14] Unlike Crane, who gathers together the poetic alter egos in the poem (Columbus, Pocahontas, Rip Van Winkle, the pioneer woman, hoboes riding the rails, sailors, gay men, et al.) in a coherent subjectivity, Rukeyser allows the women who have connected their maternal care with political activism to take on the collective mythic identity of Isis and thereby to herald a utopian reconception of our social relation to nature.

In his reading of the sixteenth poem of *The Book of the Dead*, "Power," Kalaidjian contends that Rukeyser departs from "proletcult's almost homoerotic investment in the industrial workplace of men and machines" in favor of a "more holistic setting 'midway' between nature and the dynamo."[15] What he means by "midway" is a bit confusing or misleading, because what Rukeyser argues is that modernization and industrialization should be evaluated in terms of the degree to which they realize a closer relationship between human and natural realms, not a competitive or adversarial one. It is a romantic sentiment, such as Emerson invoked when he wrote in "The Poet": "All the facts of the animal economy, sex, nutriment, gestation, birth, growth, are symbols of the passage of the world into the soul of man, to suffer there a change and reappear a new and higher fact."[16] Rukeyser begins "Power" with a visionary account of humans and nature erotically confused:

> The quick sun brings, exciting mountains warm,
> gay on the landscapers and green designs,
> miracle, yielding the sex up under all the skin,
> until the entire body watches the scene with love,
> sees perfect cliffs ranging until the river
> cuts sheer, mapped far below in delicate track,
> surprise of grace, the water running in the sun,
> magnificent flower on the mouth, surprise

as lovers who took too long on the desired face
startle to find the remote flesh so warm.
A day of heat shed on the gorge, a brilliant
day when love sees the sun behind its man
and the disguised marvel under familiar skin.

(*The Book of the Dead*, 29)

Although claimed in the 1960s and 1970s by lesbian feminists, Rukeyser preferred to identify herself as "bisexual," and her poetry is often startlingly and complexly erotic—a modernist transumption of Whitman's romantic sexuality.[17] In this opening stanza of "Power," however, the relation of natural power is complexly figured in heterosexual terms, so that the line "love sees the sun behind its man" reminds us of the natural sources for love between man and woman.

In the poem that follows "Power," "The Dam," Rukeyser divides into separate parts the imbricated forces of woman, man, river, sun, sex, flower, mouth, and body that allow her opening pastoral in "Power" to cohere. In "The Dam," we see Rukeyser's poetic identity guided by one of the civil engineers who designed the dam and cannot help but admire its artificial beauty:

Constellations of light, abundance of many rivers.
The sheeted island-cities, the white surf filling west,
the hope, fast water spilled where still pools fed.
Great power flying deep: between the rock and the sunset,
the caretaker's house and the steep abutment,
hypnotic water fallen and the tunnels under
the moist and fragile galleries of stone,
mile-long, under the wave.

(*The Book of the Dead*, 32)

What this civil engineer admires in the ideally entropy-free system of the dam as an electrical generating system is in poetic fact already represented in the opening pastoral of the preceding poem, "Power," where the real source of the dam's energy lies: the connection of humans to their natural forces, including their labor power; its relation to sexual reproduction; and the relation of both to seasonal regeneration. Rukeyser does not condemn the civil engineer and his love of science as parts of Union Carbide's criminality; she understands the engineer's love of nature and of his own sublimated sexual energy that he sees only in the dam. In effect, Rukeyser tries to get the engineer to see "the sun behind its man," and the apparent allusion to Osiris (the Egyptian god of the sun) actually directs the reader toward the agency of resurrection in the Egyptian mythology: Isis.

In Egyptian myth, after the seasonal conflict in which Osiris's twin, Set(h), dismembers his brother (and father), Isis sails the Nile "gathering the limbs of Osiris" and fishing for the key part, his phallus, to make the biomythical parts cohere again. In this supernatural account of how the annual Nile floods bring restorative river silt to the bordering farms, Isis links nature and culture (cultivation) in a symbolic ritual that also has literal referents. Rukeyser adapts Isis to the work of her women characters in *The Book of the Dead:* Philippa Allen, Mrs. Jones, Juanita Tinsley, Rukeyser herself, and the photographer, Nancy Naumberg; this work includes not only "gathering" the bodies of the male workers killed or damaged by silicosis but also reconnecting human cultivation to its natural sources. To be sure, there is no neoagrarian rhetoric in the poem, none of the nostalgia for the Jeffersonian "yeoman farmer" that is so anachronistic in the poetry and prose of the Fugitives and Agrarians of the 1920s and 1930s. Rukeyser was still a member of the CPUSA at this time, an active leftist, and committed to "modernization" and industrialization in the proper hands of the workers. But these "workers" now include the women who have been previously excluded or ignored by leftist political and economic agendas. The male workers in Rukeyser's poem, failing to take seriously their own laboring bodies and health, disconnected by industrial capitalism from what are today standard considerations of the biomedical hazards of the workplace, are victimized and powerless.

Rukeyser's women bring to the 1930s leftist theory of labor ideas of the body, nature, and health that are inherent in the "labor" they perform every day in the domestic workplace as mothers, wives, and custodians of "family values." This feminine connection with nature, itself often employed by romantic idealists to reinforce patriarchal hierarchies, is Rukeyser's means of elevating women to positions of equality in the workplace and to special status as philosophers, poets, and adjudicators of moral value.[18] Like more recent biological archaeologists, Rukeyser and the other women activists call our attention to the effects of capitalist exploitation not simply in terms of the labor relation and the gap between exchange and surplus value but also in regard to the worker's body itself, which is as polluted by silica as the surrounding environment.[19] Going far beyond critiques of the exploitation of labor in the 1930s, Rukeyser focuses on the injury capitalism does to the subtle bond between human and physical nature, anticipating both contemporary ecocriticism and its critique of what David Harvey has termed the "globalization of the body" effected by postmodern capitalism.[20] Rukeyser writes:

> The water they would bring had dust in it, our drinking water,
> the camps and their groves were colored with the dust,
> we cleaned our clothes in the groves, but we had always the dust.
> Looked like somebody sprinkled flour all over the parks and groves,
> it stayed and the rain couldn't wash it away and it twinkled
> that white dust really looked pretty down around our ankles.
>
> (*The Book of the Dead*, 22)

In this passage, we are reminded of such later scandals as the spraying of Dow Chemical's defoliant Agent Orange in Vietnam, contaminating with dangerous carcinogens the water U.S. and North Vietnamese Army troops routinely drank and used to cook and bathe. In the poem's concluding epode, Rukeyser asks us again to remember the damage done to workers' bodies by corporate capitalism, which she also links with modern warfare. She makes this appeal seven years before the atomic blasts at Hiroshima and Nagasaki, fifteen years before Native American uranium miners in the Southwest suffered exposure to massive radiation in the mines, and eight years before Pacific Islanders began to suffer the consequences of U.S. nuclear weapons testing on Bikini Atoll and at other sites:

> These touching radium and the luminous poison,
> carried their death on their lips and with their warning
> glow in their graves.
>
> (*The Book of the Dead*, 39)

Rukeyser privileges her women characters with the ability not only to comprehend the violence done to the workers by Union Carbide's greed but also to criticize its system practically and to reform it abstractly. But it is not just women who are capable of such power. The African American worker covered with silica dust recognizes the irony that he shares equality with the white worker only in this symbolic way. Rukeyser uses this Gothic moment to positively suggest how together the white and black workers might reform a murderous capitalism:

> As dark as I am, when I came out at morning after the tunnel
> at night,

> with a white man, nobody could have told which man was
>   white.
> The dust had covered us both, and the dust was white.
>
> (*The Book of the Dead*, 22)

Ultimately much depends on the coalition politics and on the coordinated labor of workers awakened to their exploitation and capable of sustaining the broadest possible coalitions across lines of race, gender, region, and class.[21] The feminine consciousness of the poem and the legal and political activism of the wives and mothers of the Union Carbide miners merely serve as the guiding spirits or mythic presences that facilitate an awareness that Rukeyser by no means restricts to women. Her mythic Isis serves as the symbol of the natural human system for which we are responsible and that defines human labor and self-value; Isis is Rukeyser's mythic judge.[22]

> But planted in our flesh these valleys stand,
> everywhere we begin to know the illness,
> are forced up, and our times confirm us all.
>
> In the museum life, centuries of ambition
> yielded at last a fertilizing image:
> the Carthaginian stone meaning a tall woman
>
> carries in her two hands the book and cradled dove,
> on her two thighs, wings folded from the waist
> cross to her feet, a pointed human crown.
>
> This valley is given to us like a glory.
> To friends in the old world, and their lifting hands
> that call for intercession.
>
> (*The Book of the Dead*, 39)

Rukeyser's radical pacifism ("cradled dove") and her poetry and the law ("the book") combine with a woman's self-consciousness regarding her own reproductive powers ("a pointed human crown") to offer us "a glory," the transcendentalist relation of humans to the miracle of nature. It is under this banner that Rukeyser extends the struggle against Union Carbide to the international stage, connecting this protest with the contemporary leftist protest against the rise of fascism that was resisted in the Spanish Civil War ("friends in the old world . . . / [who] call for intercession").

In the final poem of *The Book of the Dead*, Rukeyser claims for poetry itself the "rhythm" and "system" that imitate the virtually unrepresentable bonds between human, physical, and biochemical natures. Poetry at its best achieves some imitation of or isomorphism with this utopian (and romantic) ideal, but never in its own right and always in conjunction with other modes of protest, expression, and activism. The conclusion of the poem is an appeal to the reader not to reproduce Rukeyser's "truth" or interpret her poetic "mystery" or "logic of metaphor," but rather to continue the work in which poetry plays only a part:

> Carry abroad the urgent need, the scene,
> to photograph and to extend the voice,
>   to speak this meaning.
> Voices to speak to us directly. As we move.
> As we enrich, growing in larger motion,
>   this word, this power. . . .
> communication to these many men,
> as epilogue, seeds of unending love.
>
> (*The Book of the Dead*, 40)

It is this communication that typifies Rukeyser's mythic Isis and the power of her poetry, which modestly claims to be little more than a montage and documentary assemblage of other voices and forgotten powers. Yet in allowing these voices to be heard and these powers to be felt, Rukeyser's poetry actively contributes to, even as it does not exclusively constitute, the work of justice.

In contrast to the Jamesian central consciousness and Pound's epic thrones, Rukeyser's poet records and orchestrates the variety of voices necessary to bring about social change and to challenge laws whose authority and justice do not adequately meet new social demands. *The Book of the Dead* is, of course, a recognizably modernist poem, and it responds to the working and social conditions of an industrial economy. By finding common terms, often suggested in the poem by such mythemes as Isis, that link together the poet, mother, worker, minority, and political activist while respecting their different social functions, Rukeyser recognizes the important agencies of people other than poets and institutions other than the aesthetic in the work of social critique and reform. Insofar as the characters of her poem are capable of analytical, critical, expressive, and interpretive acts that extend far beyond poetry, Rukeyser declares that poetry is only one among many different discursive practices and institutions that can be used to challenge the dominant ideology. In this modesty about her own poetic contribution to social change, however,

Rukeyser revived the interest and relevance of literature at the very moment at which it was particularly challenged by the competitive claims of mass media, film, corporate management and marketing (including "damage control"), and political rhetoric. Whereas the modernist aesthetic I discussed in the previous chapter depends upon absorbing and controlling social and cultural differences into a masterful figure (author, interpreter, or text), Rukeyser's poem invites and encourages other voices, in many cases learning from people whose lives and experiences are decidedly unpoetic.

Rukeyser's leftist and feminist modernism in *The Book of the Dead* also allows me to draw some conclusions about how the new American Studies might contribute to the current scholarly debates about culture's role in the pursuit of social justice. Insofar as American Studies has a long tradition of social critique, its practitioners should help recast debates about social justice that are often curiously abstract and detached from tangible political, social, and ethical problems. Rukeyser teaches us that aesthetic discourses can contribute to the work of social justice, but they can best do so when they work in conjunction with other discourses and actions. Poetic writing and reading in and of themselves are usually insufficient to effect social changes, but this does not mean that such acts are absolutely powerless.

In this regard, I wish to further elaborate my critique of "aesthetic dissent" in *At Emerson's Tomb: The Politics of Classic American Literature* (1997). In that work, I defined aesthetic dissent as "the assumption that the rigorous reflection on the processes of thought and representation constitutes in itself a critique of social reality and effects a transformation of the naive realism that confuses truth with social convention."[23] I want to extend this critique to include the sort of philosophical reflection on justice that is typified by Jean-François Lyotard's observations in *Au Juste* (1979), in which he tries to think abstractly about concepts of justice and injustice. Lyotard's nonfoundational approach relies on what he terms "the pragmatics of obligation" that keeps the "game of the just" open and thus defines "absolute injustice" as anything that "prohibits ... the question of the just and the unjust [from being] raised."[24] Such an approach cannot go beyond this tacitly tautological definition. We must instead examine concrete historical instances of the relationship between justice and injustice if we want to understand the "pragmatics of obligation." Such instances are not "examples" that will serve as philosophical predicates of a wider definition of justice and injustice; these instances constitute our historical understanding of these terms. Rukeyser's *Book of the Dead* is not itself such an instance, but a way of framing the complex legal, medical, political, economic, and psychological consequences of Union Carbide's corporate crime. In so framing that crime, Rukeyser's poem becomes a part of its history, thereby rendering the poet and reader, among others, responsible for the historical consequences of an injustice that is not readily subject to judgment. By joining (and identifying) others, like Mrs. Jones, who seek justice in response to such injustice, Rukeyser and the reader make this particular poem do historical and ethical work.

What can be said of such instances of the relationship between justice and injustice in general is only that they will (a) establish just such a relationship between justice and injustice; (b) do so in a rigorously historical manner; and (c) refuse (or confuse) the authority of a singular medium—the law, government, social convention, aesthetics, scholarly truth, or any other—for establishing such a relationship. In other words, these instances that shape the historicality of the relationship between justice and injustice are not discrete "texts"; they are themselves more usefully understood as complex intertextual events whose multiple discursive and performative functions must be respected. "Judgment" is our interpretation of these instances and their historical relations; beyond these features, we cannot judge, and there can thus be no thought of justice. The relationship between such "judgment" and these "events" is what constitutes history. Understood in this way, literary and other cultural "events" have significant roles to play in the pursuit of social justice and its historical definition. Insofar as American Studies is interested in understanding the historicality and morality (or immorality) of such cultural production, the field has much to teach us about social justice and the limitations of merely formal and abstract treatments of its practice.

8.

Metavideo

Fictionality and Mass Media in
Our Postmodern Economy

> What was projected psychologically and mentally, what used to be lived out on
> earth as metaphor, as mental or metaphorical scene, is henceforth projected into
> reality, without any metaphor at all, into an absolute space which is also that of
> simulation.
> **—Jean Baudrillard, "The Ecstasy of Communication"**

Symptomatic of our difficulties as American Studies scholars in dealing
with the impact of poststructuralist theories and the consequences of
postmodern social and economic conditions is our treatment of nonprint media, especially those like television, film, and video that have
assumed economic and cultural prominence in the postindustrial era.
In many respects, American Studies has led other disciplines in addressing how different media have shaped cultural and social values. From
programs in American Studies that insist upon training their students
in several different media to scholarship that emphasizes the interrelation of visual, aural, oral, and print media, our field has anticipated and
subsequently cooperated with new academic programs and scholarship
in television and film studies and even more recently has formed programs in visual studies. American Studies scholars should be proud
of these accomplishments and should continue to work with colleagues
in these allied fields, especially as we broaden the geopolitical scope
of American Studies to include the western hemisphere and relevant

border regions or "rims" as discussed in the introduction and chapters 1 and 3.

Yet these testaments to American Studies as a multimedia and multi-disciplinary field do not tell the whole story. The core of the discipline remains stubbornly, if understandably, print oriented, so much of American Studies' scholarship in electronic and digital media continues to follow the linguistic, rhetorical, and hermeneutic assumptions of written texts. In those periods and societies in which written language serves as the dominant medium, there is considerable justification for using such methodologies. Yet in those contexts in which nonprint media centrally shape social values, we may unintentionally misinterpret these media by tacitly relying on the criteria and values of written language. These contexts are not limited to premodern and postmodern societies; they include societies, communities, and groups that rely on other media while functioning within or in proximity to print-dominated societies.

Many Native American societies struggling with Euro-American imperialism are good examples of communities that rely on oral and performative media in the neighborhood of and often in direct conflict with a dominant society that privileges written language and print culture.[1] For many reasons, including the slavocracy's ban against African American reading and writing in the antebellum South, African American communities have traditionally drawn on music, dance, oral folktales, and nonprint forms of social representation in central ways. Although written language and print forms have also played crucial roles in African American societies, they have not always been the primary models for cultural representation. As Lindon Barrett points out, since the European Enlightenment the equation of literacy with competency in written language and print forms helped rationalize cultural and racial hierarchies: "In the Western mind, the lack of literacy . . . provides the strongest evidence of the marginal or lesser human status of Africans and their descendants. Literacy becomes simultaneously the mark of African lack and Western mastery."[2] In the Euro-American colonization of native peoples, the imposition of written language and the insistence upon standards of literacy identifiable with the written word played crucial roles in the fragmentation of tribal life and social coherence. Early ethnographers and subsequent anthropologists played central parts in this destructive process of colonization, and we should learn to avoid their mistakes by critically examining the historically recent and socially specific privileging of written language and the print media.

When we reconsider this modern history of literacy as competency in writing and print, it makes such radical poststructuralist claims as Derrida's privileging of writing *(écriture)* over speech appear quite conventional, even decidedly ideological.[3] Of course, there is much in Derrida's work that challenges fundamental Enlightenment assumptions about reason, language, and nature, but to a great extent Derrida operates within the framework of Western modernity and inevitably reproduces many of its key concepts even in his most strenuous attempts to deconstruct them. The first generation of poststructuralist theories, epitomized by Derrida's writings in the late 1960s and early 1970s, did not adequately address changes in the dominant media in postmodern societies, such as the United States and France, that were already well underway by that time.

It is now a commonplace to define the deconstructive enterprise in terms of two related strategies: first, the demystification (or critical reading) of the formal integrity and thus the discrete presence of the signified; second, the analysis (or genealogical interpretation) of the relative motivations of previous significations in determining the locus of the particular utterance. The first strategy is by far the most common and has had the most dramatic effect in academic discussions: Jacques Derrida, Paul de Man, Geoffrey Hartman, J. Hillis Miller, and many others have effectively staged readings in which the apparently established meanings of a classic literary or philosophical text have been turned against themselves, brought to a point of contradiction or antithetical meaning, and then used to open the work's formal closure to an intertextual history whose ultimate limit is the history of language. In the course of such interpretations, the deconstructive critic has often suggested alternative meanings and unexpected textual associations to demonstrate the connotative richness made possible by such an active antiformalism. Less often has the deconstructive critic attempted to read the ways in which this intertextuality is repressed for the sake of particular utterances and denotative meanings. Although deconstruction has rigorously, even relentlessly, exposed the contradictions in what Derrida has called the Western metaphysics of presence, it has been considerably less vigilant in accounting for how such contradictions have disguised themselves as coherent and commensurable truths.

In academic discussions, this question is often answered quite simply and glibly. The repression of the irreducible play of signifiers is made possible by establishing some extralinguistic domain of thought, nature, or empirical fact that precedes and exceeds the presumably secondary representation of the signifier. Nietzsche and Foucault have taught us that such an abstract answer is inadequate and must be supplemented by

the specific historical conditions shaping such concepts as thought, nature, and fact. Within the specific historical conditions of the postindustrial, postmodern United States, I would contend that the conventions of
thought, nature, and fact—indeed, of any extralinguistic reference—no
longer exert much influence. These are the concepts of nineteenth-century
and early twentieth-century modern Western societies. The postmodern
United States has thoroughly accommodated itself to its irreducibly intertextual character; repression and ideological control—as social concerns, not just academic terms—operate by means of such intertextuality
rather than by repudiating it in favor of some presentable truth or self-
evident fact. Yet the best examples of such intertextuality are not radical
scholarly or avant-garde literary texts, but electronic media that employ
several different semiotic and affective modes, including image, sound,
text, and performance.

There are two reasons that poststructuralists have had trouble dealing
with electronic media in contemporary Western societies, and they are
problems American Studies scholars should address as they deal more
centrally with poststructuralist theories and with postmodern conditions. First, these media have been theorized in terms that best apply to
industrial economies, in which relatively clear distinctions can be made
between basic modes of production and the ideological strategies by
which economic practices and related social behaviors are justified. Second, electronic media serve primarily commercial purposes and are ap-
propriately understood as "mass media," whose economic purposes govern their production and distribution. Insofar as such mass media have
adapted the methods and styles we recognize as deconstructive, the commercial purposes and economic values of such features must be assessed.
In the case of the first problem, poststructuralists may be criticized for
having failed to take into account the significant semiotic changes occasioned by the shift from industrial to postindustrial production in the
West; this is a blindness they share with Frankfurt School theorists, who
pioneered critical studies of the media in the 1920s and 1930s that continue to influence our interpretations of the media. In the case of the second
problem, however, poststructuralist naïveté is more willful and defensive.
Like postmodern literary experimenters, deconstructive critics are often
unwilling to acknowledge the self-conscious rhetorical strategies of the
mass media, precisely because such strategies pose a genuine challenge to
the claims for ideological critique made by both postmodern writers and
deconstructionists. Indeed, the self-consciousness of the mass media is
so pervasive and powerful, albeit serving the very different purposes I

will try to illustrate, that it virtually negates the deconstructionist's claim to the special authority of demystification as a critical practice. In this postmodern and postindustrial economy, demystification is already a conventional rhetorical device that contributes significantly to the commercial success of these media as well as to the maintenance of certain normative ideological values.

In "Requiem for the Media" in his *For a Critique of the Political Economy of the Sign* (1972), Jean Baudrillard criticizes Hans Magnus Enzensberger's "optimistic and offensive position" with regard to the popular media. Baudrillard argues that Enzensberger's attempt (in "Constituents of a Theory of the Media") to theorize the media as parts of "a simple 'medium of distribution'" ignores the fact that in a postindustrial economy the mass media are themselves vital modes of production.[4] Enzensberger's notions of the "consciousness industry" and "the industrialization of the mind" betray his assumption that the mass media are primarily offshoots, by-products, of a familiar industrialism.[5] As a consequence, Enzensberger can rather optimistically imagine the relatively unproblematic transformation of this "medium of distribution" into "a true medium of communication."[6] For Enzensberger, "immaterial exploitation" is still a function of material production: "Material production must camouflage itself in order to survive; immaterial exploitation has become its necessary corollary."[7] Still imagining that the mass media might be employed by the Left as "popular media," as Brecht had hoped in *Theory of Radio* (1932), Enzensberger reaffirms the materialist distinctions between production and distribution, between economy and ideology. The consequence is an optimism regarding the future of the media that is as curious today as were McLuhan's fantasies of a "global village." Enzensberger accepts the "immateriality" of the media as a major means by which the Left might attack the materialism of late capitalism: "The media produce no objects that can be hoarded and auctioned. They do away completely with 'intellectual property' and liquidate the 'heritage,' that is to say, the class-specific handing-on of nonmaterial capital."[8] Baudrillard believes that Brecht and Enzensberger merely demonstrate the inapplicability of classical Marxism to postmodern capitalism, in which "The media are not *coefficients,* but *effectors* of ideology."[9]

As Jean-François Lyotard has argued, in postmodern society knowledge is a function or effect of the ultimate product of information. Evaluative criteria for the "performative efficiency" by which such information is judged and knowledge is constituted are part of the language games that determine production as surely as does the machinery of industrialism.[10] "Information," "service," "postindustrial products," and "technological products," as crude as these terms are at this stage of analysis, share a common feature: whatever materiality may be involved (computer hardware, telematic machinery, and offices and vehicles for "services") is subordinate to the essential immateriality of the product. Marketing firms, consulting agencies, computer analysts and programmers, and the like may be supported by elaborate and seemingly indispensable hardware and technicians, but these recognizably material tools and skills are subordinate to the a priori law of postmodern capitalism: the immateriality of production (or the production of immateriality). "Getting results," "increasing production," and "maximizing profits" no longer refer as clearly and simply as they once did to the increased numbers of objects manufactured and sold. The production of immaterial goods like information and services depends not so much on the simple volume of such goods and the quantification of surplus value as on the potential of such goods for subsequent production. In this view, the classical Marxian conception of surplus value would have to be redefined, perhaps incorporating the differential becoming and heterogeneity so prized by counter-cultural critics from William James to Jacques Derrida, from James's pluralistic, "unfinished" universe to the Derridean supplement and dissemination.[11]

Contemporary electronic media typify this mode of immaterial production and make such productivity an integral part of their formal system. The signifying system of these media relies upon the total subsumption of use value by exchange value. Rather than confuse the verbal sign with the special characteristics of the televisual and cinematic sign, in the rest of this chapter I shall refer to the media image. By the term "image," I mean the combination of graphic, aural, oral, performative, and visual elements that is operative especially in television and film. The media image depends upon and emphasizes its immateriality and the manner that such immateriality governs the material mechanisms and technologies employed to present it. Although material elements are part of the production of the image, the immateriality of the image governs and determines the sorts of material mechanisms required. Thus the subsumption of use value by exchange value is not a covert, furtive process constantly in danger of demystification. Whereas the rhetorical logic of industrial capitalism requires material exploitation to disguise itself by way of "immaterial" mystifications (the "illusions" of ideology), the immateriality of the media image is openly acknowledged and even celebrated as the essence of postmodern social reality. As Baudrillard has written: "Use value and needs are only an effect of exchange value. Signified (and referent) are only an effect of the signifier. . . . Neither is an autonomous reality that either exchange value or the signifier would express or translate in their code. At bottom, they are only simulation models, produced by the play of exchange value and of signifiers."[12] Whatever use value the immaterial image might appear to possess is merely the effect of the repression of its exchange value (i.e., the potential for exchange and circulation) that constitutes the image.

The electronic media have their own histories, in which the transvaluation of the customs of print culture and modern materialism took place gradually (even amid the notorious acceleration of the postmodern age) and amid significant contradictions. I cannot hope to reproduce that history with any thoroughness in this chapter, so I shall simulate a kind of figurative history by looking briefly at the metafictional assumptions of various popular television programs from the 1950s to 1980. In that period, a significant change occurred in the attitudes and values of network television with respect to its own medium. These changes, I would add, cast deconstructive conceptions of intertextuality and avantgarde claims for literary self-consciousness in an extremely different light. Preliminary and incomplete as this television history must be, I intend it to serve as an example of how American Studies might better address the social and cultural influences of one important electronic medium in the postmodern era.

In *The Honeymooners* (1955–56), Ralph Kramden (Jackie Gleason) and Ed Norton (Art Carney) quite consistently express the wistful yearning of the exploited working class for the magical powers of the capitalist.[13] Ralph, in particular, falls for every get-rich-quick scheme that wafts through the tenement window, despite his wife Alice's (Audrey Meadows) insistence that he has a "good job" as a bus driver. Norton takes particular pride in his technical expertise as a sewer worker for the Department of Sanitation, but Ralph is disgusted with such stupidity and usually convinces Norton to share the enthusiasm, expense, and folly of his various "enterprises." The conclusion of a typical episode is paradigmatic: Alice or Norton helps Ralph "cut his losses," get back his job with the Gotham Bus Company, and restore his self-esteem. Of course, it is his surviving pride in his abilities to rise above his working-class conditions that allows the complications of the next episode to arise, so it is fair to say that Ed and Alice (as well as Ed's wife, Trixie) serve quite directly the interests of capitalist exploitation of the working-class imaginary. In keeping with the basic structure of the situation comedy, *The Honeymooners* resolves problems for the sake of reproducing them in subsequent programs.

Ralph's problem, besides his working-class situation, is his failure to distinguish between a legitimate businessman and a con man. Even so, there are many examples of benign businessmen in this series, many of whom (such as Ralph's boss) help extricate him from his various problems. Businessmen and bosses have their idiosyncrasies, but they are recognizable by their patronizing understanding of the follies of the working class.[14] Dressed in sober suits, balding and elderly, they help the worker negotiate the often vast distance between their knowledge of his abilities and his desires. In one episode, Norton is offered an office job by the city, which Ralph persuades him to accept over Norton's strong reservations. His first day on the job, Norton accidentally locks the safe before putting the day's cash receipts away. The incident comically replays Hurstwood's "accident" at Fitzgerald and Moy's in Dreiser's *Sister Carrie,* and Norton, as if recalling the novel, immediately fears he might be suspected of embezzlement should he take the money home for the night. Something of this sort does occur, complicated by Ralph's unhelpful advice, but Norton's character as an essentially honest bumbler is recognized in the end by those who "know" how to read working-class behavior. Returning to his subterranean world of the sewers, Norton is again happy to play his invisible role in the maintenance of urban order, knee-deep in the waste products of late capitalism.

The representation of the media is altogether a different matter than the representation of the business world in *The Honeymooners.* Some of Ralph's most fantastic schemes involve him and Norton in television and film ventures. Directors and producers more closely resemble the sleazy con men who exploit Ralph and Ed than do the kindly businessmen and government officials who help extricate them from their problems. Caricatures, these agents of the media appear dressed in berets, wearing scarves, smoking cigarettes in long holders, and otherwise fulfilling working-class suspicions of those who openly trade in illusion. Even so, Ralph is particularly drawn to the fabled riches of the mass media, and he is willing to mime their dress and mannerisms for the sake of his dreams of power and authority.

Yet the consequences of Ralph's behavior in the television and film studios are quite different from the consequences of his other escapades. Whereas Ralph and Ed never threaten the stability of legitimate business for more than a brief moment, both of them often create utter havoc in the world of mass media. In one famous episode, "The Chef of the Future," Ralph and Norton stumble on the "opportunity" to do television commercials for a multipurpose kitchen tool: the fabled slicer/dicer/ricer of 1950s advertising.[15] As Norton demonstrates the time-consuming process of coring an apple with a paring knife or opening a can with a conventional opener, Ralph is supposed to follow each of Norton's laborious tasks with a swift demonstration of the kitchen gadget's labor-saving efficiency. The result, of course, is perfectly predictable: Norton pares and cores the apple in one swift motion, while Ralph fumbles and bumbles, drops the apple, trips on it, and freezes in complete and utter stage fright (while Norton is continuing to talk and perform with the bravura of a television chef). In the various efforts by director, stagehands, and Norton to save this live television commercial, they push and nudge Ralph back into action, but this time he weaves like a drunkard across the set, waving the kitchen gadget menacingly, and crashes into the fake plywood kitchen counter, sink, and appliances. The false-front kitchen begins to come apart as Ralph and Norton, wrestling manically with each other, topple into the very walls of the set. As the director screams desperately, "Cut! Cut!" the commercial ends with a shot of the heap of plywood and dust to which Ralph and Norton have reduced the world of illusion.

Ralph and Norton unwittingly expose the fragile, fabricated world of the mass media. Norton's technical skill with paring knife and can opener remind us of how intricately entangled television, Madison Avenue, and the new technologies are. A proper tool is merely an extension of the arm or hand, and no technological innovation is better than the man who uses it. Ralph's psychological inability to perform on this stage (Ralph's stage fright is a convention of the series) dramatizes the split between his desires and his very human limits. As an obese Jackie Gleason plays the role, of course, the undeniable materiality of the working-class man (Ralph is fat; Norton is dirty) crashes through the immaterial world of television advertising.

The real world for working-class men like Ralph and Norton is an industrial world, even though the Great Depression has caused both of them to be employed in the vast service industries of the postmodern age.[16] The working-class identity of both characters is perfectly compatible with that of the nineteenth-century industrial worker. As an increasing number of working-class people entered service industries in America in this period, they could identify with characters like Ralph and Norton, who still do work that dirties the hands and exhausts the body. It is thus not difficult to understand why *The Honeymooners* consistently portrayed its own medium in such frivolous ways and as composed of such fragile illusions. Hollywood and Madison Avenue were not real for the viewers, and they were explicitly contrasted with the more substantial character of everyday labor, which then included those public services without which urban production would have been impossible.

The Honeymooners is thus not metafictional in its essence, as so many subsequent television shows would be. Dreams of success on the stage, on television, or in film are occasional complements to Ralph's more varied imaginary, and thus his contest with the media is merely one more instance of the show's moral imperative: the acceptance of the inherent values of one's working-class position in a period during which the very concepts of work and class were changing and often ambivalent. Rather than working monologically to impose the same truth on its enthralled audience, ideology functions dialogically to adapt its controlling terms to new historical circumstances that it has helped to produce. Thus the accommodation of Ralph and Ed to their new roles in public services draws upon stereotypes of the working class—hard physical labor, dreams of opportunity—and determines a new antagonist in the mass media that profit from illusion rather than concrete labor.

Postmodern television is more thoroughly prefigured, however, in shows like The George Burns and Gracie Allen Show (1950–58) and "I Love Lucy" (1951–57), in which theatricality, celebrity, and performance are the central concerns of form and content.[17] In "Situation Comedy, Feminism, and Freud: Discourses of Gracie and Lucy," Patricia Mellencamp has convincingly shown how these two situation comedies employed their comedy to contain women within the space of post–World War II domesticity: "In situation comedy, pacification of women occurred between 1950 and 1960 without a single critical mention that the genre's terrain had altered: the housewife, although still ruling the familial roost, changed from being a humorous rebel or well-dressed, wise-cracking, naive dissenter who wanted or had a paid job—from being out of control via language (Gracie) or body (Lucy)—to being a contented, if not blissfully happy, understanding homebody (Laura Petrie)."[18]

What Mellencamp terms "containment through laughter—a release which might have held women to their place, rather than 'liberating' them in the way Freud says jokes liberate their tellers and auditors"—depends crucially on the theatrical situations of both shows (Mellencamp, 87). George Burns plays "husband as television critic, solo stand-up comic, female psychologist, and tolerant parent/performer" to Gracie, who is subject to unsettling non sequiturs and potentially subversive nonsense (Mellencamp, 83). Ricky Ricardo plays Cuban bandleader and professional entertainer to Lucy, an aspiring performer who makes disastrous efforts to break into the "industry." Mellencamp concludes that the otherwise subversive gestures of Gracie's speech and Lucy's performances are allowed comic release *in order* to be controlled: "For Lucy, Gracie, and their audiences, humor was 'a rare and precious gift.' Given the repressive conditions of the 1950s, humor might have been women's weapon and tactic of survival, insuring sanity, the triumph of the ego, and pleasure; after all, Gracie and Lucy were narcissistically rebellious, refusing 'to be hurt.' On the other hand, comedy replaced anger, if not rage, with pleasure. . . . Whether heroic or not, this pleasure/provoking cover-up/ acknowledgement is not a laughing but a complex matter, posing the difficult problems of women's simulated liberation through comic containment" (Mellencamp, 94).

Mellencamp argues that the ideological effect of such containment is heightened considerably by the theatrical situation governing both domestic comedies: "Image/person/star are totally merged as 'himself,' the 'real' is a replayed image, a scene, a simulation—what Jean Baudrillard calls 'the hyperreal'" (Mellencamp, 88). For Mellencamp, the equation of person, personality, and performer in George, Gracie, Lucy, and Ricky, for example, lends special legitimacy and even universality to the specific social circumstances of each show: "Living in suburban, affluent Beverly Hills Gracie was certainly unlike TV's nurturing-yet-domineering mothers who dwelled in city apartments" (Mellencamp, 82). Gracie's upper-middle-class or Lucy's middle-class circumstances thus help repress the economic fact that after World War II, "[m]ost women over 35 remained in the paid work force; when allowed, instead of building battleships, they took other jobs" (Mellencamp, 81). The cliché of postwar American social history—reinforced by the recent nostalgia for the 1950s—has been that American women in this period were best defined by middle-class domesticity. Popular television not only delivered this message with a vengeance; it also employed the message to legitimate its own medium.

Mellencamp shows that the feminist issues cannot be separated from questions of race and class. "Lucy's resistance to patriarchy," for example, "might be more palatable because it is mediated by a racism which views Ricky as inferior" (Mellencamp, 90). I would add that the conflict between racism and feminism is complicated further by Ricky's status as a professional entertainer. Although the con man and trickster still haunt the worlds of the nightclub, theater, and film, Ricky Ricardo's efforts to make his way in the "industry" as a Cuban bandleader accord with the basic capitalist values of hard work, self-reliance, and initiative. Ambivalently poised between working-class immigrant and entertainment professional, Ricky uses the media to minimize the challenge he poses to working-class and middle-class viewers alike, at the same time that his character heightens interest in an otherwise conventional domestic sitcom. The role of Cuban bandleader satisfies the most obvious ethnocentric stereotypes, even as it allows him to pursue the American dream within a profession that reflects popular racial attitudes toward Cuban Americans.

The normality of Ricky's professional world, however, is what seems startling and still relatively contemporary to the rerun addict or television scholar. As *"I Love Lucy"* evolved into *The Lucille Ball–Desi Arnaz Show* (1958–60), Ricky's job was the convenient vehicle for introducing various celebrity guests.[19] On the one hand, Ricky is just a small businessman who relies on his technical and organizational skills to confront the daily problems that are presumed to plague the bourgeois viewer: closing the deal, being on time for appointments, networking, balancing the demands of work and family. At once an owner and a white-collar worker, an immigrant and a typical American husband, a slick musician (typified by loose morals and fast living) and a devoted family man, Ricky seems to be a perfectly malleable and duplicitous character. Yet in his professional life, the stress falls primarily on his consistent denial of clichés about Latin lovers who hang out in nightclubs. Ricky's flashy clothes are costumes; Latin lover is an occasionally convenient pose. Above all, it is clear that the fast times of the musician's life are much exaggerated once the viewer is allowed to see behind the surfaces of the media's machinery for illusion making. Entertainment is constantly justified as a necessary complement to the serious business of everyday work, and it quite clearly shares the values of proper work: discipline, motivation, self-reliance, initiative, and talent.

Mellencamp points out that "Ricky is not given equal, let alone superior, time" to the real star of the show, Lucy: "He constantly leaves the story, and his departure becomes the cue for comic mayhem and audience pleasure." Mellencamp judges this another instance of how Lucy's domesticated feminism works through the racism directed at Ricky "with his Cuban accent (constantly mimicked by Lucy)" (Mellencamp, 90). By no means contradicting this racism, Ricky's absences from the chaos of Lucy's attempts at theatrical performance reinforce it, but in an ideologically complex manner. Ricky goes away to work in the fundamentally prosaic world of the nightclub. Without substantial property, living in an apartment owned by a kindly but befuddled landlord, Fred Mertz (William Frawley) and his wife, Ethel (Vivian Vance), Ricky and Lucy are on the make. By the end of *"I Love Lucy,"* Ricky has indeed acquired property, but of the sort that expresses well the ambivalence of "owner-ship" in this transitional age; the Cuban bandleader at the Tropicana buys the place and renames it The Ricky Ricardo Babalu Club.[20] The Cuban immigrant, anxious to be assimilated, has been accepted by U.S. capital-ism and its ethos of dedication and hard work. By implication, Lucy's weekly failures as a professional performer may be less a judgment of her lack of talent (she is, after all, obviously talented as Lucille Ball), but of her failure to work at it. For Lucy and Ethel, entertainment is adventure, romance, and fun; for Ricky, it is business. At the same time, television has succeeded in subtly shifting conceptions of business, work, and prop-erty to legitimate its own fragile medium. In *The Lucille Ball-Desi Arnaz Show,* those parental surrogates, Fred and Ethel, leave behind their own property in New York and take to the road with Lucy and Ricky. Foils now for the celebrity guests (and dazzled by them), Fred and Ethel, albeit still parenting in ambivalent ways, also play servants to the rising aristoc-racy of a new landed gentry.

Lucy and Ricky both represent the shift from material production to the immaterial production of a postmodern, postindustrial economy. And yet each character works to reproduce in our viewing experience the familiar distinctions we inherited from nineteenth-century industrialism between domestic woman and working man, privacy and publicity, fami-ly and world. Even as Lucy outperforms Ricky, she testifies to the fact that real life is even more fantastic and unpredictable than the most elaborate stage production or nightclub act. The incredulity that we experience in this simulated world of the everyday finally is less a function of a world out of joint than of Lucy's failings. The pleasure offered by her comic re-siliency encloses Lucy in the space of the home by demonstrating how in-capable she is of inhabiting the world of work and discipline. As Ricky's success seems to teach us, illusion is serious business, best left to men.

By the last half of the 1960s, popular television had significantly changed its representation of gender and class in order to meet chal-lenges and alternatives to the nuclear family. Once again, the medium's self-consciousness may be used as an index of such change as well as an indication of how much the immaterial had come to penetrate everyday life. In ABC's domestic comedy *Bewitched* (1964–72), Elizabeth Mont-gomery played a witch, Samantha, struggling to escape her supernatural heritage and to find normality with Darrin Stevens (Dick York and later Dick Sargent), her utterly conventional, middle-class ad executive hus-band.[21] The condition of their marriage—that Samantha will not use her magical powers to affect their ordinary lives—is the taboo repeatedly violated in each episode. In virtually every program, Samantha must use her powers to resolve domestic problems no longer susceptible to mortal solutions. In most cases, "mortal" refers primarily to Darrin, who seems incapable of carrying out his customary duties as husband and wage earner without extraordinary assistance from his wife. Although in some episodes it is Samantha's supernatural relatives who cause the problems—most often out of very mortal motives (bourgeois clichés about troubled relations between a husband and his in-laws are all rehearsed again and again), most often Samantha "saves" Darrin from himself; from his exploitative boss, Larry Tate (David White); or from unreasonable clients.

Samantha's powers are quite obviously the narrative occasions for technical special effects designed to hold the viewer's interest in a show with an otherwise shopworn format. The sitcom is a transparent spin-off of *I Married a Witch*, René Clair's popular 1942 film starring Fredric March and Veronica Lake. When Samantha makes chairs move, people disappear, doors open, dogs meow, and cats bark, she is both literally and fictionally directing the representational medium of television. Lucy never quite breaks into show business; Samantha *is* show business. In episode after episode, her power over the representation of ordinary reality is presented as her compensation for an otherwise tedious, repetitive, and unrecognized life as housewife. Quite literally the woman behind the man, Samantha keeps the otherwise accident-prone Darrin from hurting himself or their marriage. By implication and repetition, *Bewitched* makes it clear that Samantha's magic is not much different from the imaginative feats required of the ordinary housewife trapped in a world of incompetent men.

In one especially explicit episode, Samantha is transported by one of her perverse relatives back to 1869 Charleston, where she awakens to the ambivalent role of a postbellum Southern belle. In her conversations with her African American servant, an African American mother and child on the street, her imaginary relatives, and her aristocratic and domineering husband, she discovers an affinity between the continuing servitude of recently emancipated Southern African Americans and the dependency of the Southern belle. The Hollywood romance she desires and the viewer yawningly expects is thoroughly dismissed. Even after Samantha has returned with relief to Darrin, their daughter, Tabitha, and her Westport, Connecticut, tract house, she still notices uncanny traces of her dream in her bourgeois circumstances.

Samantha's witchcraft not only gives her a compensatory power, often employed as a form of revenge against her otherwise impotent social role; it is also a strategic self-consciousness. Whether wielded by Samantha or her kin, such supernatural power customarily reveals the unconscious of ordinary reality. That such an unconscious is in its very essence fantastic, magical, and unreal generally says less about magic in the modern age than it does about the primarily fantastic substructure of bourgeois life. Men are only apparently competent, authoritative, and responsible; in the reality of Samantha's supernatural world, such men reveal themselves as grasping, jealous, and incompetent buffoons. Women are only superficially dependent, emotional, romantically deluded, and sexually servile; in the logic of Samantha's magic, they can transcend their historical circumstances, author their destinies, and comprehend with a certain pity the frailty of mortal men.[22]

The fact that Samantha continues to play this game of appearance and reality by agreeing to suppress her magic powers for the sake of domestic normality tells us a good deal about the conscious purpose of *Bewitched:* to legitimate bourgeois domestic relations at a particularly critical moment in the history of the U.S. family. In *I Married a Witch,* Jennifer (Veronica Lake) commits herself to Wally Wooley (Fredric March) by promising, "I'll try so hard to be a good wife, and I'll only use witchcraft to help you." In fact, Jennifer uses her powers to help Wooley win the race to be the governor of New York.[23] In contrast, Samantha always returns to her family and reaffirms her marriage vows by pledging never again to use her powers to affect their lives—until the next episode, that is. The cultural unconscious of *Bewitched,* however, betrays the growing consensus that the apparent normality of the bourgeois family is sustained by social customs that are at root fantastic and can be rendered acceptable only by the most elaborate magic.

Samantha's supernatural powers realize Lucy's dream of the stage and the liberated performing self, and they transcend the servile magic of Jeannie (Barbara Eden) in the NBC competitor (from 1965 to 1970), *I Dream of Jeannie.*[24] In that situation comedy, Jeannie's "master," Captain Tony Nelson (Larry Hagman), often undoes her magic, using his own technological skills as a NASA astronaut to counter her misguided wizardry. In the midst of U.S. troop build-ups in Vietnam and Pentagon forecasts of a quick end to the war by virtue of U.S. technological and military superiority, *I Dream of Jeannie* supports such foreign policies while utterly ignoring the Vietnam War itself. *Bewitched*'s Samantha is a decidedly more contemporary woman than Jeannie, whose cloying "Yes,

Master" and bared midriff (the censors covered her navel in 1968) trade shamelessly on older stereotypes of feminine erotic dependency. Even so, Samantha is hardly a liberated woman, although her character is conceived in the spirit of television's efforts to respond to the women's rights movement. By locating the supernatural at the center of the U.S. living room—both dramatically and in the viewer's experience—*Bewitched* argues that personal power and agency depend on our abilities to manipulate the imagery and spectacle of everyday life.

Samantha is in fact a producer and director; what attracts the viewer to her is her capacity to live comfortably with the fantastically metamorphic qualities of postmodern life. Ralph and Ed are unhappy with the fantastic, even as they live full of impossible dreams. Lucy is unhappy, perhaps even schizophrenic, hopelessly divided between the dazzling reality of the theater and the tedious nightmare of the kitchen. Jeannie is a fragile anachronism, always liable to vanish at the will of the more powerful magic of U.S. technology. Samantha triumphs—pyrrhically, of course—by adapting her powers to the work of television.[25]

My final example from network television is relatively random but strategic, insofar as it shifts our attention from the domestic situation comedy to the detective genre. As well as any popular series in the latter half of the 1970s, *The Rockford Files* (1974–80) epitomizes the fundamental *intertextuality* of television, in ways as complicated as a sophisticated literary work and yet doing different ideological work.[26] The show parodically trades on many of the conventions of the private eye narrative, from those of Dashiell Hammett and Raymond Chandler to their early television imitators. *Rockford* star James Garner's identification with the successful 1960s series *Maverick,* arguably the comic end to the television western, helped establish him in his role as the engagingly ironic private investigator who is often amazed at the fantasy world of Southern California. On the face of it, the detective or private eye form seems a world apart from the domestic sitcom, but it is precisely the confusion of these two television genres that distinguishes the postmodernity of television in the second half of the 1970s.

A spin-off of *Harry O,* a campy series about a marginal private investigator (David Janssen) living at the beach in San Diego, *The Rockford Files* weaves recent television history together with more venerable literary forms and types. Rockford is a reformed confidence man, in the best tradition of the American literary hero, who has served time for his crimes. We are never quite sure whether we are to believe Rockford that he was "framed," so the original "crime" allows him to operate both inside and outside the formal legal structure. In many other ways, Rockford occupies the cultural margin so often crowded with rogues, madmen, and prophets in the Western literary tradition. As a consequence, he possesses a certain insight into the nature of postmodern California, which is best expressed by his characteristic irony.

Rockford's wit is his saving grace in a world that has gone undeniably mad, and it is virtually identical to the playful irony that for some critics has been the impasse of the literary experimentalists of the late 1960s and early 1970s.[27] Always capable of telling a good story on himself, Rockford often verges on the brink of self-loathing, because he recognizes how intimately he is involved in the world he observes. Surrounded by the most meretricious extravagance and conspicuous consumption, which are clearly the symptoms of modern criminality, Rockford lives modestly in a rusting trailer on the beach in Malibu at Paradise Cove. On the one hand, his domestic circumstances seem counter-cultural, an extension of the 1960s counter-culture's rejection of bourgeois values for the sake of neo-ruralism. Rarely finding the time to fish from the pier or take a walk with a client-lover on the beach, Rockford dreams of escape from fantastic Los Angeles even as he knows that the city is his reality. Rockford's irony recalls that of Hammett's Nick Charles and Chandler's Philip Marlowe, but it also borrows from the ironic characters of the domestic sitcom, such as Lucy and Samantha. What Rockford's sordid underworld reveals is just what is repeatedly exposed and then repressed in the therapeutic narratives of those sitcoms: the contradictions of bourgeois, urban life.

Rockford's rebellion against middle-class life is not so much a rejection of his heritage as an ambivalent effort to rediscover his working-class roots. His father, Rocky (Noah Beery Jr.), is a trucker who shares his son's love of fishing, cooking, and the outdoors. Rockford's nearly hopeless project is to convince his father that his profession as a private investigator is legitimate and deserves the respect that Rocky grants to material labor. For Rocky, Rockford is simply playing at life, as his mysterious work, messy trailer, and bachelor circumstances all seem to prove. In contrast, Rocky lives in a substantial LA bungalow, neatly and traditionally furnished, surrounded by mementos of his dead wife.[28]

In many ways, the character of Rockford is simply a television cliché, a variation on the good-hearted tough guy. Rocky and Rockford's clients (in the cases involving female clients, Rockford's father almost always establishes a sympathetic relation, often hoping to match them with his son) are generally out of touch with reality, condemned to some twilight zone in which their common-sense values fail to accord with life as it must be lived in Los Angeles. Understanding as he does both worlds, Rockford mediates, serving as a version of Joseph Conrad's Marlow, who protects innocence with a strategic lie and still vigorously combats the deceptions that he knows constitute daily experience. There is, of course, nothing postmodern about such a narrative situation.

What is postmodern about *The Rockford Files* is the decidedly textual quality of this new world of "experience," that domain so unfamiliar to Rocky and Rockford's clients. Each episode opens with the same photo montage of Southern California's gaudy variety while a voice-over of Rockford's answering machine replays the messages of his day. Ordinary messages from irate bill collectors, jilted lovers, and neglected clients build to the message that establishes the plot. The ordinary and the extraordinary belong to the same textual reality, and technology only reinforces this association. The crimes that Rockford investigates are often quite conventional—missing persons, homicides, extortion, blackmail—but Rockford's investigations always follow his postmodern modus operandi. Rockford gathers "facts" and follows "leads" by way of strategic deception—posing as a state auditor to gain access to corporate records, playing the officious carpet cleaner to get into an office, disguising himself as a door-to-door salesman to enter a private home. In his car, Rockford keeps a portable printing press, where he turns out new business cards and documents according to his needs.

The series is called *The Rockford Files* because the stories are supposedly drawn from Rockford's professional records, but he has no office, secretary, or bulging filing cabinets. Lacking even the grubby trappings of professionalism of a Philip Marlowe, Rockford relies on nothing but his metamorphic "character," his changeable personality as trickster, *homo ludens*. In his car or in his trailer, Rockford is Southern Californian transience personified. His gold Firebird is his office, and each episode involves at least one choreographed car-chase scene, from which Rockford generally emerges triumphant. His car, his printing press, his masks, and his trailer are his best weapons.[29] Rockford is the consummate Hollywood actor, who prepares for his next scene in his trailer on the set. When he "solves" the crime, he does so most often by changing the script he has been given and substituting his own text for that of his antagonist, thereby producing rather than discovering the solution to the crime.

Living outside this world—fishing in the woods, settling down to a secure bourgeois existence—has undeniable attractions for Rockford, but he knows that to do so he would have to unmake himself. His girlfriend, Beth Davenport (Gretchen Corbett), is his lawyer, and both vow not to marry. It's not surprising, then, that Rockford's trailer is *neither* an office nor a home, but some unstable and temporary combination of the two. Although its shabbiness belies the comparison, his trailer prefigures the home office of the 1980s: that imaginary condo in Century City where the young tycoon does his business by phone, modem, computer, and fax. Living in this world, Rockford must play the theatrical game better than his antagonist and produce a more convincing (marketable) product. Rocky trusts his working-class friends and extends this trust to the rest of the world, often at the risk of his son's career and life. Rockford trusts no one, rejecting at the very last even those innocent victims for whom he has battled. Least of all does he trust himself, for he knows that he is nothing but a composition of all the characters he has experienced in this fantastic world. Thus Rockford's irony is not simply his final defense, but his form of self-consciousness, the way that he knows himself as nothing but the roles he is compelled to play.

Interpreting a television character like Jim Rockford in such decidedly ponderous ontological terms may at first appear absurd, but television shows in the 1970s seemed increasingly to make certain philosophical claims about the order of things and people. As television became the primary medium of social exchange, it also began to assume a certain philosophical authority. Like the artist heroes of the high modern novel, Rockford is an essentially classless figure whose understanding of reality encompasses and transcends different classes and social groups. Nostalgically attracted to his working-class origins, fitfully entranced by middle-class respectability, Rockford actually aspires to the sort of power and authority that he combats each week. Although he denies his criminal past, Rockford actually wants to become the sort of criminal who lives outside the law or who, better yet, makes the law while escaping its confinement.

The Rockford Files marks the historical moment in which television replaced the novel as a philosophical medium, just as the modernist novel had replaced formal philosophy and even lyric poetry as the cultural medium for introspection and abstract thought. I make such a hyperbolic claim without in any way judging the artistic qualities of *The Rockford Files* relative to *Absalom, Absalom!* or *The Great Gatsby.*[30] Putting aside for the moment such aesthetic criteria, forgetting even the crucial issue of audience, I would still contend that a show like *Rockford* marks a special turn in U.S. cultural representation. Fully at home in a world of utter theatricality, Rockford makes no strenuous effort to expose the lies of this world, except in his struggle to make his own fictional production commercially successful and competitive.

As a consequence, *The Rockford Files* encourages the viewer not only to accept the conditions of the postmodern U.S.—a society remade in the image of Southern California—but also to actively participate in this basic economy. Charmed by Rocky's quaint variations on the father's perennial advice to his children—"Get a *real* job!"—the viewer still sides with the son, who knows that a hard day's work in this world requires a good script. Ed Norton and Ralph Kramden bring the fragile walls of the soundstage tumbling down, but Lucy, Samantha, and Jeannie rebuild them more solidly to become the four walls of our family rooms. Jim Rockford builds the walls out further, until they assume the airy shapes of the postmodern city.

From the cult of show business celebrity and the weekly sitcom to the "talk show," television history reveals the growing self-reflexivity of the medium. Peter Conrad explains Johnny Carson's success in terms of Carson's understanding of television's explicit appeal to its unreality: "Being on television is about being on television. If you forget the medium and its unreality, you fail."[31] As Conrad realizes, however, the medium's irony about its own illusion—an irony that could turn the "blooper" into a genre—hardly subverts or demystifies the medium. Rather, it increases its power by claiming for it a "hyperrealism" that well fits our postmodern situation. Unlike such high cultural and avowedly counter-cultural forms as the serious novel, television has not claimed such self-reflexivity as the unique and distinguishing characteristic of its forms. Instead, television has increasingly claimed that the fictionality and style of even its most extravagant programs merely follows the rhetoric of everyday life. Effacing itself, claiming a humble, albeit unfamiliar realism, popular television has aligned itself with the productive laws of a postmodern economy.

In the 1970s, network television assumed an increasingly serious air even in its most frivolous productions. In that decade, television dramas and sitcoms took on a certain pedagogical mission to teach us how to interpret our own personal relations to an irreducibly theatrical world, and it is an educational claim that structures the "reality television" of the twenty-first century. I am not referring here to the shallow bids for social relevance made by virtually every new television melodrama or to the host of documentaries, docudramas, and "news magazines" that crowd the pages of the bulging TV guides. Family shows and "white papers," talk shows and interviews, civil rights sitcoms and feminist police shows are mere by-products of the deeper philosophical, hermeneutical, and economic authority of television. Understanding the claims to social authority made by electronic media like television will require far more work than the brief and somewhat formalistic analyses of selected programs I have offered in this chapter. Just how U.S. society and its conventions of self-representation are transformed by such media, today sources of significant portions of the gross national product, will require histories of the economic, historical, institutional, and reception factors that have elevated these media to such positions of authority.

9.

"Bringing It All Back Home"

U.S. Recyclings of the Vietnam War

To put the old names to work, or even just to leave them in circulation, will always, of course, involve some risk: the risk of settling down or of regressing into the system that has been, or is in the process of being, deconstructed. To deny this risk would be to confirm it: it would be to see the signifier—in this case the name—as a merely circumstantial, conventional occurrence of the concept or as a concession without any specific effect.

—Derrida, "Outwork," in *Dissemination*

That the "old name" of Vietnam has been put to work by U.S. culture in ways that have kept it circulating, like some ceaselessly rubbed and fingered coin, needs hardly to be argued or demonstrated. No bibliography could cover the enormous representational productivity of this war: the war has left us with an unparalleled volume and variety of texts, images, stories, studies, and products. It continues to be interpreted as a war of information, interpretation, and representation, even though such academic words must sound foolish and hollow to those who fought it. It was the most chronicled, documented, reported, filmed, taped, and—in all likelihood—narrated war in history, and for those very reasons, it would seem, the least subject to understanding or to any consensus.

The war remains radically ambiguous, undecidable, and indeterminate for the U.S. public, and the heterogeneity of what we name either "Vietnam" or the "Vietnam War" (the terms have become troublingly

173

interchangeable) seems to grow even more explicit and tangled with every new effort to "heal" the wounds, with every new monument, parade, film, book. Marxists have interpreted the war as a postmodern war whose contradictions turned apparently stable ground into the quagmire secretly at the base of capitalist theories and practices. Poststructuralists have ingeniously argued that the war was conducted by the National Liberation Front (NLF) by means of a postmodern military strategy that understood the hermeneutic possibilities of booby traps and surprise attacks.[1] No Western literary experimentalist could match the ingenuity of the NLF soldier who could turn a C ration tin and a hand grenade into a lethal booby trap or the terrible technology of the Bouncing Betty mine, which destroyed the lower limbs and genitals and attacked the myths of manhood and heroism of the U.S. military. Following curiously the same line of argument, politically conservative, revisionary historians have claimed that the Vietnamese played both the antiwar movement in the United States and the insecurity and unfamiliarity with Vietnam of U.S. troops as if they were syncopated parts of a carefully composed tune.

It is just half a step from the poststructuralist arguments concerning the uncanny bricolage of the guerilla and the neoconservative arguments regarding the NLF's exploitation of the ambiguities of the war to a familiar old conclusion concerning the "mystery" of the Orient, with its thinly veiled master narrative of the cynical, amoral, wily, and manipulative Asian. Likewise, the arguments, such as Frances FitzGerald's, that insist upon the radical philosophical, religious, and cultural differences between U.S. and Vietnamese citizens as sources of the war reinforce popular conceptions of a strange, impenetrable "East"—an ethnocentrism reinforced by a U.S. foreign policy that has kept postwar Vietnam out of the news, except when events in Southeast Asia appear to justify our earlier policies. The familiar ethnocentrism and racism of imperialism, then, are reinforced, even reinvented, with a difference by way of claims for the radical ambiguity and undecidability of the Vietnam War, especially in terms of its significance for U.S. culture.

This is hardly a popular view, even among academics, for the convention has been that since Truman the U.S. government and other agents of ideology have been intent on stonewalling the issue of Vietnam, sticking to a story that the complex realities and historical events seem to name just that: a "story" to cover the bungling, ignorance, and human waste of the war. This has prompted the critical and alternative perspectives on the war of feminists , ranging from nurses' accounts of publicly unrecognized service "in country" to feminists' deconstructions of the patriarchal myths informing our policies in that and other wars; politically active veterans' groups, such as Winter Soldier and the Vietnam Veterans of America; and Vietnamese Americans, who have their own accounts of the war and its representations. These and other perspectives seemingly have added a pluralism to the name of "Vietnam" that was once cynically imagined to be a fragile edifice constructed by the military-industrial complex.

Linked to other, often subversive, discourses—those of feminism, Marxism, poststructuralism, and postmodernism—"Vietnam" has escaped the control of ideology and has become the changeable referent for a process of complex cultural dissemination. Recycled and rechanneled, Vietnam has become one commonly used index—the "Vietnam effect"— of social change that our failure in that war certainly demanded. In the 1980s, changing U.S. attitudes toward the Vietnam War and toward war in general were evident in popular oral and epistolary histories of soldiers' and noncombatants' experiences in and out of combat, such as *Bloods: An Oral History of the Vietnam War by Black Veterans* (1984) and *Brothers: Black Soldiers in the Nam* (1982); Lynda van Devanter's (with Christopher Morgan) *Home before Morning: The Story of an Army Nurse in Vietnam* (1983), Patricia Walsh's fictionalized account of her work as a nurse in a Vietnamese civilian hospital, *Forever Sad the Hearts* (1982); and minority films of the "third cinema," such as *Ashes and Embers*.[2] These and other works provided important alternative readings of the Vietnam experience, especially in their attention to the specific ways gender, race, and class shaped the war experiences of the groups represented. A common theme of these works, for example, is the irony that U.S. minorities were drafted to fight a war of imperialist aggression against other subaltern peoples. This is, of course, an old concern of liberal critiques of the war. In Peter Davis's documentary *Hearts and Minds* (1974), a Native American veteran of the war is interviewed, dressed casually in jeans and work shirt, sitting on a rock above the New Mexico desert : "In boot camp, I was called 'Ira Hayes' or 'Blanket Ass,'" he says, "depending on the drill sergeant's mood. I knew all about racism long before I went to Vietnam, yet I went anyway. From early on, I had been taught that the Marines were the best, the warrior class in this country, and I wanted to be a part of that."[3] Van Devanter writes of the treatment of U.S. nurses by U.S. soldiers, who often mixed sexist clichés about the easy morals of nurses with racist stereotypes applied to Vietnamese prostitutes. Accounts of the Presidio riots in San Francisco and other racially motivated riots among troops in Vietnam have stressed the ways that the war foregrounded

American racism as one of the motives for the war itself as well as one of the factors contributing to our military failure in Vietnam.[4]

In the 1970s and 1980s, the Vietnam Veterans of America and the Winter Soldier organization, which conducted its own trials of U.S. officials for war crimes, represented the significant political activism of Vietnam War veterans. Well into the 1980s, small guerilla theaters were run by veterans in many urban centers, as well as ensemble companies, such as the Vietnam Veterans Ensemble Theater Company in New York. Plays such as John di Fusco's *Tracers* (1980) emerged from marginal theater groups to have successful popular runs in traditional theaters.[5] Written, directed, produced, staged, and acted by veterans, such plays reflected the political solidarity that many veterans considered their only means to redress such specific grievances as the medical consequences of the military's widespread use of the Agent Orange herbicide/defoliant in Vietnam and the psychological effects of PVS (post-Vietnam syndrome) or PTSS (post-traumatic stress syndrome), as well as the more general consequences of U.S. foreign policy and the cultural repression of Vietnam as a sociopolitical entity. The work of such groups often incorporated symbolic forms into larger political projects. Thus the New York Vietnam Veterans Memorial Commission collected and published *Dear America: Letters Home from Vietnam* (1985) as one part of its collective effort to shape the memory of Vietnam in the public conscience. Taken together, the memorial itself, covered with portions of letters and other documents from the Vietnam War, and *Dear America* constitute a single work of political art and activism.[6] All of these countercultural efforts on the part of marginal groups affected by the war can be said to have been motivated by genuine commitments specifically at odds with the dominant ideology. Yet what is remarkable about U.S. ideology is the speed with which it can incorporate a wide variety of critical perspectives into an enveloping rhetorical system designed to maintain traditional order and values.

In 1985, CBS television initiated a new project aimed at the home market: *The Vietnam War,* a series of videotapes culled primarily from the war coverage of the *CBS Evening News.*[7] The overall organization of the series (eleven tapes of approximately one hour each were produced) and the internal organization of each tape are a confused mixture of thematic treatment and historical record. The third tape, *The Tet Offensive,* seems to suggest a purely historical approach, but the first two, *Courage under Fire* (concerned with the various means ground troops used to deal with the psychological pressures and physical dangers of an unpredictable war) and *Fire from the Sky* (about the air war), trace their themes in a loosely chronological manner. The curious combination of theme and history allowed the editors of this series to make some interesting revisions to the war. In *Courage under Fire,* for example, the selections proceed from 1965 to 1971, except for the final and longest selection. Nearly half of the entire tape (30 of the tape's 61 minutes) is devoted to Charles Kuralt's famous "Christmas in Vietnam," originally presented as a TV special filmed in 1965 and concerned with the daily lives and deaths in one military company along the demilitarized zone (DMZ). In this episode of the tape, whose length and formal organization make it stand out from the rest of the selections, the perspective is that of Sergeant Bossulet, a handsome and extremely capable African American officer who shows profound concern for his men's lives and his military duties. The dramatic action focuses on one of Bossulet's best enlisted men, José Duinez, a specialist in mines and booby traps, who is from Guam, where he fought the Japanese during the occupation of Guam. In the hour-long *Courage under Fire,* we see absolutely no Vietnamese—no civilians, no members of the Army of the Republic of Vietnam (ARVN), the National Liberation Front (NLF), or the North Vietnamese Army (NVA)—either living or dead. Duinez dies while looking for enemy mines, following the orders of Sergeant Ray Floyd, a blustering, macho white soldier who insists that they "look for ourselves" for an elusive sniper who has daily been attacking the camp from just beyond the tree line.

My bare description already suggests some of the peculiarities of Kuralt's 1965 mini-drama of Vietnam. The victimized Vietnamese people are erased from the entire tape, only to be replaced by a victimized U.S. soldier, represented as capable and admirable by his African American commanding officer, who has our full sympathy. Duinez, a native of Guam, is from a Western perspective indistinguishable from the Vietnamese, and his tragic death, mourned by Bossulet, concludes "Christmas in Vietnam," displacing concern for the Vietnamese and the political issue of American imperialism. Duinez's struggle with the Japanese on occupied Guam and the generally unquestioned heroism of U.S. troops in the Second World War are invoked to shape our attitudes. That perception, however, is complexly mediated by our sympathies for Bossulet, who betrays no hint of racial self-consciousness as an African American officer in this war and who epitomizes the ideals of a democratic leader intent on fulfilling his responsibilities to each man in his company. Even so, a quick interlude with Bossulet's wife and five children in California, who are trimming the Christmas tree, is accompanied by Charles Kuralt's explanation that Bossulet moved his family from New York, where he had grown up, to Seaside, California, just before being shipped out to keep his children from experiencing the urban violence in which he had been raised.

It goes without saying that the ethnocentrism of U.S. imperialism in Southeast Asia and of racism at home are reinforced by such a narrative. Our admiration for Bossulet and Duinez is conditioned by their military discipline, as if to say that the fate of so many disadvantaged minorities in the United States—military service—is just what the advertisements say it is: an opportunity for these minorities to lift themselves up by their own bootstraps. That these two men have uncritically lent their life stories to the task of legitimating such institutions as the military and the bourgeois family and such cultural myths as self-reliance and leadership is central to my claim that U.S. ideology recognizes the dissemination of Vietnam into other critical discourses and employs the rhetoric of these discourses for its own conservative purposes.

Even more interesting in the video *Courage under Fire* is the way that history is subtly revised using countercultural criticisms of the war. The historical argument represented in the video is constantly emphasized by Walter Cronkite's voice-over narration and occasional appearances, next to a map of Vietnam and a U.S. flag, to provide historical transitions and explanations. His authority in this video series is based on his experience as the anchor of the *CBS Evening News* during much of the war, and in the CBS Video Library tapes that authority has transformed him from newscaster to professional historian. With the map and flag as props, Cronkite plays the role of a professor, teaching us a history he only read while doing the *Evening News*. In the organization of *Courage under Fire,* this history forms a circle, beginning with black-and-white combat footage from 1965, the year of our first troop landings at Da Nang, then moving forward through the succeeding years and finally back to the 1965 "Christmas in Vietnam," filmed along the DMZ. In these selections from 1965, the U.S. soldiers have an air of innocence that is starkly absent, except for purposes of irony, from such later documentaries as Peter Davis's *Hearts and Minds* (1974) or even such establishment documentaries as *Vietnam: A Television History* (1983) and *Vietnam: The Ten Thousand Day War* (1984). The confusion of the soldiers, their fear, and yet their consistent sense of unquestioning duty, as yet undisturbed by antiwar demonstrations back home or by the public exposure of government lies, are immediately evident in the "Christmas in Vietnam" segment. Like the U.S. soldiers in Eugene Jones's documentary *A Face of War*, filmed during the ninety-seven days Jones and his camera crew lived with the Third Company of the Seventh Marine Battalion in 1966, "Christmas in Vietnam" was designed to represent the honest confusion and "equivocal realities" of U.S. attitudes toward the war in the mid-1960s.[8] To have made such an argument in 1965 or 1966, as Eugene Jones did, is perhaps understandable as a consequence of the specific confusions of that historical moment. It is an entirely different matter for the CBS Video Library to draw upon the ironies and confusion of 1965–66 in a 1985 history of the war. This revisionary history achieves its ends not so much by returning us to a more innocent time but, more insidiously, by *incorporating* those very countercultural challenges that are aimed at bringing about searching reexaminations of social attitudes and public policies.

Even though *Courage under Fire* concludes sentimentally with a 1965 episode of war, this video nonetheless appears to offer a short history of U.S. military heroism during the most difficult battles of the war. Yet at critical moments of that history, the video is carefully composed to avoid criticism of our foreign policy and military conduct. For example, brief news clips and commentary by Cronkite refer to President Nixon's military incursions into Cambodia, beginning in April 1970. More than any other events during 1970 and 1971, the U.S. invasion of Cambodia brought public pressure on the Nixon administration to end the war. None of this protest is represented on the video, just as none of the crucial history is even narrated, such as Nixon's troop reductions in April (100,000) and November (another 139,000) or the nine-point North Vietnamese peace proposal made to Henry Kissinger in June and Kissinger's revised peace plan in October, calling for the withdrawal of U.S. forces within six months.

Instead, Cronkite turns from the military incursions into Cambodia to the "courage of young American women in Vietnam." The tape's account of the year 1971 is thus fully occupied with CBS News interviews of nurses at the Ninety-first Hospital and with medics during a Medevac operation at Hawk Hill. These interviews seem to indicate that CBS News was concerned with the situation of women in Vietnam long before feminists connected women in Vietnam with the more general issue of women and war. Anyone who watched the *CBS Evening News* in the years 1970 and 1971 is aware that "women in Vietnam" was a question of little consequence to the network, an issue treated merely to provide local color or "filler." Re-viewed partly in light of feminists' challenges to patriarchal culture, partly in light of the exploitation of women in war (for many feminists *the* social phenomenon best suited to expose the irrationality and arbitrariness of patriarchal values), this segment on women in Vietnam served the CBS Video Library not just as the means of appearing current but as a means to accommodate the very feminist challenge to the cultural history being rewritten by patriarchy itself.

It is, of course, no revelation that marginal, countercultural, critical discourses are used in this manner in more popular forms of representation. The common conclusions about such borrowings, however, are that they function clumsily and obviously in the manner of what was once termed "radical chic" and that they thus even more readily betray the contradictions at work in that rhetoric of domination. When military fatigues and boots migrate from soldiers to antiwar demonstrators and then to high-fashion models, the path of metonymic displacement is hardly direct or simple. Such semiotic drift also involves complex combinatory (metaphoric) processes that help prepare a market for such by-products as the Saturday morning cartoon series *Rambo.*[9] The rediscovery of the military "hero" in such 1980s films as *An Officer and a Gentleman* (1982), *Top Gun* (1986), *Rambo: First Blood* (1982), *Rambo: First Blood, Part II* (1985), *Commando* (1985), *Heartbreak Ridge* (1986), and a host of other less publicized films is often judged merely a transparent recycling of familiar stereotypes out of Hollywood's mythopoeia of the 1940s and 1950s, as well as of the various nineteenth-century cultural sources of such heroism that informed cinematic mythmaking.[10] One plausible motive for this revival of the military hero in the 1980s was the U.S. government's manipulation of the cultural mythology to condition public support for new military ventures in the Caribbean, the Middle East, and Central America during Reagan's administration and in the Persian Gulf during George H. Bush's administration.[11] Yet this ideological transparency is considerably more difficult to "see through" when we consider how centrally these heroes incorporate countercultural and critical conventions.

Sylvester Stallone's Rambo character incorporates countercultural signs in just such a complex manner, which accounts in part for the extraordinary success of the several Rambo films and spin-offs. *First Blood* (1982) opens with Rambo walking down a rural road somewhere in the Northwest. Dressed in his army jacket and carrying a bedroll, his hair long, he looks like one of the many urban dropouts who moved to rural areas, especially in the Northwest, in rebellion against the urban, technological, military U.S. What he finds at the end of this road is the homestead of his African American buddy from Vietnam, Delmar Berry. Built on the shores of a magnificent mountain lake, with a sublime backdrop of snowy peaks, the sturdy cabin, outbuildings, and other signs of frontier life are designed to replicate an earlier, more authentic United States. Delmar's wife is hanging wash, and the children are playing in the yard; she greets Rambo with suspicion. Delmar has died of cancer, a victim of Agent Orange.

From this point on, the film uses a complex set of entangled images to construct the character of Rambo: the NLF's guerilla war for liberation, the U.S. counterculture's and antiwar movement's rejection of U.S. capitalism, the self-reliance of the early settlers, the alienation of African Americans, the modern film and television western's antiheroism, and the Vietnam veteran's exploitation during and after the war. The successful refashioning of these figures, drawn as they are from radically different political, historical, and representational contexts, is achieved primarily by the overdetermined myth of U.S. self-reliance and its conventional associations with the individual's existential isolation, moral conviction, resistance to the inevitable corruptions of civilization, and reaffirmation of nature.

When Rambo enters "Holidayland," the small town where his troubles begin, he is identified not simply as a potentially troublesome drifter, but as part of the counterculture. The sheriff's first words are: "Wearing that flag on that jacket and looking the way you do, you're asking for trouble around here." In the police station, everyone in sight is wearing a U.S. flag, so we must conclude that the sheriff takes Rambo's wearing a flag on his tattered military jacket as a sign of defiance, a gesture of his sympathy with the antiwar movement. This is certainly confirmed by the sheriff's obsession to "clean him up" and give Rambo "a haircut." All the derisive chatter in the sheriff's station—"Talk about your sorry-looking humanity" and "Smells like an animal"—recalls the contempt for "hippies" that was so prevalent in the popular culture of the late 1960s and early 1970s. When the sheriff's deputies finally do force Rambo to take a bath, they hose him down with a large, high-pressure fire hose. The scene, with Rambo twisting and turning in the powerful spray, recalls scenes of civil demonstrations from Selma, Alabama, to Washington, D.C., from the civil rights movement to the antiwar movement. As Rambo flashes back to scenes of his imprisonment and torture in Vietnam, the metaphors of U.S. civil disobedience are associated with him. The brief images of Rambo's Vietnamese captors are clearly modeled—as they are even more explicitly in the sequel to this film, *Rambo, First Blood, Part II*—after Hollywood stereotypes of Japanese captors in World War II. By the same token, in both films Rambo appropriates the guerilla methods the NLF employed in trying to achieve precisely those aims we would never allow them to achieve: freedom from despotic rule and irrational authority.

Rambo's arrest, his escape from the sheriff's station, and the rapid escalation of violence sparked by these events play ambiguously upon conservative defenses and liberal criticisms of U.S. foreign policies. Arrested for vagrancy and as a potential troublemaker, Rambo can identify with minorities such as Native Americans, African Americans, and counter-cultural hippies, who are routinely hassled by the police without good reason. When he breaks out of the sheriff's station, Rambo acts out the heroic fantasy of a prisoner of war escaping the notorious "Hanoi Hilton." And when the National Guard is called out to help the incompetent sheriff, the "escalation" of the conflict reminds viewers of the rapid U.S. troop buildups that occurred in Vietnam as the ARVN betrayed its incompetence to cope with the guerillas in the NLF. Rambo may thus represent multiple identities—oppressed minorities and hippies, prisoners of war, and the "Viet Cong"—in the dramatic action of the film, enabling viewers from different groups to identify with him in different ways. Taken together, these identities produce a contradictory "character," but there is nothing incoherent in its representation in the film. We are able to follow and understand Rambo's actions without any serious cognitive dissonance.

The survival equipment that Rambo takes with him into the Northwest woods reminds us of his training in the Special Forces at the same time that it suggests the transcendentalist's aim of reducing life to its lowest terms. His cruel-looking double-edged knife is, of course, a technological token, but it is a version of the Bowie knife and contains in its handle a compass, needle, and thread. The technology that invented this knife belongs to the inventiveness of the frontiersman, not the wizardry of the computer engineer. Dragging their sophisticated assault rifles through the woods, tripping over their bazookas, the police and National Guardsmen who track Rambo epitomize alienated, postindustrial man. The targets of Rambo's furious violence are not primarily people, but the objects of technology: he uses his survival skills not only to outwit the National Guard troops who have him trapped in a cave, but to overcome the sophisticated weaponry they use to try to seal the cave's mouth.[12] The tools and weapons he employs in his rebellion, with the exception of his body and his knife, have been taken from his antagonists, in perfect imitation of the tactics of the NLF, whose booby traps and mines were often made of salvaged and captured U.S. military equipment.

Stumbling into the nightmare of Holidayland in *First Blood,* instead of finding the society he had sought with his friend, Delmar Berry, Rambo gathers together a complex set of signs from high literature, popular culture, and film to figure the U.S. desire for a purifying (and thus often violently cathartic) return to first principles and original revolutionary zeal. In Peter Davis's documentary *Hearts and Minds*, Bostonians dressed as Revolutionary War soldiers for a Fourth of July celebration are interviewed concerning their views of the revolutionary struggle of the Vietnamese. One modern Minuteman reflects: "Yeah, I guess there's kind of a parallel there. They're fighting a foreign invader; they're fighting on their home soil. But the analogy stops about there. I mean, Oriental politics? You got to be kidding me!" Davis's argument that the Vietnam War was not a civil war between North and South, but a revolutionary war against French, Japanese, and U.S. colonizers was a common one among antiwar activists. Rambo's patriotism is not a straightforward expression of right-wing politics.[13] By linking Rambo with the strategies and politics of the National Liberation Front, as well as with conventional images of an earlier, revolutionary colonial America, the filmmakers transform the victory of the North Vietnamese into a useful trope for U.S. nationalism.

Thus when Rambo returns to Vietnam to rescue American prisoners of war in *Rambo: First Blood, Part II* (1985), we are fully prepared for him to reject the authority of the U.S. military in favor of his own revolution. Armed with the most sophisticated military hardware, Rambo is forced to cut himself free from most of this gear when the crew flying him in botches his parachute drop from a camouflaged corporate jet. As he cuts the cords binding him to the plane, Rambo is born again out of the necessity that has always fueled his frontier spirit and powers of self-reliance. Reassured that his safety will be protected by an elaborate computer command center, Rambo proclaims: "I've always believed that the mind is the best weapon." The sentiments are a bit shopworn by now, but they are perfectly recognizable as derivative of the U.S. transcendentalist tradition.

"Man thinking" may be a strange motto for Rambo, but it is this claim that prevents his characteristic silence from signifying the mere stupidity and brute physicality he represents for most of the Americans in the film (and watching the film, as well). His meditativeness is frequently linked to his sympathies for the exploited and victimized. When he first meets the Vietnamese woman Co, they greet each other in Vietnamese.[14] Both are dressed in clothing that resembles what popular U.S. culture of the war years derisively termed the "black pajamas" of the NLF. Co's first words in English are: "Did not expect a woman, no?" Yet for all his macho, Rambo is no sexist; "We better go," is all he answers, as if to imply that he believes the individual will always prove himself or herself according to actions, not the class, gender, or race with which he or she is associated. When Co tells her personal story, it is as simple as possible: "My father . . . killed; I take his place." Like Rambo, Co is liberated by necessity, in the burning fire of experience that dissolves national, class, racial, and gender distinctions. Co acts most daringly and bravely when she dons the garb of a prostitute and plays the coquette with the Vietnamese guards to gain entrance to the POW camp. The "enemy"—U.S., Soviet, or Vietnamese—views women as prostitutes, playthings for male desire. Thus when she opens fire on the camp guards and tosses Rambo his weapon, her violence is doubly, uncannily legitimate. As the conventional hero's "girl," she buys into sexist clichés about women who would die for love; as the sexually abused woman, she joins a host of feminine characters in 1980s films who turned their victimization by men into motives for violent revenge.

By associating Rambo with the frontier spirit, transcendentalist self-reliance, twentieth-century neoruralism, the antiwar and civil rights movements, the revolutionary zeal of the National Liberation Front, and the politicized Vietnam veteran, Stallone's first two Rambo films incorporate these different and clearly critical discourses into the general revisionary view of the Vietnam War. In histories and novels, films and plays, the revisionary argument ranges from specific criticism of our military strategies in Vietnam to a more general indictment of the failure of our national will. In *First Blood, Part II,* the Soviets have arrived in Vietnam as quickly and pervasively as the most strident anticommunist from the McCarthy era had predicted. They have arrived for the same reasons the conservatives had claimed they would: the creeping immorality and weakness of the U.S. people. The cynicism and expediency of the men conducting the "Delta Force" mission that Rambo joins are, with the exception of Colonel Trautman, Rambo's last link to the "old Vietnam," and they exemplify the moral and physical weakness that allowed us to accept defeat at the Paris Peace Talks. Even Trautman, of course, betrays his own name and reputation, caught as he is between the radical individualism of Rambo and the military bureaucracy he represents. In German, *traut* literally means "dear" or "intimate," but *die Traute* used colloquially means "guts" or "courage"; both senses are combined in the veteran's conventional belief that his comrade in arms was his intimate just insofar as they shared the courage needed to survive the war. Even so, it is not antiwar activists, bleeding-heart liberals, weeping mothers, or lazy minorities who have brought about this corruption of U.S. values in the semiotic code of the two films. Aligning himself with all of these marginalized groups, Rambo directs his rage against the military-industrial complex, thereby turning genuine dissent into an affirmation of the very nationalism that took us to Vietnam in the first place.

The Vietnamese and the Soviets are unequivocal enemies, even if the Soviets express more admiration for Rambo as a man than do members of his own Delta Force. In a "fair fight," Rambo can beat the most extravagant odds, as he does in his guerilla war inside Vietnam, in an uncanny replay of the NLF's extraordinary military victory over the United States. Before he leaves, Colonel Trautman tells him, "Let technology do most of the work," but it is just this technology that is Rambo's real enemy. Co's father "worked for intelligence agency" and was killed as a consequence; Co may be taking his place, but she does so as a warrior rather than as a spy. *First Blood, Part II* marshals countercultural arguments against new technologies in the United States to claim that the war in Vietnam would have been better conducted by freedom fighters like Rambo and Co, both of whom represent the best virtues of their respective cultures. Although each of them seeks the "quiet" life, both are ready to protect the right of each individual to such a life by force of arms.[15] By claiming that our failure in Vietnam was caused by leaders far from the scenes of battle who blindly relied on technological representations of the war, *First Blood, Part II* diverts our attention from such obvious political issues as U.S. anticommunism after World War II and our commitment to outdated foreign policies related to the balance of power. But this diversion is by no means simply achieved, insofar as it works through codes stolen from liberal critiques of the war and contemporary U.S. society.

The general distrust of representation in the two Rambo movies and many other popular works suggests an interesting twist on the metaliterary concerns of much postmodern literature. Rambo's preternatural silence, his preference for actions over words, and his undeniable physicality clearly set him apart from his commanders, who are distinguished primarily by their computer literacy. Rhetorical duplicity belongs to technology, and in this regard the first two Rambo films align themselves with those antiwar activists who judged as our greatest immorality in the Vietnam War the lies by which our leaders kept the public deluded for so long. Rambo is not too far removed from the laconic countercultural characters in *Easy Rider* (1969), who clearly prefer immediate impressions to words and texts. Yet this clear distinction between action and representation diverts us from the complex means the first two Rambo films employ to establish their hero. Both films are full of scenes of data gathering in rooms full of computers, telephones, and information-processing equipment that have the same status as technologically sophisticated weaponry. These very sites are invariably the scenes of Rambo's most violent rage. He smashes the instruments of representation with the same zeal with which the filmmakers repress their own representational borrowings. The conventional scene of "literary self-consciousness" is transformed into an apocalyptic moment in which the machinery of technological man is repudiated, even though the viewer is perfectly aware that the cameras are still running. The consequence is a film, like *First Blood, Part II,* that appears unabashedly popular, nakedly trading on the easiest and most obvious sentiments, and thus appealing to a kind of folk art stylization.

John Hellmann has persuasively argued that the virtual artistic silence on the subject of Vietnam from 1968 to 1974 was filled in part by the "Vietnam western or antiwestern, epitomized by Ralph Nelson's *Soldier Blue* (1970) and Arthur Penn's *Little Big Man* (1971)."[16] Bringing the war literally back home, especially by way of such equivocal mythic conventions as those associated with Manifest Destiny, served certain critical needs in those years, especially when it seemed so difficult to address the war without recourse to some historical explanation. That the antihero of Penn's film and Thomas Berger's novel finds his only genuine social attachment with the Lakota Sioux seemed an unequivocal indictment of the urban, technological United States in 1971. As Hellmann points out, "[T]he Vietnam western was a short-lived genre," but the "war at home" narrative is one that persisted well into the 1980s.[17] In the 1990s, it metamorphosed into the high-technology action film, a new cinematic form dominated by Sylvester Stallone and Arnold Schwarzenegger. The critical perspectives of such works seem invariably liberal, leftist, or otherwise minority oriented, at least at the levels of design and intention, but they have also served some unintended ideological purposes that are part of the general appropriation and refashioning of Vietnam. Above all, works such as these that displace the Vietnam War to the United States invariably turn a war of imperialist aggression into one of domestic conflict. Films like *Little Big Man* may qualify this generalization slightly, insofar as "Vietnam westerns" concerned with westward expansion connect the pioneers with the more general project of European imperialism. Even so, this memory is quite faint in works dealing with nineteenth-century Manifest Destiny; few invoke the sort of imperialist zeal that can be readily found in documents of that period.[18] And of course, no "Vietnam western" could completely ironize the western conventions established by several decades of Hollywood productions aimed at glorifying and thus rationalizing westward expansion.[19]

Adventure narratives testing urban man against nature have appeared in various forms and with considerable frequency in the past three decades. Walter Hill's *Southern Comfort* (1981) employs this motif to connect the Vietnam War with U.S. domestic racial and social questions, albeit without making any overt reference to Vietnam.[20] The convention of the belated rite of passage works with special irony in this film to suggest that those who missed the war still have all the motives and qualities to sink us in some other imperialist quagmire. National Guardsmen on weekend maneuvers in the Louisiana swamps run afoul of secretive Cajuns who have built their stills and shacks in the protective mazes of the bayous. Although these weekend soldiers are not supposed to carry live ammunition, one of them has brought along a couple of live rounds. Killing a Cajun more out of their own fear than because of the threat he poses, the Guardsmen bury the body, burn the shack, and hope the bayou will providentially cover their tracks. Cajun society, it turns out, is considerably more tightly knit than these soldiers had expected, and a rather conventional plot of revenge develops as the dramatic means of exposing the ineptitude of these urban soldiers in conforming to the ways of nature and man.

The conventional plot, with its frequent allusions to *Deliverance* (1971), the film based on James Dickey's novel, and its use of virtually every popular cliché about Cajuns, bayous, and the Southern Gothic, makes possible an extended meditation on a hypothetical war at home.[21] The Cajuns are generally invisible, at best seen through mists or as hidden parts of the wilderness, especially because the camera follows the perspectives of the soldiers. Like the NLF, these backwoodsmen appear primarily as corpses or shadows. The Guardsmen are particularly unsettled by the unfamiliarity of a region so close to home and by their accidental discovery of the reality behind the myths of U.S. subculture. Picked off one by one by Cajun snipers and guerillas, the soldiers begin to fight among themselves, replaying our popular notions of dissent among combat troops in Vietnam. When two surviving soldiers find their way out of the swamp and into a Cajun settlement, the analogy with Vietnam is made particularly explicit. A festival is underway, and Cajuns from the surrounding bayous arrive with cooked food and live animals as music and informal celebrations begin. Uncertain who their actual enemies are, the two soldiers are jumpy and paranoid because the dialect of the villagers is incomprehensible to them.

The conventional narrative of the patrol in Vietnam generally ends in a village, where the troops try to overcome local, linguistic, and political differences to determine just who might be the enemy.[22] In *Southern Comfort*, the climactic scene in the Cajun village is a sort of nightmarish reversal of the Vietnam patrol; the two survivors are perfectly aware that they have blundered into a foreign culture that appears to threaten the dangers they have just barely escaped. As it turns out, these two survivors, whose very survival indicates that they are cannier than their fellows in the ways of the woods as well as in the ruses of foreigners, are not just paranoid; the "enemy" appears in the back room of one of the shacks and silently attacks them, and the two soldiers barely survive in a graphically violent scene of self-defense. This attack unites the two soldiers in a camaraderie that for one urgent moment transcends their very different backgrounds and values, just as we have heard that combat soldiers in Vietnam found a special fraternity in battle.

The messages of this film are explicit and unequivocal regarding the significance of Vietnam. The democratic United States consists of many different subcultures, each of which has internal customs and practices that must be tolerated as part of a healthy multiculturalism. By extension, our respect for this diversity ought to be applied in our foreign policies as well; we are, after all, a nation composed of most of the other peoples of the earth. The blunders of the National Guardsmen in this film repeat the larger cultural errors of the government in the conduct of the Vietnam War.

Even so, *Southern Comfort* ironically turns against its own intentions or allows those intentions to be employed in the larger revisionary project of at last "winning" the Vietnam War. The Cajuns are U.S. citizens after all, which is why these weekend soldiers must learn to tolerate their different cultural values. As the two survivors hurry toward the helicopter landing zone, repeating the common scene we remember from the evening news coverage of the Vietnam War, they acknowledge the inevitable separateness of this subculture. Their "understanding" of this "foreign" culture has been primarily a matter of survival, not the means of cultural recognition. Leaving the Cajuns well enough alone, the soldiers, like U.S. popular culture after 1973, suggest that such "foreigners" want nothing more than their privacy. Yet this film, released in 1981, appeared at a moment when some critics of the Vietnam War were calling for U.S. recognition of the Vietnamese government and thus the beginning of normal diplomatic relations that would lead to economic assistance, a foreign policy that the U.S. would not adopt until 1995. Arguments in favor of providing economic assistance to Vietnam were often made in the context of reparations the United States might reasonably be said to owe a country that it had devastated economically, environmentally, and politically. On the other hand, U.S. journalists like Stanley Karnow who returned to Vietnam in 1985 on the tenth anniversary of the fall of Saigon showed particular interest in reporting the demonstrable "failures" of the Vietnamese to rebuild their country.[23] Leaving Vietnam alone over the past twenty-five years has certainly helped us shape a self-fulfilling prophecy of economic difficulty for that country. As Frances FitzGerald wrote in *Fire in the Lake,* understanding Vietnamese history and multiculturalism involved our recognition that Vietnamese culture is fundamentally different from our own, an argument that in 1972 might have seemed in the best interests of the Vietnamese, at least in the eyes of the antiwar movement in this country.[24] A decade later, however, it was clear enough that our deliberate laissez-faire policy with respect to Vietnam could be justified on precisely FitzGerald's and *Southern Comfort*'s terms. As Edward Said has shown us, the claim of the *radical otherness* of another culture belongs to the rhetoric of Orientalism; neglect or repression, even in the guise of tolerance of differences, is as much an imperialist policy as military intervention, as the economic misfortunes of contemporary Vietnam testify.

In still other ways, *Southern Comfort* evokes Vietnam only to Orientalize it yet again. The film takes account of what we might term the phenomenology of the individual's ideological values, insofar as we see the Cajuns only from the mediated perspectives of the National Guardsmen. Although these Guardsmen come from different classes and backgrounds, they are primarily from urban areas, and they share certain simple stereotypes of their antagonists. We see nothing but cultural clichés, then, such that the final appearance of the enemy takes the form of two vicious "crackers" such as haunt northern tourists in the South. While dancing, talking, and eating go on undisturbed in the village square and houses, the back room is filled with the violent unconscious of Cajun subculture. In this scene of recognition, the enemy reminds us that these Cajuns support themselves with homemade "white lightning," petty theft, and the law of the rifle. The smiling women and helpful farmers look away when those more truly authorized attempt to apply their violent law to outsiders. Like the crackers who kill and sodomize the inept but finally decent suburbanites in *Deliverance* and the NVA soldiers who force their captives to play Russian roulette in Michael Cimino's *The Deer Hunter,* these Cajuns are perversions of the natural law. The encounter with the Other in *Southern Comfort* is supposed to be cathartic; it shows us otherness only to remind us of its terrors and thus allows us once again to estrange and repress it.

The violence of representation operates in the rhetorical uncanniness of U.S. ideology, which can and does turn just about anything to its purposes with a sensitivity to the connotative and figural qualities of language unmatched by the subtlest artist, the cleverest critic. In the aftermath of the Vietnam War, U.S. ideology has managed to live up to Jean-François Lyotard's definition of the postmodern as "the presentation of the unpresentable."[25] For U.S. society the unpresentable is just what the play on words suggests—what cannot be made present because it exceeds the conventional boundaries of representation, what is for that very reason improper, unpresentable under the formal requirements of that system of representation. "Vietnam" unpresentable? In a sense, of course, that was the case in the United States during the Reagan and George H. Bush administrations, when historical, political, and cultural understanding was desperately needed.[26] "Vietnam" remains the name that cannot be properly uttered, even though we continue to translate it into very presentable terms, very recognizable myths and discourses.

One vehicle for such discourses was the popular television series *Miami Vice.* At the beginning of the October 3, 1986, episode of the show, teenagers huddled around their television sets, buzzing about Sonny Crockett's (Don Johnson's) new Ferrari.[27] His black Daytona has been blown up by some African American weapons smuggler in a shocking but necessary demonstration of a handheld rocket launcher. Word that a new car is on the way has been reported on the evening news. Stories in the *Los Angeles Times* have recounted Enzo Ferrari's threat of a lawsuit over the use of the old car (though it turns out to be a replica; originals are too expensive). At ten o'clock the prologue ran, but the disappointed teenagers watched documentary footage from Nicaragua spliced together with a docudrama of a cameraman and reporter recording U.S. troops fighting in a small Nicaraguan village. At the close of this prologue, a Nicaraguan woman carrying her dead child walks into the camera's eye.

From 1984 to 1989, *Miami Vice* succeeded by playing upon the popular notion that greed and cynicism were "good," but its amoral posture was suddenly replaced by explicit political commentary. Between the prologue of this episode and Crockett's desperate and futile efforts, along with his partner, Ricardo Tubbs (Philip Michael Thomas), to get this videotaped "evidence" of U.S. military support of the Contras on the major network news, the Ferrari appears to rev up the interest of yawning teenagers. Most of the hour-long program, however, is devoted to Ira Stone (Bob Balaban), Crockett's old Vietnam buddy, who shot the tape in Nicaragua. Stone, who had first appeared on the "Back in the World" episode of *Miami Vice* aired on December 6, 1985, was a cheap hustler, sometime photographer, and Vietnam veteran who had uncovered a scam to recover and sell heroin smuggled into the United States in body bags.[28] The scam is being carried out by Stone's and Crockett's former commanding officer in Vietnam (played by G. Gordon Liddy), who is now operating as "Captain Real Estate." "Back in the World" cynically manipulated popular conventions of the Vietnam War and its veterans merely for the sake of a new, interesting story. The plot of that episode had been borrowed from Robert Stone's *Dog Soldiers* (1974); even the name of the character Ira Stone had seemingly been casually borrowed from the author of that novel.[29]

In this particular episode from 1986, however, Liddy returns as the head of a paramilitary organization, funded by wealthy Nicaraguans living in Miami, that sends mercenaries to help the Contras. Liddy makes it clear that their purpose is to make enough Contra military success possible to convince Congress to provide more extensive and formal military assistance. The drama of the show revolves around problems of textuality. Crockett does not believe even his own eyes when he views Stone's tape, assuming that Stone must have staged the events as part of yet another confidence scheme. Convinced only after he has been beaten up by one of Liddy's henchmen, Crockett has to use the tape to bargain for Stone, whom Liddy has kidnapped. An African American woman reporter for a major network—the only such reporter who is willing to take a chance on Stone's shady reputation—is killed and the tape erased (a powerful magnet is used for both tasks) by one of Liddy's men. In the end, Stone is killed, Liddy escapes, and Crockett and Tubbs arrive too late as a transport plane full of mercenaries takes off for Nicaragua. Assuring the dying Stone that his tape will be aired on the six o'clock news, Crockett returns to his boat to listen to the news on the radio (fashionably countercultural, he does not own a TV), which reports events recorded on Stone's tape but claims that they are new atrocities committed not by the Contras, but by the Sandinista government.

Culture critics must have seen this episode as representing a new phase in popular television. Until that time, *Miami Vice* had represented Latin Americans almost universally as canny but brutal Bolivian, Colombian, or Venezuelan drug dealers wearing woolen caps and riding in custom Mercedes (Ricardo Tubbs's presence as a hip Afro-Cuban American vice officer had seemed to permit the unlicensed representation of other people of color as either sexy women or utterly amoral criminals). This sudden shift from flagrant ethnocentrism and racism to political self-consciousness worked back by way of Vietnam, linking our illegal support of the Contras in Nicaragua with our conduct in Southeast Asia. Liddy, as both political personality and born-again actor, made that connection unavoidable. The program's sympathies with the Sandinistas and its opposition to U.S. support for the Contras were beyond any doubt, as was the episode's studied self-consciousness regarding the political content of every popular medium from the evening news to *Miami Vice* itself.[30] The fact that the program did not quite represent Liddy's organization as an extension of the CIA seemed perfectly understandable and acceptable. *Miami Vice*, after all, could go only so far with such flagrant political commentary; direct indictment of the CIA would have led to a scandal that network television never would have risked.

Two days after this October 3, 1986, episode aired, on October 5, a private U.S. cargo plane loaded with arms and munitions was shot down in Nicaragua. Eugene Hasenfus, a U.S. citizen from Wisconsin and a Vietnam veteran, survived the crash and claimed to be a mercenary working for an organization fronting for the CIA. Vice President George Bush, Secretary of Defense Robert Schultz, and a host of other government officials denied any involvement in the affair, attributing it to overzealous private citizens supporting the Contras. As we can see with hindsight, *Miami Vice* supported the government's claims. Some latter-day G. Gordon Liddy, master of renegade dirty tricks, was undoubtedly behind this abortive venture. Was this just another parable for paranoiacs? Or was this crossing of popular television and foreign policy an event or coincidence that still speaks of the power of ideology to draw upon the slippery figures of its own representational machinery? As the Iran-Contra scandal unfolded in the months that followed and Oliver North's testimony before Congress revealed the extent of the National Security Council's involvement in what came to be called "Irangate," the purchase of the cargo plane carrying Hasenfus was traced to funds the National Security Council had raised by illegally selling arms to Iran and then laundering the money through Swiss banks.

At the 1968 Democratic National Convention in Chicago, antiwar activists staged a host of symbolic acts, claiming that their symbols were finally more powerful than the facts of the government's policies in Vietnam. Yippies at the 1967 antiwar March on Washington circled the Pentagon and chanted mantras to "levitate" the building, which many later claimed had "really" lifted off the ground. In those innocent days, the playful, heterogeneous discourse of the U.S. counterculture fought the referential claims of government experts. That was modernism. Postmodernism began with the discovery that the violence of representation, the unhinging of meaning, the free play of signification, and the heterogeneity of language are means by which U.S. ideology maintains itself, always speaking in someone else's voice, never appearing as such, always more true to itself as it wanders from its apparent way.

10.

Elián González, Cuban American Détente, and the Rhetoric of Family Values

Ideology is a "representation" of the imaginary relationship of individuals to their real conditions of existence.
—Louis Althusser, "Ideology and Ideological State Apparatuses" (1970)

The U.S. Immigration and Naturalization Service was within the outside border of reasonable choice when it ruled that Juan Miguel González could speak for his son, Elián.
—U.S. 11th Circuit Court of Appeals (June 1, 2000)

When six-year-old Elián González was picked up by fishermen while lying faceup in a black truck tire inner tube off the coast of Fort Lauderdale, Florida, he had already crossed numerous borders and was about to cross even more fantastic boundaries generated by U.S. neocolonialism in the Caribbean. Drifting off Florida where the Caribbean Sea meets the Atlantic, not far from the infamous "Bermuda Triangle," where ships and planes have vanished as does matter in galactic "black holes," Elián hovered between life and death, one of the three survivors of a capsized seventeen-foot open boat, having become separated from his mother, Elizabeth Brotons, and her boyfriend, Lazáro Rafael Munero, both of whom had drowned, and also from his father back in Cuba.[1] The territorial, geographic, existential, and kinship boundaries Elián had to cross in that critical moment were also economic, national, political, cultural, legal, and linguistic borders. Even Elián's name crosses the borders of kinship, gender, and custom, combining his father's given name, Juan, with his mother's, Elizabeth.[2] In the U.S. mass media, Elián's name was routinely mispronounced to sound like *alien*, reinforcing the many different borders he had not only crossed, but threatened. His mother and Munero had fled Cardenas, Cuba, ostensibly for the economic opportunities available in Florida and for the "better life" greater earning power invariably signifies in the U.S. media. More than forty years of the U.S. embargo against Cuba and of the Cuban emigré community in the United States, especially South Florida, have produced distinct differences between Cuban and Cuban American cultures. Spanish may be the principal language in both Cardenas and Miami, but there are also distinct differences between the Spanish spoken by Cuban Americans in the United States, where English is the dominant language (and monolingualists continue to clamor for it to be legally designated the "official" language), and Cuba, where Spanish is the language of everyday communication.

Once within the territorial boundaries of the United States, Elián embodied old sectional differences between states' and federal rights, historically associated with the conflict between the regions of South and North, and reminded cultural historians of nineteenth-century fights over slavery—battles fantastically restaged in the very different semiotic register of Cuban Americans pitted against the Immigration and Naturalization Service (INS) and U.S. Attorney General Janet Reno. Herself the favorite target of antigovernment zealots as diverse as neo-Nazi survivalists and white supremacists, libertarians, and religious cultists and separatists, Reno helped embody the curious crossing of Cold War rhetoric—anticommunist xenophobia and either isolationism or hawkish endorsement of military intervention around the globe—with the emerging rhetoric of our new "warm war" era, in which the United States either engages in or negotiates (often in the media as much as through diplomatic channels) ceaseless "low-key" conflicts to fulfill its role as global policeman. Like other right-wing immigrant groups—such as the Vietnamese Americans who in the spring of 1999 protested in Westminster, California, the video store owner, Truong Van Tran, who displayed the flag of the Republic of Vietnam and a photograph of Ho Chi Minh—the Cuban Americans immediately confused U.S. nationalism with dedication to their cause: the military, diplomatic, or political defeat of Castro and the restoration of Cuba to the halcyon "democracy"— or at least to the property rights and laissez-faire capitalism—of the regime of Fulgencio Batista y Zaldívar (1933–59), noted for its close ties with U.S. organized crime.[3]

Janet Reno, caricatured on television talk shows such as *David Letterman* (CBS) and Jay Leno's *Tonight Show* (NBC) as a man in women's clothing (a transvestite), a butch woman (a lesbian of the old "butch-femme" model), an oversized woman (an unfeminine woman and thus somehow deformed or disabled), and always over- or undersexed (and therefore always the object of sexual jokes and innuendo), as U.S. attorney general was constructed as a mass-mediated image of the liberalism—what Rush Limbaugh used to deride as the "feminazism"—of the Clinton administration.[4] In the matter of Elián, the Cuban American activists in South Florida challenged the legal authority of the U.S. attorney general by appealing both to Florida courts and to the U.S. Congress in ways that quickly confused the jurisdictional question with the ongoing struggle in the U.S. public sphere over family values.[5] Janet Reno claimed that the U.S. attorney general had proper jurisdiction over the case, because Elián had been shipwrecked in international waters and then rescued by U.S. citizens. In her judgment, this was not a legal case that could be adjudicated in Florida's state or municipal courts, because it involved international law. Political observers will recall that the religious Right appealed to family values in both the 1992 and 1996 presidential campaigns, urging the Republican Party to take a stand on this issue in ways that many believe cost the Republicans both elections. Indeed, in the 1992 election campaign Bill Clinton had succeeded in convincing the majority of voters that family values were best represented at the end of the twentieth century by the ethnic and structural diversity of American families. Some pundits have argued that Clinton's affair with Monica Lewinsky so damaged the Democratic Party's credibility with regard to "family values" that Al Gore's bid for the presidency in 2000 was doomed to failure.

The contradictions and discrepancies visible in this confusion of U.S. and Cuban emigré nationalism surrounding Elián were narratively worked through in terms of a rhetoric of family values that was manipulated by Castro, the U.S. government, partisan politicians jockeying for power in the 2000 presidential election, and the anti-Castro Cuban American National Foundation (CANF). Castro relied on Elián's father, Juan Miguel González, and stepmother, Nelsy Carmenate; his six-month-old half-brother; and his two Cuban grandmothers, Raquel Rodriguez and Mariela Quintana—dramatis personae on whom the U.S. government would also depend. The CANF would employ Elián's extended family of aunt and uncle (Lazáro González), assorted uncles and cousins in Miami, and the Catholic Church.⁶ Both the Democratic presidential front-runner, Vice President Al Gore, and the Republican, Texas Governor George W. Bush, patriotically reaffirmed U.S. nationalism, condemned Cuba for its violation of human rights, and agreed that the custody issue would be better settled in a "state family court," as if Elián were already a U.S. citizen.⁷ Of course, this is not a new story. Robyn Wiegman, Dana Nelson, Amy Kaplan, and Lauren Berlant have written in recent years about the confusion of domestic and national romances in nineteenth-century U.S. culture, reminding us that the family and the nation share certain ideological terms that have indissolubly linked public and private, foreign policies and personal behaviors, from that century to the present.⁸

When Elián's father found that Elián was alive but stranded not only in a foreign country but one with legal restrictions against travel to and from and trade with Cuba, he appealed to his Uncle Lázaro, who had lived for many years in Miami, both to take care of Elián and to help negotiate with the U.S. government his return to Cuba. But this proxy family, assisted by the CANF, worked to legitimate its claim not only to Elián but, more important, to the political and cultural capital with which he was quickly invested. In their efforts to transform Elián into a symbol of the political interests of one segment of the Cuban emigré community in the United States, the family and the CANF also relied on the rhetoric of family values. Elián's cousin Marisleysis was presented as his surrogate mother, and legal arguments included reference to Elián's attachment to his cousin in just this capacity, playing on his need for such surrogacy in the wake of his mother's drowning. Marisleysis herself played this role consistently, insisting not only that she was the proper surrogate mother for Elián but that she herself needed Elián for the sake of her own (admittedly new) identity as "mother." When she checked into a Miami hospital for "nervous exhaustion," the event seemed to reinforce, rather than call into question, her maternal rights.⁹ Subsequently, the twenty-one-year-old Marisleysis, always accompanied by her father, Lázaro, insisted that Elián was being held by the INS against his will and that he would "run to" his Miami family if he were able.¹⁰

Since the Gulf War in 1991, rapid adjustment by all parties to the dominant rhetoric in the news media has characterized cultural representation. With the fall of the Berlin Wall and the breakup of the Soviet Empire in Eastern Europe after 1989, many people thought we were witnessing a new "border crossing" in which inexpensive access to video and computer technologies was equalizing the playing field of cultural representation. In our still modernist imaginations, we deluded ourselves that populist access to such technologies would threaten state hegemonies and promise greater democracy. Indeed, the much touted radical democracy theories of the late 1980s seemed realizable in "peoples' revolutions" undertaken in part by activists astutely using computer, telematic, and video technologies to rebel against the Soviet Empire, the People's Republic of China, and the Marcos dictatorship in the Philippines, among many other regimes in the grassroots revolutions of the late 1980s and early 1990s. But such promises of populist revolution and radical democracy now have to be qualified by the ways that both "the state" and "the people" are constructed symbolically and with great speed by these same inexpensive technologies. Both the state and the people have the potential for an ideological overdetermination that makes the old polarities suspect and thus suggests that yet another boundary has been transgressed.

Both Fidel Castro and Janet Reno responded to the family values that Elián's Cuban American relatives, obviously coached by the CANF, claimed as their symbolic capital. For Castro to appeal for the preservation of the nuclear family as his best means of criticizing his enemies in the Cuban American community and the U.S. federal government seemed particularly absurd. Consulting with Elián's father, Juan Miguel González, in a "secure" government location outside Havana, Castro seemed to betray basic Marxist critiques of the nuclear family as the locus of bourgeois capitalism.[11] Sanctioning González's visit to the United States, even encouraging and funding travel by his new wife and baby, Castro accepted the language game of family values as fully as the U.S. government did. Hardly less absurd than Castro's touting González's virtues as a father were Janet Reno's praising González as a "good father" and images of her and the Cuban father posing for cameras like some postmodern "odd couple," fueling yet again the humor of the professional comics who play significant roles as political interpreters in the contemporary U.S. public sphere.[12] The denouement of this little episode of confused and subverted boundaries was the curious tableau of Elián playing with a "rainbow coalition" of children on the immaculate lawns of New Wye Plantation, a plantation worked by slave labor in the antebellum period and now refurbished as an elegant and "enlightened" conference center amid the still racist and wealthy enclaves of Maryland's Eastern Shore.

The boundary between "family" and nation, state, or identitarian community was deliberately confused in all three narratives of Elián's story, yet in consistent ways. To be a good family member, one must follow the cultural conventions of the nation, state, or community in which the family resides, and the argument tacitly proposed was that such a good family member (father, mother, sibling, aunt, uncle, or cousin) knows the consensually accepted meaning or definition of the United States, Cuba, or Cuban America. What should have become manifestly clear in the public struggle over Elián González's cultural and political capital was the utter fictionality of all three states and of the "families" intended to support each of them, these postmodern Laputas.

Cubans and Cuban Americans refashioned a variety of folktales and historical incidents to mythologize Elián. Cuban Americans speculated that Elián was yet another manifestation of the "boy on the dolphin," a reappearance of early Christian legends of an apocalyptic second coming. This time, of course, the Catholic sign of Christ's epiphany was linked with fantasies of Cuban emancipation, the end of Castro's rule, and the return of Cuban American emigrés to their homeland. In March, the Miami relatives "fighting to retain custody" of Elián claimed that "an image in an oval mirror that hangs in a bedroom in their home depicts the Virgin Mary, offering evidence that he is blessed and should remain in the United States."[13]

The Cuban rumors were no less fantastic and revolved around the legend of "las Niñas," or the children kidnapped and sacrificed to the Afro-Cuban god Changó. The association of Elián with this folklore was strengthened by the proximity of the date of his rescue or "kidnapping," November 22, to December 4, the feast day of the Catholic Santa Barbara and her Afro-Cuban equivalent, Changó.[14] Stephan Palmié traces the modern history of "las Niñas" to the widely publicized murders of Cuban children in November and December of 1904. Afro-Cubans were accused of the murders, which were rumored to have involved ritual mutilation for purposes of "brujería" ("witchery"). Palmié argues that the "savagery" attributed to Afro-Cubans and the demonization of Santería and other Afro-Cuban religions was part of an effort by early twentieth-century Cuban nationalists to dissociate Cuba from its Afro-Cuban heritage.[15] As Palmié argues, the real antagonists in the legend of "las Niñas" were not Afro-Cubans but Spanish colonialism and U.S. neocolonial commercial interests, each of which had at different times "kidnapped" and enslaved Cuba's future. If Palmié is right, the Cuban rumors linking Elián with the legend of "las Niñas" are strangely appropriate, insofar as his "kidnapping" by Cuban Americans seemed to many Cubans yet another instance of U.S. neocolonial interference in Cuban national interests.[16] The folklore of "las Niñas" was also used by Cuban Americans to suggest that Elián's return to Cuba would constitute "kidnapping" by Fidel Castro, a suggestion tacitly made in much of the anticommunist rhetoric. Shortly after the legal decision that ensured Elián's return to his father in Cuba, a pamphlet was circulated in Miami that claimed Castro would ritually sacrifice Elián on his return.[17]

It was hardly this fictionality, however, that turned most U.S. citizens against the anti-Castro Cuban emigré community and aligned them quite curiously with Castro's socialist state and with Reno's and Clinton's federal government. Instead, it was the apparent reality of the "natural family" and an insistence upon honoring "blood relations" and proximity of descent that allowed the U.S. attorney general and Fidel Castro—two of the unlikeliest heroes, let alone allies, in the annals of world literature—to defeat the claims of Elián's extended family and overcome Janet Reno's and Fidel Castro's faulty authority for their versions of the story. Reno's Waco-style predawn assault on the home of Elián's extended family in Miami hardly fit the script of "family values," even if the sport utility vehicle into which the young Elián was summarily tossed looked oddly like the neighborhood carpool vehicle, if the viewer could matte out the INS agents in full body armor and toting guns seemingly inspired by those in the science fiction film *Men in Black*. In his own way, Castro also displayed his unfamiliarity with the conventions of family values by sending Juan Miguel González, his new wife, Nelsy, and their baby dressed "equally" in the black uniforms of mournful Cuban peasants crushed by the successful U.S. embargo.

Despite these diegetic blunders, these lapses in media taste and form, Castro and Reno succeeded where Elián's Cuban emigré relatives and the CANF failed, because the latter stressed family ties as a consequence of social construction rather than direct descent and thus "nature." Uncle Lazáro's "adoptive family" was typified by its endorsement of postmodern capitalism and its ontological reliance on consumerism. In a videotape made by his Miami family in which Elián González lectured his father on his desire to remain a free citizen of the United States and never return to Cuba, Elián appeared bedecked with gold and surrounded by the relative wealth of the furnishings in his aunt and uncle's bedroom, where he appeared to rely on the "family" produced by consumer capitalism.[18] As I have already pointed out, both Castro and the U.S. government entered the competition with the Miami relatives and the CANF to commodify Elián: Castro took Juan Miguel González to a state-owned mansion outside Havana, where the two debated global politics and parenting like old friends who were equals; the Clinton administration whisked the liberated

Elián from Miami to the New Wye Plantation, where he played with an ethnically mixed group of instant friends.

Despite efforts by the Miami relatives and the CANF to suggest that Elián's father had been abusive and thus had violated the rights of the natural family, the argument of blood kinship won the day for both the Cuban and the U.S. governments.[19] Elián's grandmothers, Raquel Rodriguez and Mariela Quintana, bravely faced reporters in New York City and Washington, D.C. as part of the coalition formed by Castro and the U.S. government to defend the father's rights to custody of his child. When the grandmothers visited Elián for a bare ninety minutes, they confessed that he was "not the same child" he had been and insisted upon his rescue from his Miami "abductors."[20] Nevertheless, the authority of the grandmothers was never tested against the circumstances of Elián's conception and birth, both of which had occurred after Juan Miguel González and Elizabeth Brotons had divorced.[21] It is very likely that Elián's *illegitimacy* would have negatively affected González's custody rights in U.S. public opinion, which was running strongly against the Miami relatives and the CANF. In any case, this technicality stresses the fact that public opinion was based on a spurious understanding of González's natural rights to custody of his son, Elián. His only natural right would have been to custody of Elián as a "natural son" under the law, which is to say a bastard. In fact, the father's relationship to his son was as socially and legally constructed as the claims made by the extended family in Miami.

While the Cuban nuclear family stayed, like leisure-class tourists, at the New Wye Plantation pending the outcome of the circuit court of appeals decision regarding Elián's request for political asylum in the United States, the outcome of this much-publicized psychodrama had already been decided in the public debates in this country and Cuba. In effect, the cooperation between the Cuban and U.S. governments contributed to détente and perhaps accelerated the demands of the U.S. public that the government lift the economic embargo against Cuba and normalize political relations (and foreign travel).[22] This surprising result was produced in part by public opinion, supported by the major news media, which effectively demonized the Miami relatives and conflated all Cuban Americans with the CANF and its demonstrators massed outside Uncle Lazáro's Miami home. Months after Elián had reunited with his family in Cuba, Florida International University polled "1,975 Cuban Americans in Miami-Dade County" and "found that 82% of those polled believed the Elian [sic] case hurt the interests of the Cuban American community."[23]

The same poll indicated that "Cuban Americans were in favor of engaging in dialogue with Cuba, even though they remain dead set against easing the trade embargo."[24]

Signs of macropolitical détente beginning on the popular level may be encouraging, but such positive signs were accompanied by negative consequences, including what some view as "ethnic and racial divisions in Miami-Dade County between Cuban Americans and whites and blacks," as well as other non–Cuban Americans who felt "disenfranchised by Cuban American elected officials who sided with Elian's [sic] relatives in their standoff with federal authorities."[25] By the same token, some pollsters estimated that as many as "5% to 10% of the Cuban American vote in the presidential election was motivated by a desire to punish Al Gore for the way the Clinton administration" handled the case.[26] If they are right, the Elián González case may well have decided the 2000 U.S. presidential election.

Cubans expressed outrage at the conduct of Elián's Miami relatives, the conspiracy of the CANF, and the delays of the U.S. government and legal system and reaffirmed the rights of the natural family. Even the Colombian writer Gabriel García Márquez, who tries in his "Shipwreck on Dry Land" primarily to report Cuban public opinions about the crisis as a corrective to the massive U.S. news media campaign, cannot help demonizing Elián's natural mother, Elizabeth Brotons, and her boyfriend, Munero, in the interests of reasserting the family rights of Juan Miguel González.[27] Drawn into the international war of words and images, Cubans from Castro to the general public seem to have realized that media spin will be crucial to the next stages of its "warm war" with the United States.

I shall make no judgment whatsoever about the rights of any of the parties involved, except to point out that the confusion of family, community, state, and national rights was the deliberate work of each interested group, including the news media, in the narrativization of "The Elián González Story."[28] I do not write this title, suitable for a made-for-television movie, ironically, because television and film production companies have already approached Juan Miguel González and Elián to make just such a film of their relatively brief public "life-stories." I know nothing of the relative rights of the families, communities, states, and governments involved to determine the identity and history of Elián González. What I do know is that the incredible transgression of boundaries that Elián González's recent history involved is a consequence of postmodern mobilities (not all of which are the result of technological wizardry) and of the growing instability of conventional borders not only in the minds of intellectuals (for whom such borders have always been fictional) but also in the public imagination. And I know that such instability is likely to be met with repressive measures in the names of security and legality and what now appears to be a nearly inevitable reversion to national authorities to adjudicate what are certain to be increasingly complex, ambiguous, and numerous cases of border crossings.

There are no magical or simple solutions to these problems, but certainly one recourse would be to take up such issues in international tribunals, like the World Court in the Hague, and political organizations, like the United Nations. Both are frequently, albeit differently, criticized as ineffective or incompetent, usually by those interested in reasserting some sort of national authority (too often, it is sad to say, that of the United States as the new imperial power in world affairs). We have certainly entered a transnational and postnational era in which global capitalism and its related technologies have played significant parts in destabilizing the geopolitical borders of nations and the equally powerful boundaries of language, law, culture, race, kinship, class, education, and many areas. Such destabilization has produced and will continue for some time to produce reactions in the names of the nation, ethnic or cultural identity, religious faith, historical affiliation, even ancient monarchical rights and feudal fealties that have already led to terrible human and ecological violence. We must not be foolish enough to believe that anything as abstract and unreal as history, the market, technology, or even reason can negotiate and adjudicate these differences. Now, more than ever, some transnational political and legal organization is desperately needed to address just such problems as the Elián González story dramatizes.[29]

Just as necessary as new institutions for adjudicating such transnational incidents will be cultural interpretations of such events, which seem increasingly frequent and politically explosive. Negotiating the curious combinations and displacements of the Elián González story or the cultural significance of the Vietnam War requires far more than merely common sense or good analytical skills. The scholar-critic of the new American Studies will have to be attentive to the strange intersections of politics, law, mass media, popular folklore, literary rhetoric, history, and economics that allow such events to be understood. Such scholars will have to be wary of conventional interpretations and attentive to the subtlety with which old ideas can be transformed or "morphed" by the dizzying, competitive mass media. For example, in the Elián González case an appeal to "family values" was not used simply to reaffirm the presumed normality of Middle America, "home and hearth," conventional gender hierarchies, bourgeois respectability, and patriotism.[30] This appeal to "family values" was also used by Fidel Castro, Janet Reno, and Cuban American immigrants to bolster very different political agendas. Cultural narratives undergo constant changes, especially those narratives that have some success, which is to say circulation (or "air time"). In order to understand the stories told by the mass media, the new scholar-critic will have to respect their complexity and be able to *work fast*, in keeping with the accelerated pace of our age.

Notes

Introduction

1. Gene Wise, "'Paradigm Dramas' in American Studies: A Cultural and Institutional History of the Movement," *American Quarterly* 31:3 (Bibliography Issue, 1979), 314.

2. See Charles Bernheimer, ed., *Comparative Literature in the Age of Multiculturalism* (Baltimore, Md.: Johns Hopkins University Press, 1995), and J. Hillis Miller, "Literary and Cultural Studies in the Transnational University," *"Culture" and the Problem of the Disciplines*, ed. John Carlos Rowe (New York: Columbia University Press, 1998), 45–67.

3. Wise, "'Paradigm Dramas,'" 337, for example, refers to the "new cultural studies" of the 1970s as promising evidence of new vitality in the field, anticipating the cultural studies model of the 1990s. By the same token, contemporaries and admirers of Wise's work, especially this famous essay, have expressed strong objections to cultural studies, often viewing it as a threat to American Studies. See Jay Mechling, "Some [New] Elementary Axioms for an American Cultur[al] Studies," *American Studies* 38:2 (Summer, 1997), 12–18, in a section entitled "The Poverty of Cultural Studies." Despite Mechling's insistence that he holds no "antipathy" to "cultural studies," this section is replete with anxieties regarding the threat of cultural studies to the traditional fields and aims of American Studies (28, n. 13).

4. Günter Lenz, "'Ethnographies': American Culture Studies and Postmodern Anthropology," *Prospects* 16 (1991), 1–40, does an admirable job of reminding us of the progressive aims of earlier American Studies scholars and schools, especially with respect to their treatment of "culture" as a concept and organizing field of study.

5. My reference to the "nations" of Canada includes Quebecois nationalist movements and Canadian Indians who claim national sovereignty. For an excellent account of the importance of Canada in the new comparative American Studies, see Adam Weissman, "Reading Multiculturalism in the United States and Canada: The Anthological vs. the Cognitive," *University of Toronto Quarterly* 69:3 (Summer 2000), 689–715.

6. Lawrence Buell, "American Literary Emergence as a Postcolonial Phenomenon," *American Literary History* 4 (1992), 411–42.

7. Julia Kristeva, *Nations without Nationalism*, trans. Leon S. Roudiez (New York: Columbia University Press, 1993), 10.

8. Ibid., 11.

9. Ania Loomba, *Colonialism/Postcolonialism* (London: Routledge, 1998), xiv.

10. Gesa Mackenthun, "America's Troubled Postcoloniality: Some Reflections from Abroad," *Discourse* 22:3 (Fall 2000), 37. See also C. Richard King, ed., *Postcolonial America* (Urbana: University of Illinois Press, 2000), 10, who explains the diverse purposes of his edited collection to provide "multiple, perhaps even conflicted, visions of the shape of postcolonial America, its connections with postcoloniality as some sort of global condition, and its implications for prevailing critiques of U.S. imperialism."

11. See Werner Sollors and Marc Shell, eds., *The Multilingual Anthology of American Literature* (New York: New York University Press, 2000), and my discussion of their work in chapter 3.

12. See chapters 1 and 3 for discussions of Mary Louise Pratt. Paul Jay, in "The Myth of 'America' and the Politics of Location: Modernity, Border Studies, and the Literature of the Americas," *Arizona Quarterly* 54:2 (Summer 1998), 181, writes: "[Paul] Gilroy's location approximates what Glissant has called a 'cultural zone,' a space between national borders where identity and culture have evolved in syncretic patterns that are traceable in literature and other forms of expression." Valuable as Jay's adaptation of Glissant's "cultural zone" is for the new American Studies, it is too literary and needs further theoretical elaboration and practical illustration to serve as a category for cultural semiotics.

13. Norman R. Yetman, "American Studies from Culture Concept to Cultural Studies?" *American Studies* 38:2 (Summer, 1997), 5.

14. Ibid.

15. Günter Lenz, "Periodization and American Studies," in *Grolier Encyclopedia of American Studies*, 4 vol., ed. George Kurian, Miles Orvell, Jay Mechling, and Johnella Butler (New York: Grolier Press, 2001), 3: 293–96.

16. John Carlos Rowe, *At Emerson's Tomb: The Politics of Classic American Literature* (New York: Columbia University Press, 1997), 1–16. See also Larry Reynolds, *European Revolutions and the American Literary Renaissance* (New Haven, Conn.: Yale University Press, 1988).

17. Amy Kaplan, "'Left Alone with America': The Absence of Empire in the Study of American Culture," in *Cultures of United States Imperialism*, ed. Amy Kaplan and Donald E. Pease (Durham, N.C.: Duke University Press, 1993), 5–11.

18. Russell J. Reising, in *The Unusable Past: Theory and the Study of American Literature* (New York: Methuen, 1986), p. 56, writes: "Thus Miller's Puritan resembles the existentialist's isolated man, tragically alone in the world and responsible for facing reality without mediation."

19. See Joseph N. Riddel, *The Inverted Bell: The Counter-Poetics of William Carlos Williams* (Baton Rouge: Louisiana State University Press, 1974), and John Carlos Rowe, *Through the Custom-House: Nineteenth-Century American Fiction and Modern Theory* (Baltimore, Md.: Johns Hopkins University Press, 1982).

20. See, for example, Jonathan Arac, Wlad Godzich, and Wallace Martin, eds., *The Yale Critics: Deconstruction in America* (Minneapolis: University of Minnesota Press, 1983).

21. Jay, "The Myth of 'America,'" 174.

22. Ibid.

23. Ibid.

24. Stuart Hall, "The West and the Rest: Discourse and Power," in *Modernity: An Introduction to Modern Societies,* ed. Stuart Hall, David Held, Don Hubert, and Kenneth Thompson (Cambridge, Mass.: Blackwell Publishers, 1996), 221. In an interesting section of this essay, "'In the Beginning All the World Was America,'" Hall suggests that the exceptionalist discourse of conquest and colonization is critically revealed by studying the Americas and Canada in the context of western modernization.

25. Frederick Buell, *National Culture and the New Global System* (Baltimore, Md.: Johns Hopkins University Press, 1994), 12.

26. Ibid.

27. Kristeva, *Nations without Nationalism,* 50.

28. Buell, *National Culture and the New Global System,* 341.

29. Donald E. Pease, "New Perspectives on U.S. Culture and Imperialism," *Cultures of United States Imperialism,* 26.

30. Francis Fukuyama, *The End of History and the Last Man* (New York: Avon Books, 1992).

31. Buell, *National Culture and the New Global System,* 119.

32. Houston Baker Jr., *Modernism and the Harlem Renaissance* (Chicago: University of Chicago Press, 1987); Cary Nelson, *Repression and Recovery: Modern American Poetry and the Politics of Cultural Memory, 1910–1945* (Madison: University of Wisconsin Press, 1989); Michael North, *The Dialect of Modernism: Race, Language and Twentieth-Century Literature* (New York: Oxford University Press, 1994); Sieglinde Lemke, *Primitivist Modernism: Black Culture and the Origins of Transatlantic Modernism* (New York: Oxford University Press, 1998); Lindon Barrett, *Blackness and Value: Seeing Double* (New York: Cambridge University Press, 1999).

33. See, for example, Gerald Vizenor, ed., *Narrative Chance: Postmodern Discourse on Native American Literature* (Albuquerque: University of New Mexico Press, 1989).

34. Randy Bass, *Engines of Inquiry: A Practical Guide for Using Technology to Teach American Culture,* a collaborative publication of the American Crossroads

Project (Washington, D.C.: Georgetown University Press, 1997); Mark Poster, *The Second Media Age* (Cambridge, Mass.: Polity Press, 1995); N. Katherine Hayles, *How We Became Posthuman: Virtual Bodies in Cybernetics, Literature, and Informatics* (Chicago: University of Chicago Press, 1999).

35. Poster, *The Second Media Age*, 11.

36. I am thinking of the influence of the Puritan Origins school on work from F. O. Matthiessen's *American Renaissance: Art and Expression in the Age of Emerson and Whitman* (New York: Oxford University Press, 1941) to Sacvan Bercovitch's *The Rites of Assent: Transformations in the Symbolic Construction of America* (New York: Routledge, 1993). For an excellent critical and historical account of this scholarly genealogy, see Reising, *The Unusable Past*, 49–92.

37. I double majored in history and English at Johns Hopkins University, from which I graduated in 1967, and I earned my Ph.D. in English from the State University of New York, Buffalo, in 1972. My decision to enter the graduate program at Buffalo, instead of the American Civilization program at Brown, was based on financial need and impulse, not on intellectual grounds.

38. See, for example, Joyce Appleby, Lynn Hunt, and Margaret Jacob, *Telling the Truth about History* (New York: W. W. Norton, 1994), and Mark Poster, "Textual Agents: History at 'The End of History,'" in *"Culture" and the Problem of the Disciplines*, ed. John Carlos Rowe (New York: Columbia University Press, 1998), 199–227, for differing accounts of how poststructuralism has influenced contemporary historiography.

39. This is precisely my effort in *Literary Culture and U.S. Imperialism: From the Revolution to World War II* (New York: Oxford University Press, 2000).

40. See Lenz, "'Ethnographies,'" and James Clifford and George Marcus, eds., *Writing Culture: The Poetics and Politics of Ethnography* (Berkeley: University of California Press, 1986).

41. Buell, *National Culture and the New Global System*, 259.

42. Mechling, in "Some [New] Elementary Axioms," 12, writes: "Cultural Studies, as currently practiced, tends to have impoverished understandings (or undertheorized versions) of several key concepts, among them 'culture,' 'history,' 'discourse,' and 'class.'"

43. See Etienne Balibar and Immanuel Wallerstein, *Race, Nation, Class: Ambiguous Identities*, trans. Etienne Balibar and Chris Turner (New York: Verso Press, 1991); Masao Miyoshi, "Ivory Tower in Escrow," *Boundary 2* 27:1 (2000), 41–42.

44. Bart Moore-Gilbert, *Postcolonial Theory: Contexts, Practices, Politics* (London: Verso, 1997), 203.

45. Bruce Robbins, "Introduction," in *Cosmopolitics: Thinking and Feeling beyond the Nation*, ed. Pheng Cheah and Bruce Robbins (Minneapolis: University of Minnesota Press, 1998), 12–13.

1. A Future for American Studies

1. William Bennett's *To Reclaim a Legacy: A Report on the Humanities in Higher Education* (Washington, D.C.: National Endowment for the Humanities, 1984) was

his mandated 1984 report to Congress as director of the National Endowment for the Humanities. Dinesh D'Souza, *Illiberal Education: The Politics of Race and Sex on Campus* (New York: Free Press, 1991).

2. In "The New Pedagogy," *South Atlantic Quarterly* 91 (Summer 1992), 765–84, I argue that the conservative attacks on "political correctness" should motivate progressive critics and teachers at many different levels and representing a wide range of different methods and approaches to find terms of agreement and consensus rather than continuing the often divisive debates among ourselves that have given conservatives in the United States further grounds to criticize the "incoherence" and "fragmentation" of "liberal educational" curricular reforms. I think that such political unity among progressive educators in the fields of American literature and American Studies is part of this overall project, which still remains a crucial task both in response to continuing attacks on "political correctness" and as an integral component of liberal education.

3. Homi Bhabha, "DissemiNation: Time, Narrative, and the Margins of the Modern Nation," in *Nation and Narration*, ed. Homi Bhabha (New York: Routledge, 1990), 314.

4. Paul Lauter, "The Literatures of America: A Comparative Discipline," in *Redefining American Literary History*, ed. A. LaVonne Brown Ruoff and Jerry Ward Jr. (New York: Modern Language Association, 1990), 9–34.

5. Paul Lauter, *Canons and Contexts* (New York: Oxford University Press, 1991); Paul Lauter, general ed., *The Heath Anthology of American Literature*, 3rd ed., 2 vols. (Boston: Houghton Mifflin Co., 1998).

6. Mary Louise Pratt, "Arts of the Contact Zone," *Profession 91*, 33–41; Mary Louise Pratt, "Linguistic Utopias," in *The Linguistics of Writing: Arguments between Language and Literature*, ed. Nigel Fabb, Derek Attridge, Alan Durant, and Colin MacCabe (Manchester: Manchester University Press, 1987), 48–66.

7. Lauter, "The Literatures of America," 9. Page numbers subsequently cited in the text refer to this essay.

8. The problem of "cultural definition" was effectively solved by world literature comparatists by accepting the self-definitions of nation-states. The title of Homi Bhabha's collection, *Nation and Narration*, is entirely familiar to comparatists who have worked in the "world literature" model. It is thus perfectly understandable why Erich Auerbach's *Mimesis: The Representation of Reality in Western Literature*, trans. Willard R. Trask (Princeton, N. J.: Princeton University Press, 1953), which was originally published in German in 1946, should occupy such a central position in the "world literature" paradigm for comparatism, because it so eloquently demonstrates the emergence of different national (read also "modern," because the terms are obviously the same) "literatures" out of broader mythic and aesthetic resources in the West that offer the common substrate for these different and differing cultures. By identifying in the manifest differences of national literatures (French, German, English, and Spanish) their shared Western aesthetic (and mythic) heritage, Auerbach was able to reconcile the cosmopolitan, transnational aims of European modern artists and critics with the revival and reaffirmation of nationalist sentiments and

curricula in the years after World War II. To be sure, Auerbach's intentions were transnational in the best spirit of the high moderns (among whom he certainly should be counted as an important figure). Like so many other modernist works, however, *Mimesis* offers its own space (or narrative) as an alternative to a nationalism many moderns hoped might have a limited history. Nevertheless, the moderns who demonstrated how certain nationalities found their specific identities in and through a common "Western tradition" often helped legitimate nations and their aesthetic ideologies those moderns may have considered provincial, as did many U.S. expatriates, such as Henry James, T. S. Eliot, Gertrude Stein, and Ernest Hemingway.

9. Pratt, "Arts of the Contact Zone," 34. Page numbers subsequently cited in the text refer to this essay.

10. Pratt's account of this text, together with Rolena Adorno's reintroduction of it to the scholarly community in her *Guaman Poma de Ayala: Writing and Resistance in Colonial Peru* (Austin, Texas: University of Texas Press, 1986), are fascinating and instructive examples of the arts of the contact zone in their own rights.

11. Pratt points out that Guaman Poma's text was discovered in 1908 by "a Peruvianist named Richard Pietschmann" who "was exploring in the Danish Royal Archive in Copenhagen" and came across the manuscript. Lest we take this for simply one more of those New Historicist "anecdotes" about some fabulously uncanny text from everyday social life, Pratt connects the text's "neglect" with the scholarly reception it received when it was "introduced" to the scholarly community: "Pietschmann prepared a paper on his find, which he presented in London in 1912, a year after the rediscovery of Machu Picchu by Hiram Bingham. Reception, by an international congress of Americanists, was apparently confused. It took twenty-five years for a facsimile edition of the work to appear, in Paris. It was not till the late 1970s, as positivist reading habits gave way to interpretive studies and colonial elitisms to postcolonial pluralisms, that Western scholars found ways of reading Guaman Poma's *New Chronicle and Good Government* as the extraordinary intercultural tour de force that it was. The letter got there, only 350 years too late, a miracle and terrible tragedy" (33–34).

12. Hirsch's *Cultural Literacy* (Boston: Houghton Mifflin Co, 1987) has not been associated unequivocally with the conservative attacks on "political correctness," but the very concept of "cultural literacy" depends both on the singularity of "national culture" and on nationalism's monolingualism. The following passage is representative: "Although nationalism may be regrettable in some of its world-wide political effects, a mastery of national culture is essential to mastery of the standard language in every modern nation. This point is important for educational policy, because educators often stress the virtues of multicultural education. Such study is indeed valuable in itself; it inculcates tolerance and provides a perspective on our own traditions and values. But however laudable it is, it should not be the primary focus of national education. It should not be allowed to supplant or interfere with our schools' responsibility to ensure our children's mastery of American literate culture. The acculturative responsibility of the schools is primary and fundamental. To teach the ways of one's own community has always been and still remains the essence of the education of our

children, who enter neither a narrow tribal culture nor a transcendent world culture but a national literate culture" (18). The unwitting ethnocentrism in this passage is bound up with an unreflective commitment to "American literate culture" that simply begs the question of what constitutes "one's own community" and "our children" in the demonstrably multicultural United States today. Rather than smugly condemn the provincialism and anachronism of such sentiments, however, we need to develop clearer examples of the alternatives to "communities" other than "narrow tribal culture," "transcendent world culture," and "national literate culture" that already exist.

13. As Pratt points out in "Arts of the Contact Zone," pp. 33–41, one of our problems is the extraordinarily abstract "speech-act" model we have for communication. Monolingual and monocultural nationalisms are also subtly reinforced by "monolinguistic" paradigms. Speech acts are obviously different in structure and function according to the intercultural situations in which they occur.

14. Myra Jehlen, "Why Did the Europeans Cross the Ocean? A Seventeenth-Century Riddle," in *Cultures of United States Imperialism*, ed. Amy Kaplan and Donald E. Pease (Durham, N.C.: Duke University Press, 1993), 54.

15. Henry Louis Gates Jr., *The Signifying Monkey: A Theory of African-American Literary Criticism* (New York: Oxford University Press, 1988); Gloria Anzaldúa, *Borderlands/La Frontera: The New Mestiza* (San Francisco: Spinsters/aunt lute, 1987); and Cherríe Moraga and Gloria Anzaldúa, eds., *This Bridge Called My Back: Writings by Radical Women of Color* (Watertown, Mass.: Persephone Press, 1981). In her review of *Borderlands/La Frontera,* "Algo secretamente amado," in *Third Woman: The Sexuality of Latinas,* ed. Norma Alarcón, Anna Castillo, and Cherríe Moraga (Berkeley: Third Woman Press, 1989), p. 151, Moraga notes that "the revelation of the fundamental alienation of the brown woman reflects a radical departure from traditional Chicano letters." Moraga criticizes Anzaldúa for "jargon" and "laborious" or "strained" stylistic gestures, but she acknowledges the book as "a kind of blueprint for *la nueva cultura* that Anzaldúa envisions" for "*mestiza* consciousness" (155). Lisa Lowe, *Immigrant Acts: On Asian-American Cultural Politics* (Durham, N.C.: Duke University Press, 1996).

16. Donna Haraway, "A Manifesto for Cyborgs: Science, Technology, and Socialist Feminism in the 1980s," in *Feminism/Postmodernism,* ed. Linda J. Nicholson (New York: Routledge, 1990), 191.

17. Auerbach ends *Mimesis* with an appeal for "a common life of humankind on earth" (552). To be sure, Auerbach's transnational dream still belongs to modernism, as I noted earlier, but it is an anticipation as well of the multicultural ideals and models we are now beginning to theorize and, one might hope, practice in the wake of nationalism. What Auerbach imagined to be "the approaching unification and simplification" may have lent itself too readily to the arguments we hear today for a return to a "common culture," but Auerbach also understood from his own experience the borderlands and arts of the contact zone I have tried to develop in this chapter. The famous "signature" of *Mimesis* remains a testament to that bordering: "Written in Istanbul between May 1942 and April 1945. First published in Berne, Switzerland, 1946."

2. Postmodernity and the New American Studies

1. John Enck, "Interview with John Barth," *Contemporary Literature* (Spring 1967), 34.

2. John Barth, "The Literature of Exhaustion," *The Atlantic* (August 1967); rpt. in *The Friday Book: Essays and Other Non-Fiction* (New York: G. P. Putnam's Sons, 1984), 72.

3. John Barth, "The Literature of Replenishment," *The Atlantic* (January 1980); rpt. in *The Friday Book,* 193–206.

4. John Barth, *Lost in the Funhouse: Fiction for Print, Tape, and Live Voice* (Garden City, N.Y.: Doubleday and Co., Inc., 1968), 1–2.

5. Friedrich Nietzsche, *The Birth of Tragedy and the Genealogy of Morals,* trans. Francis Golffing (Garden City, N.Y.: Doubleday and Co., Inc., 1956), 299.

6. Theodor Adorno, *Prisms,* trans. Samuel and Shierry Weber (London: Spearman, 1967), 37.

7. See Fredric Jameson, *Postmodernism or, the Cultural Logic of Late Capitalism* (Durham, N.C.: Duke University Press, 1991), ix–xxii.

8. See Russell Jacoby, *The Last Intellectuals: American Culture in the Age of Academe* (New York: Basic Books, 1987).

9. Eugenio Donato, "The Two Languages of Criticism," and Jacques Derrida, "Structure, Sign and Play in the Discourse of the Human Sciences," in *The Languages of Criticism and the Sciences of Man: The Structuralist Controversy,* ed. Richard Macksey and Eugenio Donato (Baltimore, Md.: Johns Hopkins University Press, 1970), 89–97, 247–64.

10. A "revision" that Lacan himself offered on numerous occasions, despite the popularity of the slogan and its simile. "In Agency of the Letter in the Unconscious," in *Ecrits: A Selection,* trans. Alan Sheridan (New York: W. W. Norton Co., 1977), 170, Lacan argues: "The unconscious is neither primordial nor instinctual; what it knows about the elementary is no more than the elements of the signifier."

11. The advertising copy that Derrida wrote for Editions Galilée to promote *Glas* describes the text in this manner: "In the first place: two columns. Truncated above and below, cuts also in their sides: incisions, tattoos, incrustations. At first reading, it seems as if two texts are set up, one against the other or one without the other, without communication between them. And in a certain deliberate fashion, that is true, as far as pretext, object, language, style, rhythm, and law are concerned. A dialectic of one side, a galactic [motion] of the other, heterogeneous and indiscernibly dependent on their effects, sometimes nearly hallucinatory. Between the two, the bell clapper of another text, speaking an other 'logic': in proper names of obsequy, penetration, restriction, taboo, . . . of death" (my translation). Elizabeth Bruss, *Beautiful Theories: The Spectacle of Discourse in Contemporary Criticism* (Baltimore, Md.: Johns Hopkins University Press, 1982).

12. For an excellent critical reading of the "Yale School," see the essays collected in *The Yale Critics: Deconstruction in America,* ed. Jonathan Arac, Wlad Godzich, and Wallace Martin (Minneapolis: University of Minnesota Press, 1983).

13. The most familiar examples of the "new realism" on television of this period are *All in the Family*, which explored the working-class family's complicity in the perpetuation of racism and sexism, and *Maude*, which focused on the impact of feminism on the bourgeois family. For the recent influence of the documentary on the development of docudrama, see my "From Documentary to Docudrama: Vietnam on Television in the 1980s," *Genre* 21 (Winter 1988), 451–77.

14. In "The Race for Theory," *Cultural Critique* 6 (Spring 1987), 67–79, Barbara Christian argues that the elitism of critical theory, especially in its poststructuralist versions, is integral to its arguments and methods and that the noted "difficulty" and "sophistication" of deconstruction are means of preserving "critical theory" as a white, ethnocentric discipline. Christian criticizes both the "New Philosophers" (Lacan, Foucault, Derrida, et al.) and the Continental feminists, the latter for imitating the styles and arguments of those "New Philosophers" even as they criticized their blindness to issues of gender. Christian's argument is, perhaps designedly, undialectical. By stressing the inherent racism of poststructuralist theory rather than the failure of poststructuralism to elaborate the implications of its own theories for a critique of race and gender, Christian invalidates the valuable work by many contemporary feminist and African American scholars that has been significantly influenced by poststructuralist theory. Further, Christian's call for a "return" to the literary work and the self-evident values of "expressive" writing is based on a misunderstanding of the political aims of the postmodern critique of "literature" as a discrete mode of representation.

15. Maxwell Geismar, "Introduction," *Soul on Ice* (New York: Dell Publishing, 1968), xii.

16. Richard Slotkin's trilogy about the ideology of Westward expansion— *Regeneration through Violence: The Mythology of the American Frontier, 1600–1860* (Middletown, Conn.: Wesleyan University Press, 1973), *The Fatal Environment: The Myth of the Frontier in the Age of Industrialization, 1800–1890* (New York: Atheneum, 1985), and *Gunfighter Nation: The Myth of the Frontier in Twentieth-Century America* (New York: Atheneum, 1992)—has often been criticized for its relative neglect of the role of women in such an ideology. Richard Drinnon's *Facing West: The Metaphysics of Indian-Hating and Empire Building* (Minneapolis: University of Minnesota Press, 1980) is yet another classic work of American Studies that is notable for its neglect of gender relations and hierarchies in the periods studied. Annette Kolodny, in *The Lay of the Land: Metaphor as Experience and History in American Life and Letters* (Chapel Hill: University of North Carolina Press, 1975) and *The Territory before Her: Fantasy and Experience of the American Frontiers, 1630–1860* (Chapel Hill: University of North Carolina Press, 1984), has examined critically the various ways writers in the United States have "feminized" nature, thus combining the aims of patriarchal and territorial domination, gender hierarchies, and the ideology of imperialism.

17. Henry Louis Gates Jr., ed., *Black Literature and Literary Theory* (New York: Methuen, 1984); Henry Louis Gates Jr., ed., *"Race," Writing, Difference* (Chicago: University of Chicago Press, 1986); Henry Louis Gates Jr., *The Signifying Monkey: A*

Theory of Afro-American Literary Criticism (New York: Oxford University Press, 1988); Henry Louis Gates Jr., ed., *African and African American Literature,* special issue of *PMLA* (January 1990).

18. James Clifford and George E. Marcus, eds., *Writing Culture: The Poetics and Politics of Ethnography* (Berkeley: University of California Press, 1986).

19. Henry Louis Gates Jr. and Nellie McKay, eds., *The Norton Anthology of African American Literature* (New York: W. W. Norton Co., 1996); Henry Louis Gates Jr., ed., *Black Literature, 1827–1940,* CD-ROM (Alexandria, Va.: Chadwyck-Healey Inc., 1994–).

20. Susan Jeffords, *The Remasculinization of America: Gender and the Vietnam War* (Bloomington: Indiana University Press, 1989).

3. Postnationalism, Globalism, and the New American Studies

1. Werner Sollors, "For a Multilingual Turn in American Studies," *American Studies Association Newsletter* (1997), also posted for discussion on the web site for Randy Bass's American Crossroads Project (http://www.georgetown.edu/crossroads), where Sollors describes the anthology that would be published as *The Multilingual Anthology of American Literature,* ed. Marc Shell and Werner Sollors (New York: New York University Press, 1998).

2. E. D. Hirsch Jr., *Cultural Literacy: What Every American Needs to Know* (Boston: Houghton Mifflin Co., 1987), 70–93; Arthur Schlesinger Jr., *The Disuniting of America: Reflections on a Multicultural Society* (New York: W. W. Norton, 1992).

3. In his response to discussion of his essay on the American Crossroads web site, Sollors notes: "It is also simply not true that monolingualism reduces illiteracy or technological ineffectiveness. . . . It is a myth that bilingualism lowers language performance in first languages. . . . It seems doubtful to me whether 'English only' education, based on the false myths of a monolingual past and of better language skills of monolingual people, makes for more civic cohesion than would a fuller understanding of the pervasive multilingualism in U.S. history and society" ("From 'English Only' to 'English-Plus' in American Studies," American Crossroads [http://www.georgetown.edu/crossroads], August 2, 1997).

4. Paul Lauter, in his response to Sollors's essay on July 26, 1997 on the American Crossroads web site (http://www.georgetown.edu/crossroads), makes a particularly important point about the need to study the ideological assumptions behind the previous foreign language requirements for students seeking admission to graduate programs in American Studies. Earlier arguments favoring the so-called tool languages of French and German, usually neglecting Spanish, Portuguese, Chinese, Japanese, Korean, Vietnamese, and the many other languages crucial to the history of nations and immigrant populations in the western hemisphere and virtually repressing the study of Native American languages, except by specialists in these fields, have played their parts not only in reinforcing the monolingual ideology of the United States but also in perpetuating what I would term the heritage of Eurocultural colonialism in the United States.

5. I do not include here rigorous accounts of U.S. pragmatism as a methodology, theory, and philosophy in its own right, rather than a vaguely invoked synonym for American character. For an excellent account of U.S. pragmatism in this precise sense, see Mark Bauerlein, *The Concept of Pragmatic Mind: Emerson, William James, Charles Sanders Peirce* (Durham, N.C.: Duke University Press, 1997). For a version of how American pragmatism can be used as a substitute for American national character, see Richard Poirier, *The Renewal of Literature: Emersonian Reflections* (New York: Random House, 1987), and *Poetry and Pragmatism* (Cambridge, Mass.: Harvard University Press, 1992).

6. Leo Marx, "Rethinking the American Studies Project," in *American Studies in Germany: European Contexts and Intercultural Relations*, ed. Günter Lenz and Klaus J. Milich (New York: St. Martin's Press, 1995), 54.

7. Cary Nelson, in *Manifesto of a Tenured Radical* (New York: New York University Press, 1997), pp. 64–70, provides a concise and relevant manifesto of cultural studies, outlining what cultural studies at their best ought to achieve. Missing from his manifesto, however, is any consideration of nationalism and imperialism as central topics for cultural critics. For my own approach to cultural studies, see chapter 4.

8. See John Carlos Rowe, *Literary Culture and U.S. Imperialism: From the American Revolution to World War II* (New York: Oxford University Press, 2000), in which I develop this thesis about U.S. nationalism and imperialism from the first decades of the U.S. republic—the Alien and Sedition Acts, for example—up to the 1940s. There are, of course, many other scholars working in this area, many represented in Amy Kaplan and Donald Pease, eds., *Cultures of United States Imperialism* (Durham, N.C.: Duke University Press, 1993), and Donald Pease, ed., *National Identities and Post-Americanist Narratives* (Durham, N.C.: Duke University Press, 1994).

9. Leo Marx, "Rethinking the American Studies Project," 54.

10. Richard P. Horwitz, "Preface," in *Exporting America: Essays on American Studies Abroad*, ed. Richard P. Horwitz (New York: Garland Publishing, Inc., 1993), xv. The essays in this collection by U.S. and non-U.S. specialists in American Studies offer interesting complements to and case studies in support of my argument.

11. Jim Zwick, "Towards Critical Internationalism within U.S.-based American Studies," February 18, 1997, and my response, February 18, 1997, on the American Crossroads web site (http://www.georgetown.edu/crossroads).

12. Emory Elliott initiated this work as former chair of the International Committee of the American Studies Association (ASA). Like Paul Lauter, Elliott has visited many international American Studies programs and helped bring many international scholars to the United States for extended visits. Thanks to both Paul and Emory, American Studies specialists from Brazil, Poland, and Indonesia visited our research group.

13. As we learned from the international scholars visiting our research group and from those attending the public forums we sponsored at the ASA and California American Studies Association conventions in 1996 and 1997, American Studies may serve a wide range of different educational and intellectual purposes around the

world. Local political, cultural, and intellectual issues are often interestingly woven into the curricula and pedagogy of American Studies in non-U.S. cultures in ways U.S. scholars unfamiliar with those cultures (and their languages and histories) do not understand. Such hybridizations of local and international knowledges range from explicit efforts to circumvent repressive regimes and local censorship to subtler modes of responding to U.S. cultural imperialism by transforming the ineluctable importation of U.S. cultural "goods."

14. For example, Reinhold Wagnleitner, *Coca-colonization and the Cold War: The Cultural Mission of the United States in Austria after World War II,* trans. Diana M. Wolf (Chapel Hill: University of North Carolina Press, 1994), which critically interprets the post–World War II competition between the United States and the Soviet Union for the control of Austrian culture.

15. During her participation in the Minority Discourse Project at the University of California's Humanities Research Institute in 1993 and 1994, Norma Alarcón took colleagues on a tour of the U.S.-Mexico border, both to familiarize them with an important site of political and social conflict and to remind them that all "border studies" must be mindful of the actual border zones and their consequences for individual lives. I agree that Alarcón's purpose is an important one for us to keep in mind, but I also think that the U.S.-Mexico border was discursively constructed long before physical barriers were erected (by the Treaty of Guadalupe-Hidalgo, for example) and discursively as well as physically policed.

16. Sean Wilentz, "Integrating Ethnicity into American Studies," *Chronicle of Higher Education,* November 29, 1996, A56. Lawrence Buell, in "Are We Post-American Studies?" in *Field Work: Sites in Literary and Cultural Studies,* ed. Marjorie Garber, Paul B. Franklin, and Rebecca Walkowitz (New York: Routledge, 1996), p. 89, argues that "nation and culture aren't coextensive, but neither are they disjunct." Acknowledging that the "familiar debates about national identity vs. cultural particularism" have been replaced by "the issue of whether a model of cultural identity at any level can hold its ground against a model of cultural hybridization or syncretism" (89), Buell concludes with a markedly colonialist metaphor for the apocalypse facing American Studies scholars who abandon the nationalist and exceptionalist models of the previous generation's work: "The more decentered so-called American literary studies becomes, the more suspect the category of nation as a putative cultural unit, and the more likely United States literature specialists may be to oscillate between clinging to discredited assumptions about national distinctiveness vs. throwing ourselves wholly, *amor fati*–like, on the pyre of postnationalism (in a kind of subdisciplinary suttee)" (91). It is quite a rhetorical stretch to link postnationalist discussions with the outlawed practice of Hindu suttee, but Buell's choice of metaphors reveals his intention of suggesting thereby the "primitivism" of other cultures—a primitivism American Studies must avoid. Buell's orientalism in this instance is interestingly, albeit predictably, complemented by appeals to scientific rationality and the rhetoric of Christian belief: "[I]f we're *truly rigorous* in trying to get to whatever *empirical bedrock underlies* those assumptions while at the same time remaining atten-

tive to the distinction between culture and nation (and with this the promise of border, diaspora, and global culture studies), then we will be *faithful* to our *posts* as post-American Americanists, whatever the outcome of the culture wars" (91, emphasis mine). How extraordinary that such "rigor," "empiricism," and "bedrock" investigation should conclude in a merely rhetorical flourish, redolent of religion (now of the Euro-American Christian varieties, to be sure): "faithful to our posts as post-American Americanists"!

17. For a more general treatment of the problem of the Enlightenment university and the new modes of knowledge, see David Lloyd, "Foundations of Diversity: Thinking the University in a Time of Multiculturalism," in *"Culture" and the Problem of the Disciplines,* ed. John Carlos Rowe (New York: Columbia University Press, 1998), 15–43.

18. For a good discussion of the new regionalism that has emerged as a consequence of the new global economy, see Michael Clough, "Birth of Nations," *Los Angeles Times,* July 27, 1997, M1, M6.

19. Paul Gilroy's model of the "black Atlantic," seen in *The Black Atlantic: Modernity and Double Consciousness* (London: Verso, 1993), is one model for such pedagogical practices and curricular designs.

20. Jesse Vasquez, president of the National Association for Ethnic Studies and professor of education and Puerto Rican Studies at Queens College, responded in an understandably angry way to Wilentz's article "Integrating Ethnicity into American Studies" in his letter to the *Chronicle,* January 31, 1997, concluding an otherwise sensible critique of Wilentz's arguments by challenging: "It may be that it is ethnic studies that now should consider taking over American studies, and not the other way around" ("Opinion," B3).

21. Randy Bass and Jeff Finlay, *Engines of Inquiry: A Practical Guide for Using Technology to Teach American Culture* (Washington, D.C.: Georgetown University Press, 1997).

22. The Columbia Online Project, which makes available portions of scholarly books recently published by Columbia and Oxford University Presses, and *Literature Online* from Chadwyck-Healey, an electronic publisher, are steps in this direction, but academic presses have been slow to adapt to the electronic means of disseminating scholarly materials that are currently available.

23. Clough, "Birth of Nations," M1.

4. The Resistance to Cultural Studies in the United States

1. The critics of cultural studies often rely on such anecdotal evidence to dismiss cultural studies as a coherent movement and method, but bad examples of any viable intellectual approach can always be gathered and do not necessarily invalidate that approach. In such cases, the best response to critics is to clarify the basic assumptions and values of the approach rather than responding to particular examples.

2. Wolfgang Iser, *The Range of Interpretation* (New York: Columbia University Press, 2000), 159–63.

3. J. Hillis Miller, in "Literary and Cultural Studies in the Transnational University," in *"Culture" and the Problem of the Disciplines,* ed. John Carlos Rowe (New York: Columbia University Press, 1998), p. 63, argues that "the acceptance by the university of cultural studies has been suspiciously rapid and easy," especially when cultural studies contributes to an "antitheoretical turn" among contemporary intellectuals. Miller's point is that critical theory is more "radical" and "challenging" to traditional university structures than "cultural studies," which in its untheorized versions reinforces "an antitheoretical return to mimesis." Miller implies here that cultural studies is far more subject to a naïve "reflection theory"—wherein cultural texts merely distortedly reflect more profound social, economic, and political conditions—and can thereby relegitimate critical theory as more sophisticated in its interpretation of the relationship between culture and ideology. His position is in several instances clearly defensive; for example: "Theory of the sixties, seventies, and eighties has gone on being effective" (63).

4. Jay Mechling, "Some [New] Elementary Axioms for an American Cultur[al] Studies," *American Studies* 38:2 (Summer 1997, special issue, *American Studies: From Culture Concept to Cultural Studies?*), 15.

5. Jean-François Lyotard, *The Postmodern Condition,* trans. Geoff Bennington and Brian Massumi (Minneapolis: University of Minnesota Press), 31–34.

6. Paul de Man, "The Resistance to Literary Theory," *Yale French Studies* 63 (1982), 3–20; revised as the title essay of *The Resistance to Theory,* ed. Wlad Godzich (Minneapolis: University of Minnesota Press, 1986), 12.

7. I refer here to interview questions sent to me (and other theorists) by Fengzhen Wang (Beijing University) and Shaobo Xie (University of Calgary) addressing a wide range of issues in contemporary theory. My answers to those questions are included in "Cultural Studies Today," an interview for *Cultural Studies,* ed. Fengzhen Wang and Shaobo Xie (Alberta: University of Calgary Press, forthcoming 2002, and Beijing: Chinese Academy of Social Sciences Press, 2001).

8. De Man, *The Resistance to Theory,* 8: "Contemporary literary theory comes into its own in such events as the application of Saussurean linguistics to literary texts." But for de Man this application does not result in the subordination of "literature" to its "linguistic" infrastructure; instead, literature affirms and distinguishes itself as the best site for "thinking" (substitute here "reading") about language. It is a clever argument, but more than fifteen years in retrospect can be seen as an argument haunted by its own internal logic, its lack of historical demonstration (language is nothing if not its historical enactment), and its author's apparent ignorance of the rapid developments of "rhetoric" and "tropology" in the popular and mass media even in the 1980s (see chapters 8 and 9).

9. In *The Resistance to Theory,* de Man makes a similar point about the rhetorical deconstruction he proposes as an alternative to structuralist semiotics, New Critical aesthetic categories, and philosophical a priori in general. De Man's affirmation of "reading" as the interpretive practice of following rhetorical paths, teasing out their implications and signifying potentials rather than drawing conclusions about "meaning," is his own version of the impossibility of a metalanguage. In the place of

metalanguage, de Man frequently offers "literature": "Literature involves the voiding, rather than the affirmation, of aesthetic categories" (10). Elsewhere he asks rhetorically: "What is meant when we assert that the study of literary texts is necessarily dependent on an act or reading, or when we claim that this act is being systematically avoided?" (15). For de Man, "reading"—that is, the deconstructive mapping of rhetorical possibilities—takes the place of "systematic," "grammatical," and "logical" modes of analysis, all of which are mystified by their assumption of a metatheoretical model.

10. Such pragmatics differ significantly from de Man's distinction in *The Resistance to Theory* between the "linguistic moment" and "historical and aesthetic considerations," which for him are illusions when understood apart from their linguistic conditions of appearance (7). Such a distinction enables de Man to trivialize the "historical" and the "aesthetic," which are coded terms that refer respectively to Marxists (none is mentioned in the essay) and formalists (either New Critics or *Rezeptionsaesthetik* theorists, like Hans Robert Jauss and Wolfgang Iser, who are specifically mentioned). Cultural criticism is not, then, anything like the "theory" or "literary theory" so celebrated by de Man in "The Resistance to Theory," because cultural criticism refuses to accept the distinction de Man makes between interpretation as the determination of "meaning or value" (an illusion for de Man) and interpretation as the determination of "the modalities of production and of reception of meaning and of value prior to their establishment" (what his version of rhetorical deconstruction accomplishes) (7). According to the very "non-concepts" of a poststructuralist theory of language, the distinction cannot be maintained in any effective, pragmatic, systematic, or even functional way.

11. I am grateful to Lauren not only for this helpful phrase, but also for her public lecture and discussion in the spring of 1998 at the University of California–Irvine, during which many of these resistances to cultural theory were discussed.

12. Fredric Jameson, *Postmodernism, or the Cultural Logic of Late Capitalism* (Durham, N.C.: Duke University Press, 1991), and Neil Postman, *Amusing Ourselves to Death: Public Discourse in the Age of Show Business* (New York: Viking, 1985).

13. Cary Nelson, in *Manifesto of a Tenured Radical* (New York: New York University Press, 1997), pp. 13–28, also points out the limitations of "English as it was." Nelson and I are exactly contemporaries as far as our undergraduate and graduate educations are concerned.

14. De Man, *The Resistance to Theory*, 17.

15. John Carlos Rowe, *Literary Culture and U.S. Imperialism: From the Revolution to World War II* (New York: Oxford University Press, 2000), 97–119.

16. Paul de Man, *Blindness and Insight* (New York: Oxford University Press, 1971), 148–50; chapter 9 of this book; Susan Jeffords, *The Remasculinization of America: Gender and the Vietnam War* (Bloomington: Indiana University Press, 1989); Janice Radway, *A Feeling for Books: The Book-of-the-Month Club, Literary Taste, and Middle-Class Desire* (Chapel Hill: University of North Carolina Press, 1997); Tania Modleski, *Loving with a Vengeance: Mass-Produced Fantasies for Women* (Hamden, Conn.: Archon Books, 1982).

17. When I was asked in the early 1990s to give a series of lectures to high school

seniors at Tustin High School that would simulate a lower-division university lecture course, the English teachers proposed that I lecture on Herman Melville's *Moby-Dick*. I suggested that instead we screen *Rambo: First Blood, Part II*, on the grounds that the advanced placement English teachers at Tustin were perfectly capable of teaching *Moby-Dick* to their students but that the treatment of mass-market texts might involve less familiar theoretical and practical concerns. The lectures were successful, especially when measured by the excellent papers written by the students—papers I read and graded, with the help of Krista Walter, then a Ph.D. candidate at UC–Irvine, and by the students excited and challenged by the subject matter. But there was considerable initial resistance among them to viewing, much less writing about, such lowbrow material.

18. See Nelson, *Manifesto of a Tenured Radical*, especially chapters 1 and 4.

19. For a discussion of how popular debates regarding multiculturalism have affected curricula in higher education, especially programs in American Studies, see the introduction to *Post-Nationalist American Studies,* ed. John Carlos Rowe (Berkeley: University of California Press, 2000), 10–14.

20. John M. Ellis, *Literature Lost: Social Agendas and the Corruption of the Humanities* (New Haven, Conn.: Yale University Press, 1997); see also my review of Nelson's and Ellis's very different books in *Academe: Bulletin of the A.A.U.P.,* May–June 1998, 76–77.

21. Richard Rorty, "The Necessity of Inspired Reading," *The Chronicle of Higher Education,* February 9, 1996; see also my response in "Letters to the Editor," *The Chronicle of Higher Education,* March 8, 1996, B4. Rorty's op-ed piece is based on a longer essay, "The Inspirational Value of Great Works of Literature," which was first delivered as a lecture at the Modern Language Association's annual convention in December 1995, published in *Raritan* 16 (Summer 1996), pp. 8–17, and included as an appendix in Richard Rorty, *Achieving Our Country: Leftist Thought in Twentieth-Century America* (Cambridge, Mass.: Harvard University Press, 1998), pp. 125–40.

22. De Man, *The Resistance to Theory,* 19.

5. Hawthorne's Ghost in Henry James's Italy

1. John Carlos Rowe, "Swept Away: Henry James, Margaret Fuller, and 'The Last of the Valerii,'" in *Readers in History: Nineteenth-Century American Literature and the Contexts of Response,* ed. James L. Machor (Baltimore, Md.: Johns Hopkins University Press, 1993), 32–53. A revised version of this essay is included as chapter 1 in my *The Other Henry James* (Durham, N.C.: Duke University Press, 1998), 38–55.

2. Henry James, *William Wetmore Story and His Friends: From Letters, Diaries, and Recollections,* 2 vols. (Boston: Houghton Mifflin Co., 1903), 1: 5. Further references in the text are to this edition.

3. See Rowe, "Swept Away," pp. 37–42, for my account of how James links Fuller and the many legends and artistic representations of Beatrice Cenci that were so popular in the nineteenth century.

4. Nathaniel Hawthorne, *The Marble Faun: Or, The Romance of Monte Beni,* in *Centenary Edition of the Works of Nathaniel Hawthorne,* ed. William Charvat, Roy

Harvey Pearce, and Claude M. Simpson (Columbus: Ohio State University Press, 1968), vol. 4, 464–65. Further references in the text are to this edition.

5. In his "Textual Introduction" to *The Marble Faun* in the *Centenary Edition of the Works of Nathaniel Hawthorne*, p. xlv, Fredson Bowers explains the addition of the 1860 "Postscript" to the romance: "Shortly after March 16, 1860 . . . , a second printing . . .—called the second edition of the title—was published, containing the added postscript." For Giuseppe Ossoli's opposition to Fuller's marriage to his son, see Bell Gale Chevigny, *The Woman and the Myth: Margaret Fuller's Life and Writings* (Boston: Northeastern University Press, 1994), p. 379.

6. Here I am following the theoretical and historical argument of Scott S. Derrick in *Monumental Anxieties: Homoerotic Desire and Feminine Influence in 19th-Century U.S. Literature* (New Brunswick, N.J.: Rutgers University Press, 1997) that the "nineteenth century's ongoing efforts to essentialize and divide men and women on the basis of gender had the consequence of creating extremely powerful bonds between members of the same sex" and that a man's "powerful desire for the stuff of masculinity," especially when masculinity has been challenged, "may often create homoerotic desire for the body of the other man as its inevitable by-product" (28). Yet I confess to hedging my own claims about the power of masculine ideology in the work of producing homoerotic and homosexual desires, much as Derrick himself does when he acknowledges that "desire for other men may come from other sources, such as a primarily homosexual orientation," even if such desire has "difficulty understanding and expressing itself apart from ideas of aspiration and identification" characteristic of nineteenth-century patriarchal masculinity (28–29). The degree to which the differences between Hawthorne's and Henry James's responses to women's rights and independent women are attributable to different historical (and thus ideological) periods and to the different sexual orientations of the authors (Derrick treats James's "primary orientation" as "almost certainly homosexual" and Hawthorne's as "primarily heterosexual" [29]) can be judged only after close analyses of their respective treatments of similar historical and literary people, places, and things.

7. Rowe, "Swept Away," 48.

8. The discovery of the Venus de Milo (Aphrodite of Melos) on Melos in 1820 was only one of many spectacular nineteenth-century discoveries of classical marbles and bronzes that gave special impetus to neoclassical sculpture in this period.

9. In what follows, I am indebted generally to the excellent work of Millicent Bell, *Hawthorne's View of the Artist* (New York: State University of New York Press, 1962); Rita K. Gollin and John L. Idol Jr., with the assistance of Sterling K. Eisiminger, *Prophetic Pictures: Nathaniel Hawthorne's Knowledge and Uses of the Visual Arts*, Contributions in American Studies, No. 99, ed. Robert H. Walker (Westport, Conn.: Greenwood Press, 1991); Viola Hopkins Winner, *Henry James and the Visual Arts* (Charlottesville: University of Virginia Press, 1970); and Adeline Tintner, *The Museum World of Henry James* (Ann Arbor, Mich.: UMI Research Press, 1989).

10. Dolly Sherwood, *Harriet Hosmer, American Sculptor, 1830–1908* (Columbia: University of Missouri Press, 1991), 134.

11. Hawthorne to William Ticknor, January 1855, as quoted in Caroline Ticknor,

Hawthorne and His Publisher (Boston: Houghton Mifflin Co., 1913), 141. Hawthorne uses his complaint against the popular literary tastes in America to explain his plan to extend his stay in Europe.

12. Wayne Craven, *Sculpture in America* (New York: Thomas Y. Crowell Co., 1968), 327.

13. Ibid., 330.

14. Ibid., 333.

15. Ibid., 334.

16. Sherwood, *Harriet Hosmer*, 195.

17. Ibid., 214.

18. Ibid.

19. T. Walter Herbert, in *Dearest Beloved: The Hawthornes and the Making of the Middle-Class Family* (Berkeley: University of California Press, 1993), p. 231, notes that Lander's refusal "to respond to the 'inquiry'" did not stop the rumors, which then "became accepted as commonplace matters of fact, to which Louisa responded likewise with defiance." Herbert connects the Hawthornes' snubbing of Lander at the hint of sexual scandal with their negative reactions to "the nudity of the pictures and statues they viewed in Italy" and writes that "their minds insistently formed a judgment concerning the sexual interaction between artist and model."

20. For an excellent account of the Hawthornes' relationship with Maria Louisa Lander, see Robert L. Gale, *A Nathaniel Hawthorne Encyclopedia* (Westport, Conn.: Greenwood Press, 1991), pp. 272–73.

21. Herbert, *Dearest Beloved*, 232.

22. Lora Romero, *Home Fronts: Domesticity and Its Critics in the Antebellum United States* (Durham, N.C.: Duke University Press, 1997), 103. Hawthorne makes this reference to Fanny Fern in a letter to his publisher, Ticknor, dated February 5, 1855, as quoted in Romero, p. 103.

23. John D'Emilio and Estelle B. Freedman, in *Intimate Matters: A History of Sexuality in America* (New York: Harper and Row, 1988), pp. 157–58, discuss the influence of the "growing reticence about sexuality among the middle class" on "American artists of the antebellum period," noting that it was "acceptable to depict the naked body in European art," but that "those who exhibited in America learned that nudity and sexuality were highly controversial." Of course, such prudishness at home explains why several American sculptors worked in Europe and why several of these chose neoclassical styles and subjects in which nudity was more accepted because conventional and venerable.

24. Craven, *Sculpture in America*, 268.

25. Ibid., 116. The American abolition movement frequently invoked the long historical struggle against slavery from ancient times to the present and the international goals of abolition. Powers's sculpture develops the patience and abjection of the classically beautiful feminine figure in the manner of a recognizable Christian pathos, as denoted by the cross amid the drapery on the post on which the sculptural figure leans, invoking the sentimentalism used by Stowe, Jacobs, and other antebel-

lum abolitionists to persuade viewers and readers to bring an end to the barbarism of slavery wherever it happened to occur.

26. Craven, *Sculpture in America*, 277.

27. Ibid., 279.

28. Sherwood, *Harriet Hosmer*, 313.

29. Ibid., 25, 204. Wayman Crow, the father of Hosmer's friend and classmate Cornelia Crow, "urged the gradual, voluntary manumission of slaves" and gave his own servants their freedom in 1853, "an act that Hatty applauded when she received the news in Rome" (25).

30. See Rowe, "Swept Away," pp. 43–44, for a discussion of Fuller's treatment of heroic Greek women. In "Appendix G. Euripides. Sophocles," in *Woman in the Nineteenth Century* (New York: W. W. Norton and Co., Inc., 1971), p. 197, Fuller adopts the voice of her narrative alter ego, Miranda, to comment on the "many allusions . . . to characters of women drawn by the Greek dramatists," beginning with an invocation of "Iphigenia! Antigone!" as models for feminine vitality and independence that had been "dwarfed and defaced" by the "bad nurture" of nineteenth-century culture, concluding that "hearts like yours are in our breasts, living, if unawakened; and our minds are capable of the same resolves." I am reminded in this context of Judith Butler's "Antigone's Claim: Kinship, Aberration and Psychoanalysis," one of the 1998 Wellek Library Lectures (May 8, 11, and 12), a lecture series sponsored by the Critical Theory Institute at the University of California–Irvine, in which Butler reinterpreted Antigone—in Sophocles' *Antigone*, in Hegel's theory of tragedy, and in Lacan's Seminar XIII—as a feminist and potentially as a transgendered alternative to Oedipus and the family romance of socialization he has been used to legitimate from Sophocles to Freud.

31. Nathaniel Hawthorne, *Passages from the French and Italian Notebooks*, vol. 10 of *The Complete Works of Nathaniel Hawthorne*, Riverside Edition, 13 vols. (Boston: Houghton, Mifflin and Co., 1882), 494. Further references in the text are to this edition.

32. Arlin Turner, *Nathaniel Hawthorne: A Biography* (New York: Oxford University Press, 1980), 339. In his *Italian Notebook*, April 25, 1858, Hawthorne recounts how the sculptor Benjamin Paul Akers "conducted us to the shop of the jeweller Castellani, who is a great reproducer of ornaments in the old Roman and Etruscan fashion," where the Hawthornes saw a reproduction of "the toilet-case of an Etruscan lady . . . with her rings for summer and winter, and for every day of the week, and for thumb and fingers; her ivory comb; her bracelets; and more knick-knacks than I can half remember" (*French and Italian Notebooks*, 181).

33. William Wetmore Story, *Graffiti d'Italia*, 2nd ed. (Edinburgh: William Blackwood and Sons, 1875), 154.

34. Gollin and Idol, *Prophetic Pictures*, 94.

35. Hawthorne's image of these neoclassical sculptures burned to "quicklime" for the sake of preserving the ideal beauty of the classical *Venus de Medici* recalls, of course, Bartram's lime kiln and the allegorical tale of Ethan Brand's quest for the Unpardonable Sin in Hawthorne's "Ethan Brand" (1851). Gollin and Idol, in *Prophetic*

Pictures, p. 185, cite Hawthorne's comments on Powers's *Greek Slave* as part of their excellent section entitled "Hawthorne's Comments on Art: A Sampling."

36. D'Emilio and Freedman, *Intimate Matters*, 121: "The modern terms *homosexuality* and *heterosexuality* do not apply to an era that had not yet articulated these distinctions. Only in the late nineteenth century did European and American medical writers apply these categories and stigmatize some same-sex relationships as a form of sexual perversion. Until the 1880s, most romantic friendships were thought to be devoid of sexual content."

37. In the same passage, James elaborates: "The 'story' of the most beautiful of legends is (at least pictorially speaking) not in Andromeda, isolated and divinely bare, but in the mailed and caparisoned Perseus, his glorious gear, his winged horse and helmet and lance" (*William Wetmore Story*, II, 83).

38. Friedrich Nietzsche's *The Birth of Tragedy from the Spirit of Music* (1872) dates from the very end of the romantic classicism that James recalls in *William Wetmore Story* and thus figures as an interesting, albeit unintended, commentary on the rationalization of ancient Greek mythic nature worship in the long Enlightenment heritage that stretches from Plato and Aristotle to Kant and Hegel.

39. In a May 22, 1858, entry in his *Italian Notebooks*, Hawthorne describes a visit to Frederika Bremer's house and the tour she conducted of the Tarpeian Rock, a portion of which her Roman garden bordered. Taking her visitors to the garden side of the rock, she then conducted them through her house, into the street, "into the piazza of the Capitol," and finally to a "parapet, leaning over which we saw the sheer precipice of the Tarpeian Rock" (*French and Italian Notebooks*, 215). Bremer (1801–65) was a popular Swedish novelist who was well known in Europe and the United States for her political activism on behalf of women's rights and antislavery issues. What would otherwise be merely a trivial episode of Roman tourism is in fact full of strange coincidences and significance when read in conjunction with the legends of the Roman woman Tarpeia, for whom the rock was named; the use of the rock to execute criminals, especially traitors to the state, in ancient Rome; and Hawthorne's use of the rock as the site of Donatello's murder of the Model. In the most common legend of Tarpeia, according to Pierre Grimal's *The Dictionary of Classical Mythology*, trans. A. R. Maxwell-Hyslop (Oxford: Basil Blackwell Ltd., 1986), pp. 432–33, she was the daughter of Tarpeius, who had been charged by Romulus to protect the Capitol during the war with the Sabines. While the Sabine king, Tatius, was encamped at the foot of the Capitol, Tarpeia fell in love with him and let him and his troops into Rome on the promise that he would marry her. Instead of marrying her, Tatius had her crushed to death beneath the shields of his troops. Thus a treasonous woman who was herself betrayed is presumed to have been the origin of the Roman practice of hurling traitors from the height of the Tarpeian Rock. Bremer's association with the rock, even in Hawthorne's casual fancies as a tourist, suggests that Miriam's "mystery" involves more than just some sexual scandal, such as Nathalia Wright finds in the amorous triangle and murder mystery involving the Duc de Choiseul-Praslin, his wife, and the governess, Henriette Deluzy-Desportes, as a possible source of Miriam's

mystery (Nathalia Wright, "Hawthorne and the Praslin Murder," *New England Quarterly* 15:1 [March 1942], 5–14). Along with other extrinsic and intrinsic hints, Bremer's association with the novel gives credibility to the notion that Hawthorne seriously linked Miriam with the political revolutions of Europe in 1848, again giving some validity to Fuller as a model for her character and to her father-in-law as the "family" member in high places relative to the papacy. To be sure, Bremer's popularity as a novelist might also have provoked a certain envious reaction on Hawthorne's part, prompting his choice of the Tarpeian Rock for the particular dramatic action in *The Marble Faun*.

40. Derrick, *Monumental Anxieties*, 36.

41. Craven, *Sculpture in America*, 117. Thus "the 'Greek Slave' was to them a greater work of art than the 'Venus de' Medici' [because] it possessed Christian 'fortitude and resignation' and faith in the 'goodness of God,' in spite of the horrible circumstances in which the young girl found herself. It was perhaps as much due to the literary and philosophical content as to the artistic merits of the statue that it owed its brilliant success" (117).

42. Ibid., 281.

43. "'The poor young man has perished among the prizes that he sought,' remarked she.—'But what a strange efficacy there is in Death! If we cannot all win pearls, it causes an empty shell to satisfy us just as well. I like this statue, though it is too cold and stern in its moral lesson'" (*The Marble Faun*, 117).

44. Sheila Teahan, in "The Story in It: *William Wetmore Story* and His Intertexts," a paper delivered at the Hawthorne Society meeting in Rome (June 5, 1998), argues that James often treated ironically Story and his career as a sculptor, as well as Story's numerous (and admittedly tedious) literary works. Teahan's point does not, however, invalidate my notion that James found in Story's sculptures certain useful defenses against social and political changes, such as women's rights and abolition, which he and many others linked with changing sexual and ethnic mores.

45. Carol Holly, in *Intensely Family: The Inheritance of Family Shame and the Autobiographies of Henry James* (Madison: University of Wisconsin Press, 1995), p. 94, suggests that James uses "his biography of . . . Story" as his first effort at autobiography, aptly citing the famous letter Henry Adams wrote to James (Nov. 18, 1903) after reading *William Wetmore Story and His Friends:* "You have written not Story's life, but your own and mine,—pure autobiography."

46. Of course, the hand Count Valerio keeps in a secret cabinet in his study recalls the sculpture of Hilda's hand that Kenyon shows Miriam in chapter 13 of *The Marble Faun*, and that Hawthorne specifically notes is based on "Harriet Hosmer's clasped hands of Browning and his wife, symbolizing the individuality and heroic union of two high, poetic lives" (*The Marble Faun*, 120). The single hand Valerio retains from the unearthed classical sculpture of Juno and the single hand of Hilda that Kenyon sculpts in Hawthorne's romance suggest not only the desire for "heroic union" of the sort that will be represented in the marriage of Hilda and Kenyon at the end of the romance, but also the fracture or alienation in contemporary gender

relations that makes such "heroic union" so rare or difficult to achieve. There is yet another possible allusion in the hand Kenyon keeps in his own treasure box in *The Marble Faun*. Hawthorne comments in *The French and Italian Notebooks* on Hiram Powers's sculpture of an "exquisite . . . little baby's hand," "delicately represented in the whitest marble," based on the Powerses' daughter Luly's hand: "'Luly's hand,' Powers called it. . . . The Sculptor made it only for himself and his wife; but so many people, he said, had insisted on having a copy, that there are now forty scattered about the world" (*French and Italian Notebooks*, 308). Like bronzed baby shoes in the 1940s and 1950s, sculpted hands, especially of children, became conventions by the 1860s, and many other sculptors, including Akers, produced these sentimental sculptures.

47. Robert L. Gale, *A Henry James Encyclopedia* (Westport, Conn.: Greenwood Press, 1989), 8.

48. Henry James, "Adina," in *The Tales of Henry James*, ed. Maqbool Aziz, vol. 2: 1870–1874 (Oxford: Oxford University Press, 1978), p. 359. Further references in the text are to this edition.

49. For the story of Abraham, Sarah, Hagar, and Isaac, see Genesis 12–23. I am grateful to Professor Sharon Baris of Bar-Ilan University, Ramat Gan, Israel, who was kind enough to provide this gloss for me at the Hawthorne Society meeting in Rome. In a subsequent letter, Professor Baris notes that in Hebrew "Adinah" used as a proper name is masculine and associated with David and the tribe of Reuben, as recounted in II Kings 14:2 and I Chronicles 11:42. In Julius Fuerst and Samuel Davidson, *A Hebrew and Chaldee Lexicon to the Old Testament*, 5th ed. (London: Williams and Norgate, 1885), p. 1016, "Adinah" is defined as "preparer of sexual pleasure, pleasure-giver, rejoicer." I am grateful to Professor Baris for all of these sources and for her interpretive skills.

50. The libretto was written by Felice Romani, who based it on Eugène Scribe's *Le philtre*. The opera premiered at the Teatro della Canobbiana in Milan on May 12, 1832, and had its American premiere at the Park Theater in New York on May 22, 1844, according to David Ewen, *Encyclopedia of the Opera* (New York: A. A. Wyn, Inc., 1955), p. 134.

51. It also echoes the Old Testament story of Abraham and Sarah. Rightly fearing that the Egyptians will be dazzled by Sarah's (then Sarai's) beauty, Abraham (then Abram) smuggles her into Egypt hidden in a box. There are, of course, countless myths and legends that allegorize woman's feminine powers as a secret contained in a box or casket, which is what makes the scene of discovery in "Adina" so oddly evocative.

52. When Scrope and the narrator first examine the stone, the latter says he "bent my nose over it," and describes it as "about the size of a small hen's-egg, of a dull brown colour, stained and encrusted by long burial, and deeply corrugated on one surface" ("Adina," 352).

53. Pierre Walker, "'Adina': Henry James's Roman Allegory of Power and the Representation of the Foreign," *Henry James Review* 21:1 (Winter 2000), 16–20, convincingly points to several allusions in "Adina" to Wagner's *Der Ring des Niebelungen*.

Although Wagner's operatic cycle was not staged until 1876, two years after "Adina" was published, the cycle had been published in 1863. Walker makes important connections between the magic ring in Wagner's opera and James's use of the topaz intaglio in "Adina."

54. Herbert, *Dearest Beloved*, 226.

55. Fred Kaplan, *Henry James, The Imagination of Genius: A Biography* (New York: William Morrow and Co., Inc., 1992), 145. At the time, James was "renting a horse by the month." Harriet Hosmer was well known for her "skill at riding" and for her independence as one of the few American women to keep a horse for her personal use. Herbert, in *Dearest Beloved*, p. 236, refers to Hosmer's riding and quotes Hawthorne's statement of his uneasiness at witnessing "the spectacle of a peasant-woman riding on horseback astride," creating in Herbert's interpretation a "sexually charged gender anomaly" of the woman rider grasping the horse "between the rider's legs."

56. Henry James, "Roman Rides," *Italian Hours* (New York: Horizon Press, 1968), 234. This travel essay was first published by James in the *Atlantic Monthly* in August 1873, reprinted in *Transatlantic Sketches* (1875), and finally collected in *Italian Hours* (1909).

57. William Wetmore Story, *Nero* (Edinburgh: William Blackwood and Sons, 1875), is dedicated to the actress Fanny Kimble, whom James also notes was in the company that night listening to Story's reading. In his "Dedication" to that book, Story characterizes the period of Nero's rule as one of "cruelties and crimes which would not now be tolerated, and by passions so violent and unrestrained, that they seem to bear the taint of insanity," suggesting a progressive scheme for Western civilization stretching from the "decline" of the Roman Empire to the dawn of the new American imperium in Story's own age (vi).

58. Adina's "conversion" and "marriage" to Angelo are scenically represented for the narrator in his accidental encounter with her in a "Capuchin convent at the edge of the Alban lake," where he finds her looking fixedly and strangely "on the shining altar" ("Adina," 373). The Model in *The Marble Faun*, of course, turns out to be a Capuchin emissary of whatever Roman official or family member has a claim on Miriam, and the Model's murder by Donatello, himself nominally Catholic, seems to enact symbolically a conflict between Catholicism and Protestantism. Such echoes of Hawthorne play about the dramatic action of James's "Adina."

59. Gordon Hutner, in *Secrets and Sympathy: Forms of Disclosure in Hawthorne's Novels* (Athens: University of Georgia Press, 1988), p. 183, argues that in *The Marble Faun* "Hawthorne asks the reader to accept the kept secrets in the novel" and concludes that "art without sympathetic apprehension is incomplete." James is producing sympathy in the reader by way of a similar technique of withholding a secret, then asking the reader to keep that secret for him.

60. Derrick, *Monumental Anxieties*, 29.

61. Lee J. Siegel's omnibus review of recent books on queer theory and gay studies, "The Gay Science: Queer Theory, Literature, and the Sexualization of Everything,"

New Republic 219:19 (November 9, 1998), pp. 30–42, complains that this "sexualization of everything" is a consequence of these approaches that somehow interferes with, even destroys, our appreciation of literature. What is troubling about the backlash represented by Siegel's review is her claim that the discussion of homosexuality somehow "sexualizes everything," which implies that scholars in the areas of gay studies and queer theory can think of nothing other than "sex." This claim is obviously false, but it reveals a homophobia that goes far beyond the feminization of same-sex relationships to encompass scholarly investigations of modern sexuality, especially in the artistic and intellectual traditions of the humanities.

6. Modern Art and the Invention of Postmodern Capital

1. Jean Baudrillard, *The Mirror of Production,* trans. Mark Poster (Saint Louis, Mo.: Telos Press, 1975); Jean Baudrillard, *For a Critique of the Political Economy of the Sign,* trans. Charles Levin (Saint Louis, Mo.: Telos Press, 1981); and Jean-François Lyotard, *The Postmodern Condition,* trans. Geoff Bennington and Brian Massumi (Minneapolis: University of Minnesota Press, 1984).Further references to *The Postmodern Condition* in the text are to this edition.

2. John Gardner, *On Moral Fiction* (New York: Basic Books, Inc., 1978); Gerald Graff, *Literature against Itself: Literary Ideas in Modern Society* (Chicago: University of Chicago Press, 1979); John Aldridge, *The American Novel and the Way We Live Now* (New York: Oxford University Press, 1983); Charles Newman, *The Post-Modern Aura: The Act of Fiction in an Age of Inflation* (Evanston, Ill.: Northwestern University Press, 1985).

3. Philip Roth, "Writing American Fiction," *Commentary* 31 (1961), 224.

4. Geoffrey Hartman, "Language from the Point of View of Literature," in Jean Baudrillard, *Beyond Formalism: Literary Essays, 1958–1970* (New Haven, Conn.: Yale University Press, 1970), 353.

5. Gabriel García Márquez, *The Autumn of the Patriarch,* trans. Gregory Rabassa (New York: Harper and Row, 1976); D. M. Thomas, *The White Hotel* (New York: Viking Press, 1981); John Irving, *The World according to Garp* (New York: E. P. Dutton, 1978).

6. In *On Moral Fiction,* p. 71, Gardner uses Gass to exemplify the special concern of experimental writers with language in and for itself: "The more time one spends piling up words, the less often one needs to move from point to point, argument to argument, or event to event; that is, the less need one has of structure." Gardner clearly judges Gass's "language games," his fictional "logical positivism," as substitutes for the sorts of philosophically credible arguments conventionally offered by fiction.

7. Fredric Jameson, *Postmodernism, or, The Logic of Late Capitalism* (Durham, N.C.: Duke University Press, 1991), *Fables of Aggression: Wyndham Lewis, the Modernist as Fascist* (Berkeley: University of California Press, 1979), and *The Political Unconscious: Narrative as a Socially Symbolic Act* (Ithaca, N.Y.: Cornell University Press, 1981).

8. Jameson, *Fables of Aggression,* 55.

9. Jameson, *The Political Unconscious,* 221–22.

10. Henry James, "The Art of Fiction" (1884), in Morris Shapira, ed., *Selected Literary Criticism* (Harmondsworth: Penguin Books, Ltd., 1968), 85.

11. Isabel Archer's "vigil of searching criticism" in *The Portrait of a Lady, The Novels and Tales of Henry James*, The New York Edition, 26 vols. (New York: Charles Scribner's Sons, 1907–1917), vol. 4, pp. 186–205; Milly Theale's contemplation of the "kingdoms of the earth" from her Alpine ledge in *The Wings of the Dove*, vol. 19, p. 124; and Lambert Strether's "little study in French ruralism," when he confronts Chad Newsome and Madame de Vionnet in *The Ambassadors*, vol. 22, pp. 245–66. These are all versions of that central moment in James's fiction in which fictionality reveals itself to the central consciousness.

12. The phrase "a world elsewhere" comes from Richard Poirier's *A World Elsewhere: The Place of Style in American Literature* (New York: Oxford University Press, 1966), and is used by Poirier to suggest a uniquely American theme from the Transcendentalists to the moderns "to create a world in which consciousness might be free to explore its powers and affinities." For Poirier, such aesthetic freedom is an equivalent (or substitute) for the promise of democratic freedoms.

13. Ezra Pound, "'Blandula, Tenulla, Vagula,'" in *Collected Shorter Poems* (London: Faber and Faber, 1952), 53. K. K. Ruthven, in *A Guide to Ezra Pound's "Personae" (1926)* (Berkeley: University of California Press, 1969), p. 46, notes that "the title alludes to . . . the Emperor Hadrian's dying address to his soul" and thus anticipates Pound's identification of the poetic voice with strong rulers in his *Cantos*.

14. Canto CXVI, from "Drafts and Fragments of Cantos," in *The Cantos of Ezra Pound* (New York: New Directions, 1970), 795. Further references in the text are to this edition.

15. Pound adapted the term "throne" from the Thrones in Dante's *Divine Comedy*, who "are the angels in control of the seventh sphere," as Carroll F. Terrell notes in *A Companion to the Cantos of Ezra Pound*, 2 vols. (Berkeley: University of California Press, 1980), vol. 1, p. 143. Terrell also points out that Dante associates the Thrones with rubies and "later with a description of the surrounding brilliance of gleaming water and light." Pound associates his own historical "thrones" with the radiant light and diaphanous form that he uses elsewhere as metaphors for the energy of poetic form.

16. Jameson, *Fables of Aggression*, 110.

17. Hugh Kenner, *The Pound Era* (Berkeley: University of California Press, 1971), 532.

18. Ezra Pound, *Jefferson and/or Mussolini* (London: Stanley Nott, Ltd., 1935), 62. Further references in the text are to this edition.

19. Jameson, *The Political Unconscious*, 76.

20. Ezra Pound, *Hugh Selwyn Mauberley*, in *Collected Shorter Poems*, 208.

7. Another Modernism

1. Cary Nelson, *Repression and Recovery: Modern American Poetry and the Politics of Cultural Memory, 1910–1945* (Madison: University of Wisconsin Press, 1989), 17.

2. Ibid., 38: "The canon suggests that both literary quality and the nature of

literature's social relations are always already substantially decided, rather than being sites of continuing struggle and negotiation."

3. In particular, see Michael North, *The Dialect of Modernism: Race, Language, and Twentieth-Century Literature* (New York: Oxford University Press, 1994); Sieglinde Lemke, *Primitivist Modernism: Black Culture and the Origins of Transatlantic Modernism* (New York: Oxford University Press, 1998); Thomas E. Yingling, *Hart Crane and the Homosexual Text: New Thresholds, New Anatomies* (Chicago: University of Chicago Press, 1990).

4. Muriel Rukeyser, *The Book of the Dead*, in *Out of Silence: Selected Poems*, ed. Kate Daniels (Evanston, Ill.: TriQuarterly Books/Northwestern University Press, 1992). Further references in the text refer to this edition. Martin Cherniack, *The Hawk's Nest Incident: America's Worst Industrial Accident* (New Haven, Conn.: Yale University Press, 1986).

5. Walter Kalaidjian, *American Culture between the Wars: Revisionary Modernism and Postmodern Critique* (New York: Columbia University Press, 1993), 162–63.

6. Ibid., 163.

7. Joseph E. Stevens, *Hoover Dam: An American Adventure* (Norman: University of Oklahoma Press, 1988), 66–75.

8. As Michael Davidson points out in his chapter on Rukeyser's *Book of the Dead* in *Ghostlier Demarcations: Modern Poetry and the Material World* (Berkeley: University of California Press, 1997), p. 143, Nancy Naumberg's photographs "were not included in the first edition of *U.S. 1*," and as Davidson has personally reported to me, those photographs have not survived. It is not clear whether Rukeyser and Naumberg intended to collaborate on a poem accompanied by photographs, in the manner of Margaret Bourke-White and Erskine Caldwell's *You Have Seen Their Faces* (1937) and James Agee and Walker Evans's *Let Us Now Praise Famous Men* (1941), but the project and the poem deserve comparison with these contemporary works.

9. Philip Blair Rice, "The Osiris Way," *The Nation*, March 19, 1938.

10. M. L. Rosenthal, "Muriel Rukeyser: The Longer Poems," *New Directions in Prose and Poetry* 14 (1953), 202–39; Kalaidjian, *American Culture between the Wars*, 290–91, n. 28.

11. Kalaidjian's *American Culture between the Wars*, pp. 174–87, is particularly helpful in showing that Rukeyser's "mythic feminism" is part of a wider leftist-feminist critique of the patriarchal ideology that stretches from the dominant culture, including its monumental public works projects, to the orthodox Left and its arts (especially mural art) and that linked industrial progress with the physical strength of the male worker.

12. Constance Coiner, in *Better Red: The Writing and Resistance of Tillie Olsen and Meridel Le Sueur* (New York: Oxford University Press, 1995), pp. 39–71, and Paula Rabinowitz, in *Labor and Desire: Women's Revolutionary Fiction in Depression America* (Chapel Hill: University of North Carolina Press, 1991), pp. 17–62, both provide excellent accounts of how race and gender were marginalized by the CPUSA in the 1930s, despite impressive contributions to the Left (and the party) by peoples of

color and women. It is also important to recognize that Trotskyites of the 1920s and 1930s in the United States (as well as in Europe and in exile from the Soviet Union) were more consistent advocates of women's and minority rights as part of the "international" aims of Marxist revolution. I am grateful to Glen Motil of UC–San Diego for this observation about the overlooked influence of Trotskyites in the emergence of modern feminism and civil rights in the United States.

13. There are important echoes between "Absalom" (and other strongly elegiac poems in *The Book of the Dead*) and Whitman's use of elegy for activist purposes in his Civil War collections, *Drum-Taps* and *Sequel*. I am thinking particularly of the possible influence of Whitman's "Vigil Strange I Kept on the Field One Night" on Rukeyser's "Absalom" and of Whitman's "The Wound-Dresser" on the overall tone of *The Book of the Dead*. For a fuller treatment of Whitman's politically motivated elegies, see my *At Emerson's Tomb: The Politics of Classic American Literature* (New York: Columbia University Press, 1997), 145–61.

14. See Hart Crane, *The Bridge*, in *Complete Poems of Hart Crane*, ed. Marc Simon (New York: Liveright, 1993), 100–101 (the conclusion to "The Tunnel") and 107–8, for a comparison of complementary passages of descent, ascent, and transcendence.

15. Kalaidjian, *American Culture between the Wars*, 174.

16. Ralph Waldo Emerson, "The Poet," in *Essays, Second Series*, vol. 3 of *The Works of Ralph Waldo Emerson*, 14 vols. (Boston: Houghton Mifflin and Co., 1883), 25.

17. Rukeyser, in "Despisals," first collected in *Breaking Open* (1973), reprinted in *Out of Silence*, connects tolerance of ethnic and religious minorities with sexual tolerance: "In the body's ghetto, / never go despising the asshole / nor the useful shit that is our clean clue / to what we need. Never to despise / the clitoris in her least speech" (138).

18. I discuss the romantic idealist subordination of women in Hegel and Emerson in *At Emerson's Tomb*, 37–40 (Emerson) and 67–76 (Hegel).

19. Bioarchaeologists study the effects in the past of the natural and social environment on human and animal biologies, trying to explain changes in their health and abilities to adapt to such environments. See, for example, Theya Molleson, "The Eloquent Bones of Abu Hureyra," *Scientific American* (August 1994), 71–75. Abu Hureyra is a region in what is now northern Syria. I am grateful to Abraham Tarango of UC–San Diego for this reference and for the suggestion of bioarchaeology's relevance to Rukeyser's ecofeminism.

20. David Harvey, *Justice, Nature, and the Geography of Difference* (Cambridge, Mass.: Blackwell Publishers, 1996), 248–50.

21. Like other monumental civil engineering projects undertaken in the United States during the Depression, the hydroelectric project at Gauley Bridge, West Virginia, drew unemployed workers from all over the country. Thus the rural regionalism with which the poem begins actually ends up representing the diversity of workers (and their homes) involved in this project. See Joseph E. Stevens, *Hoover Dam: An American Adventure* (Norman: University of Oklahoma Press, 1988), for a

parallel account of the use of workers from all over the United States to build Hoover (Boulder) Dam in the same period.

22. W. E. B. Du Bois and other Harlem renaissance intellectuals used Isis as the symbol of Pan-African identity in the 1920s and 1930s, as Du Bois did in *Darkwater* (1920), included in *The Oxford W. E. B. Du Bois Reader*, ed. Eric Sundquist (New York: Oxford University Press, 1996), especially in the poem "Children of the Moon," which concludes chapter 7 and is in the voice of Isis (577–80). Du Bois also argued for the coalition of white and African American workers in ways that resemble Rukeyser's appeal in this poem. For a further discussion of these issues in Du Bois, see my *Literary Culture and U.S. Imperialism: From the Revolution to World War II* (New York: Oxford University Press, 2000), pp. 212–16.

23. Rowe, *At Emerson's Tomb*, 1.

24. Jean-François Lyotard and Jean-Loup Thébaud, *Just Gaming*, trans. Wlad Godzich (Minneapolis: University of Minnesota Press, 1985), 66–67.

8. Metavideo

1. For an example of this conflict between Native American oral and performative culture and the Euro-American print culture, see my discussion of the "Black Elk narratives" in *Literary Culture and U.S. Imperialism: From the Revolution to World War II* (New York: Oxford University Press, 2000), 217–52.

2. Lindon Barrett, *Blackness and Value: Seeing Double* (New York: Cambridge University Press, 1999), 73.

3. Derrida's special use of the term *"écriture"* to designate the differential system of language and to distinguish that system from the structural linguistic privileging of speech is by now a famous feature of his early writings, and it is best treated in *De la grammatologie* (Paris: Éditions de Minuit, 1967) and the essays collected in *L'Écriture et la différence* (Paris: Éditions du Seuil, 1967).

4. Jean Baudrillard, "Requiem for the Media," in *For a Critique of the Political Economy of the Sign*, trans. Charles Levin (Saint Louis: Telos Press, 1981), 168.

5. See in particular Enzensberger's essays "The Industrialization of the Mind" and "Constituents of a Theory of the Media" in his *Critical Essays*, The New German Library, vol. 98, ed. Reinhold Grimm and Bruce Armstrong (New York: Continuum, 1982).

6. Baudrillard, "Requiem for the Media," 168.

7. Hans Magnus Enzensberger, "The Industrialization of the Mind," trans. by Enzensberger, in *Critical Essays*, vol. 98, 11.

8. Hans Magnus Enzensberger, "Constituents of a Theory of the Media," trans. Stuart Hood, in *Critical Essays*, vol. 98, 56.

9. Baudrillard, "Requiem for the Media," 169.

10. Jean-François Lyotard, *The Postmodern Condition: A Report on Knowledge*, trans. Geoff Bennington and Brian Massumi (Minneapolis: University of Minnesota Press, 1984), 47: "Power is not only good performativity, but also effective verification and good verdicts. . . . Now it is precisely this kind of context control that a general-

ized computerization of society may bring. The performativity of an utterance, be it denotative or prescriptive, increases proportionally to the amount of information about its referent one has at one's disposal. Thus the growth of power, and its self-legitimation, are now taking the route of data storage and accessibility, and the operativity of information."

11. See my "Surplus Economies: Deconstruction, Ideology, and the Humanities," in *The Aims of Representation,* ed. Murray Krieger (New York: Columbia University Press, 1987), for a more specific translation of Marx's surplus value into postmodern terms.

12. Baudrillard, "Beyond Use Value," in *For a Critique of the Political Economy of the Sign,* 137.

13. *The Honeymooners* was developed as a CBS series out of sketches that Gleason did on *The Cavalcade of Stars* (1949–52). On his own show, *The Jackie Gleason Show* (1952–55, 1956–57, 1958–61), Gleason also incorporated sketches involving the Kramdens and Nortons. The independent series *The Honeymooners* lasted only one season (1955–56) and was judged a television failure. It is difficult to judge whether such "failure" was a consequence of the show's political sentiments or simply of its independent format or of other unpredictables. That the "sketches" were more successful when incorporated in the "variety" shows on early television that had evolved from vaudeville may support my claim that the characters linger in the sociological limbo between industrial and postindustrial America. See Vincent Terrace, *Encyclopedia of Television Series, Pilots and Specials,* vol. 1: *1937–1973* (New York: New York Zoetrope, 1986), 206.

14. As Terrace notes in *Encyclopedia of Television,* vol. 1, p. 206, Ralph entered the workforce as a fourteen-year-old paperboy, but he got his first adult job with the WPA during the Great Depression. Even though the paperboy was the clichéd prototype of the self-reliant modern American from Alger to Hollywood films of the 1930s and 1940s, this confirms that Ralph's "career" has been exclusively concerned with the media and public services rather than with explicitly industrial labor.

15. According to Terrace, in *Encyclopedia of Television,* vol. 1, p. 206, "The Chef of the Future" was Art Carney's favorite episode.

16. Ralph owes both his job and his marriage to the WPA. He met Alice when she was distributing snow shovels to WPA workers. These details remind us of how the Great Depression changed the conditions of ordinary labor, as well as the presumably "free exchange" of labor power for wages between worker and capitalist. The employment of the unemployed for large-scale public works projects helped effect the transformation of American production from primarily material goods to "goods and services" and ultimately to "representations." Terrace, *Encyclopedia of Television,* vol. 1, 206.

17. "*I Love Lucy*" ran for 179 episodes from 1951 to 1957 on CBS. Terrace, in *Encyclopedia of Television,* vol. 1, p. 212, summarizes the dramatic situation: "The recurring storyline relates Lucy's continual efforts to become an entertainer, despite Ricky's endless attempts to discourage her."

18. Patricia Mellencamp, "Situation Comedy, Feminism, and Freud: Discourses of Gracie and Lucy," in *Theories of Contemporary Culture*, vol. 7 of *Studies in Entertainment: Critical Approaches to Mass Culture*, ed. Tania Modleski (Bloomington: Indiana University Press, 1986), 81. Further references in the text are to this chapter.

19. *The Lucille Ball–Desi Arnaz Show* ran on CBS from 1958 to 1960 and was directed by Desi Arnaz. Terrace, in *Encyclopedia of Television*, vol. 1, p. 271, provides a pertinent summary of the storyline: "A continuation of 'I Love Lucy,' wherein Lucy and Ricky Ricardo, and their friends Fred and Ethel Mertz, travel to various places and become involved with a different guest star in each episode."

20. Terrace, *Encyclopedia of Television*, vol. 1, 271. At first the orchestra leader at the Tropicana Club, Ricky owns The Ricky Ricardo Babalu Club by the end of *"I Love Lucy."*

21. *Bewitched* ran on ABC for 306 episodes, from September 17, 1964, to July 1, 1972. Terrace, *Encyclopedia of Television*, vol. 1, 47–48.

22. Not surprisingly, family relations among Samantha's supernatural relatives reproduce quite precisely mortal relations, suggesting that bourgeois family relations are, in fact, universal.

23. Although Jennifer's father is an eight hundred thousand-year-old warlock, she traces her origins to 1632 and the Puritan Bay Colony. Wooley's ancestors burned witches in Salem, which is why Jennifer and her father have returned to persecute him. In fact, the real "witch" in the film is Wooley's fiancée, Miss Masterson, whose father owns a powerful newspaper and is backing Wooley's candidacy for the governorship. In this 1942 film, the witchcraft is conventionally identified with mortal women, like Miss Masterson, who reverse conventional roles of masculine dominance and feminine dependency. Both physically erotic and psychologically vivacious, Veronica Lake's Jennifer saves Wally Wooley from the castrating Miss Masterson. Transparent as the sexism of *I Married a Witch* is, it anticipates the more complex ways *Bewitched* will invest women with power on 1960s television.

24. *I Dream of Jeannie* ran on NBC for 139 episodes from September 18, 1965, to September 8, 1970. Terrace, in *Encyclopedia of Television*, vol. 1, p. 212, summarizes the dramatic situation: "During the test flight of a NASA rocket, a third stage misfires, causing it to crash-land on a deserted island in the South Pacific. . . . U.S. Air Force Captain Tony Nelson . . . finds a strange green bottle, which he opens. A pink smoke escapes that materializes into a beautiful girl dressed as a harem dancer—a genie. 'Thou ask anything of thy slave, Master. . . .' Realizing the problems her presence and powers will cause him at NASA, he sets her free, despite her desire to remain with him. When Tony returns to his home in Cocoa Beach, Florida, and discovers Jeannie hidden in his survival kit, he learns of her fate and permits her to remain with him—provided she curtail her powers and grant him no special treasures."

25. Peter Conrad, *Television: The Medium and Its Manners* (Boston: Routledge and Kegan Paul, 1982), 26: "Samantha . . . is a technological maven who can do the housework by remote control, at the twitch of a nose not the flick of a switch. Actually Elizabeth Montgomery on that show enjoyed the services of a troop of

off-camera domestic servants, who performed the dirty work her magic affected to abolish."

26. *The Rockford Files* ran on NBC from September 13, 1974, to July 25, 1980. Terrace, *Encyclopedia of Television Series, Pilots and Specials,* vol. 2: *1974–1984* (New York: New York Zoetrope, 1985), 352. CBS produced eight made-for-television films, *The New Rockford Files,* which aired between 1994 and 1999.

27. Charles Newman, in *The Post-Modern Aura: The Act of Fiction in an Age of Inflation* (Evanston, Ill.: Northwestern University Press, 1985), 131, contends that the mass media are actually reactionary imitations of realist conventions: "The media, on the other hand, through the obsessive use of the very conventions Modernism discredited, endlessly recirculates content, to produce an aura which makes the spectator experience an equally non-existent reality, employing all the conventions of Realism in the distortion of real life." Series like *Rockford,* however, demonstrate that modernist conventions are as influential in shaping popular television as realist devices. Irony, in particular, seems more pervasive in the storylines and styles of popular television of the 1980s than an unproblematic realism.

28. Even Rocky, however, is fascinated by the ways television confers reality on things and people. At the end of one episode, as Rockford and his father watch a client thank Rockford on the evening news, Rocky concludes: "I don't know much about all of this [Rockford's case and his career], but I *do know* that it *means something* to hear my boy mentioned on TV!" The two-part episode thus concluded focused on a businessman (Jackie Cooper) who was trying to build a secret international center for storing and processing information on the people of the world. Housed in an abandoned missile site outside Los Angeles, the center would be used to obtain geopolitical power.

29. Rockford is reluctant to use his gun, which he keeps in his cookie jar in the trailer. Although this trait may well be a carryover from *Maverick,* whose protagonist preferred talking and playing to shooting, it still expresses the postmodern way Rockford fights crime.

30. My literary examples are not entirely casual. Like Faulkner's Sutpen and Fitzgerald's Gatsby, Rockford dreams of power closer to that of the author than that of the merchant prince.

31. Conrad, *Television,* 16.

9. "Bringing It All Back Home"

1. As an example, see Herman Rapaport, "Vietnam: The Thousand Plateaus," in *The Sixties without Apology,* eds. Sohnya Sayres, Anders Stephanson, Stanley Aronowitz, and Fredric Jameson (Minneapolis: University of Minnesota Press, 1984), 137–47.

2. Wallace Terry, ed., *Bloods: An Oral History of the Vietnam War* (New York: Random House, 1984); Stanley Goff and Robert Sanders, with Clark Smith, *Brothers: Black Soldiers in the Nam* (Novato, Ca.: Presidio Press, 1982); Lynda van Devanter, with Christopher Morgan, *Home before Morning: The Story of an Army Nurse in Vietnam* (New York: Beaufort Books, 1983); Patricia Walsh, *Forever Sad the Hearts* (New

York: Avon Books, 1982); *Ashes and Embers*, dir. and writ. Haile Gerima (Mypheduh Films, 1982).

3. *Hearts and Minds*, dir. Peter Davis (BBS Productions, 1974; distributed in the U.S. by Warner Brothers, 1975).

4. David Cortright, *Soldiers in Revolt: The American Military Today* (New York: Doubleday and Co., 1975). Emile de Antonio's documentary *In the Year of the Pig* (Pathé Contemporary Films, 1969) focuses on the racism and ethnocentrism that motivated America's foreign policy in Southeast Asia during the Vietnam War.

5. *Tracers: A Play,* conceived by John DiFusco, written by the original cast (New York: Hill and Wang, 1986).

6. Bernard Edelman, ed., *Dear America: Letters Home from Vietnam* (New York: Simon and Schuster, 1985). See my discussion of *Dear America* and the New York memorial in "Eye-Witness: Documentary Styles in the American Representations of Vietnam," in *The Vietnam War and American Culture,* ed. John Carlos Rowe and Rick Berg (New York: Columbia University Press, 1991), pp. 148–74.

7. *The Vietnam War,* with Walter Cronkite, the CBS Video Library, 11 videotapes (New York: CBS News, 1985–87).

8. *A Face of War,* dir. Eugene S. Jones (Commonwealth United Entertainment, 1968).

9. This 1986 animated series, directed by Michael Hack, was introduced by its own "mini-series," in which Rambo helps an avuncular Latin American leader quell communist insurgents in a small Central American country.

10. *An Officer and a Gentleman,* dir. Taylor Hackford (Paramount Pictures, 1982); *Top Gun,* dir. Tony Scott (Paramount Pictures, 1986); *Rambo: First Blood,* dir. Ted Kotcheff (Artisan Entertainment, 1982); *Rambo: First Blood, Part II,* dir. George P. Cosmatos (TriStar Pictures, 1985); *Commando,* dir. Mark L. Lester (20th Century Fox, 1985); *Heartbreak Ridge,* dir. Clint Eastwood (Warner Brothers, 1986).

11. In the 1980s the U.S. military learned new ways to use financial and cultural capital to manipulate its representation in Hollywood films, television, and other media. Certainly these cultural war games prepared the U.S. military for its successful manipulation of the news coverage of the Gulf War in 1991.

12. In several places in both *Rambo* films, implicit references are made to Huck Finn and Tom Sawyer, with each of whom Rambo has certain curious affinities. Rambo's struggle to escape the sealed cave recalls Tom and Becky's escape from "Injun Joe's Cave" in *Tom Sawyer,* even though the analogy at first seems absurdly far-fetched. But Tom's escape from the cave is his special rite of passage, his means of proving his character above and beyond society. He saves Becky from the cave when her father, Judge Thatcher, cannot.

13. In the mid-1980s, Ronald Reagan referred several times to Bruce Springsteen's song *Born in the U.S.A.* as one of the his favorites, even citing its title in several speeches as evidence of Springsteen's patriotism. Obviously Reagan had never listened carefully to the lyrics, which are deeply critical of how U.S. policies work together to exploit the working class at home and the Vietnamese in a "foreign land." Unlike Reagan's misunderstanding of Springsteen's lyrics, the first two Rambo films

are not misreadings of countercultural rhetoric, but conscious efforts to transcode such discourse for explicitly conservative political purposes.

14. In *A Face of War*, Jones shows one or two of the U.S. marines speaking Vietnamese with the villagers in "No-Name Village," which the Marines are trying to protect from NLF infiltration. Jones shows these marines from so many different angles and with such frequency in the scenes shot in this village that it appears that nearly the entire company speaks Vietnamese.

15. Mark Lester's *Commando* (1985), an obvious spin-off of Stallone's *Rambo*, also invokes the virtues of the quiet, domestic family man to legitimate Colonel John Matrix's (Arnold Schwarzenegger's) violence. Like Sylvester Stallone, Arnold Schwarzenegger as a celebrity and as a character in 1980s action films endorsed conservative political positions, but did so often in terms borrowed from the counterculture and liberal politics. In the film *Commando*, his character, John, occupies a marginal position between military authority and the Latin American tyrant whose men kidnap his daughter. John aligns himself both with the traditional family and with minorities. Falling in love with an Afro Asian American woman, Cindy (Rae Dawn Chong) who, like Rambo's Co, helps John overcome enormous odds, he and his rescued daughter return to her in the final scene of the film. When his former commanding officer, General Kirby, who arrives too late to be of much use in crushing the Latin American desperados, encourages him to return to his old commando unit, John tells him: "This was the last time." Kirby argues, "Until the next time," but John, holding his daughter and casting a cinematic glance at his waiting girlfriend—a glance that virtually constitutes the three as a family, answers decisively: "No chance." In retrospect, we can see how 1980s film and television (see chapter 8) aligned the threatened nuclear family with oppressed and marginalized people as a part of a developing cultural narrative of "family values" that would play a central part in the culture wars of the late 1980s and early 1990s, as well as in the presidential campaigns of 1992, 1996, and 2000.

16. John Hellmann, *American Myth and the Legacy of Vietnam* (New York: Oxford University Press, 1986), 94–95.

17. Ibid., 95.

18. See Reginald Horsman, *Race and Manifest Destiny: The Origins of American Racial Anglo-Saxonism* (Cambridge, Mass.: Harvard University Press, 1981).

19. See Richard Slotkin, *Gunfighter Nation: The Myth of the Frontier in Twentieth-Century America* (New York: HarperPerennial, 1993).

20. *Southern Comfort*, dir. Walter Hill (20th Century Fox Film Corporation, 1981).

21. *Deliverance*, dir. John Boorman (Warner Brothers, 1972); James Dickey, *Deliverance* (Boston: Houghton Mifflin Co., 1970).

22. The cinematic scene of the U.S. military patrol arriving in a Vietnamese village often prepares for the cathartic firefight with the invisible enemy, now forced out of hiding, as in Ted Post's *Go Tell the Spartans* (Spartan Productions, Inc., 1978) and Oliver Stone's *Platoon* (Orion Pictures Corporation, 1986).

23. Stanley Karnow, *Vietnam: A History* (New York: Viking, 1983), 42: "The northern Vietnamese seem to be remarkably cheerful despite their grim poverty—

perhaps because they are disciplined after a generation under Communism, and maybe because they never knew the affluence experienced by their Southern compatriots during the America era. In an ironic twist, however, the capitalistic propensities that the Communists were supposed to obliterate in the south are instead creeping northward with alarming speed. . . . The Communists cannot easily stop the trend, having been compelled by the economic crisis to loosen up in order to spur production. . . . Private entrepreneurs are . . . emerging in Hanoi, though more cautiously than in Ho Chi Minh City."

24. Frances FitzGerald, *Fire in the Lake: The Vietnamese and the Americans in Vietnam* (New York: Random House, 1972), 3–43.

25. Jean-François Lyotard, *The Postmodern Condition,* trans. Geoff Bennington and Brian Massumi (Minneapolis: University of Minnesota Press, 1984), 78.

26. H. Bruce Franklin, in *M.I.A. or Mythmaking in America* (Brooklyn, N.Y.: Lawrence Hill Books, 1992), 127–67, implicates 1980s action films, including the Rambo films, in efforts by the Reagan and George H. Bush administrations to use the POW-MIA issue to continue the economic and political embargo of the Republic of Vietnam.

27. "Stone's War," *Miami Vice,* October 3, 1986. *Miami Vice* ran from 1984 to 1989 and was produced by Universal TV.

28. "Back in the World" episode, *Miami Vice,* Fall 1985.

29. Robert Stone, *Dog Soldiers* (Boston, Mass.: Houghton Mifflin, 1974).

30. When accused by Crockett of being an untrustworthy con man, unlikely to be interested in political issues for altruistic reasons, Stone counters: "You think you're much better? Driving fast cars, wearing fancy clothes, and making coke busts?"

10. Elián González, Cuban American Détente, and the Rhetoric of Family Values

1. Gabriel García Márquez, "Shipwreck on Dry Land," trans. Granma International, published in Spanish in *Juventud rebelde* (March 21, 2000), p. 2, describes Munero as "the local cock of the walk, a womanizer without a regular job, who learned judo not as a sport, but to fight, and had served a two-year prison sentence for armed robbery in Varadero's Siboney Hotel."

2. Ibid.: "For Cubans, Elián is just another of the many names they invent, turning their backs on the books of the saints [and making up] names, like: Usnavi, Yusnier, Cheislisver, Anysleidis, Alquimia, Dylier, Anel." Of course, Elián's cousin's name, Marisleysis, is another combinatory name that follows this Cuban tradition.

3. On January 16, 1999, several weeks before the Vietnamese lunar New Year, Tet, Truong Van Tran displayed a flag of the Democratic Republic of Vietnam and a framed picture of Ho Chi Minh in the window of his video store in a strip mall in Westminster, California. Anticommunist Vietnamese Americans quickly assembled in protest against his display, organizing both physical demonstrations outside his video store and a legal challenge to his right to display these symbols of the communist victory in the Vietnam War. For an excellent account of the larger political im-

plications of this event, see Daniel C. Tsang, "Serve the People? Challenges in Little Saigon," in *Legacy to Liberation: Politics and Culture of Revolutionary Asian Pacific America*, ed. Fred Ho, Carolyn Antonio, Diana Fujino, and Steve Yip (San Francisco: AK Press, 2000), 217–26. Chris Buzachero, "Elián González in Hyper-Space," *Ctheory: Theory, Technology, and Culture* 23:1–2 (Spring 2000), 1: "Title VI of the Helms-Burton Act places specific sanctions on Cuba for the return of stolen property to the largely white, wealthy Miami exiles. On one level, the battle over Elian *[sic]* is another chapter in the property battle between Cuba and the United States."

4. Hillary Rodham Clinton's construction by the media and by antigovernment groups is equally interesting in regard to the confusion of antifeminist, antigovernment, and more conventional partisan politics. The flexibility and curious consistency of the sexual rhetoric used to demonize public figures as different as Hillary Clinton and Janet Reno are what should interest cultural critics. Both are variously cast as "dykes," "frigid" *and* "sex-starved," women with men's ambitions, "bitches," "butches." And yet their political roles, personal appearances, and public identities are obviously drastically different.

5. Technically, it is the U.S. Department of Commerce, along with the U.S. Congress, that maintains the economic embargo of Cuba, and it is the Department of State that continues to forbid U.S. citizens from traveling to Cuba, except on the visas issued to them rarely (by the Department of Commerce, not the State Department).

6. Márquez, in "Shipwreck on Dry Land," 5, characterized the Cuban American National Foundation as "created by Jorge Mas [Santos] and sustained by his heirs," who appeared "to be spending millions of dollars to ensure that Elián is not returned to his father."

7. *Los Angeles Times*, June 2, 2000, A4.

8. Robyn Wiegman, *American Anatomies* (Durham, N.C.: Duke University Press, 1995); Amy Kaplan, "Manifest Domesticity," *American Literature* 70:3 (September 1998, special issue, "No More Separate Spheres!" ed. Cathy N. Davidson): 581–606; Lauren Berlant, *The Queen of American Goes to Washington City: Essays on Sex and Citizenship* (Durham, N.C.: Duke University Press, 1997); and Dana Nelson, *National Manhood: Capitalist Citizenship and the Imagined Fraternity of White Men* (Durham, N.C.: Duke University Press, 1998).

9. In a similar fashion, Elián's mother's decision to take her six-year-old son on a dangerous trip in an overcrowded boat was treated in the media as evidence of her "love" for her son rather than as what it would be judged in most legal systems: as an irresponsible act that called her parental rights into question. The latter view is developed by Márquez, in "Shipwreck on Dry Land," in reaching conclusions in favor of Juan Miguel González's paternal rights that are similarly biased by sentimentalism regarding the "family."

10. *Los Angeles Times*, June 2, 2000, A24.

11. Friedrich Engels's *The Origin of the Family, Private Property and the State* (New York: Viking Penguin, 1985) is the classic Marxist critique.

12. David Letterman's "Campaign 2000" skits repeatedly satirized the lack of

substantive debate in the 2000 presidential campaign, but the intent was clearly to express strong political opinions, generally supportive of the Democrats, while pretending to trivialize politics. Of particular note was the use of the much-publicized photograph of the armed INS agent discovering Elián and the "fisherman" in the closet of Lazáro González's home in Miami on the morning of the INS raid. The photograph was accompanied by the voice-over: "'Campaign 2000,' brought to you by U.S. Attorney General Janet Reno, 'Don't get up; we'll let ourselves in.'"

13. CNN News, March 28, 2000, *http://www.cnn.com/2000/US/03/28/virgin.mary/*. As the CNN report noted, this was "not the first time that the Elián story has included reports of images depicting the Virgin Mary. Just last weekend another image claimed by some to picture the Virgin Mary appeared in the window of a nearby bank."

14. Ernesto Chávez Álvarez, *El crimen de la niña Cecilia: La brujería en Cuba como fenómeno social (1902–1925)* (Habana: Editorial de Ciencias Sociales, 1991), 26–32, traces the first trial in Cuba for witchery (including charges of human sacrifice and criminal ritual) back to 1622.

15. Fernando Ortiz, "Porvenir de la brujería" [The future of witchery], in *Los negros brujos* (Habana: Editorial de Ciencias Sociales, 1995), 180–201, originally published in 1906, is a good example of the fact that early twentieth-century Cuban social scientists and ethnographers viewed Afro-Cuban religious and cultural practices as contrary to the progress of the Cuban Republic.

16. Stephan Palmié, *Wizards and Scientists: Explorations in Afro-Cuban Modernity and Tradition* (Durham, N.C.: Duke University Press, 2002), 9–22, 55–59. Márquez, in "Shipwreck on Dry Land," 5, discusses the CIA propaganda campaign of the 1960s, "Operation Peter Pan," in terms that suggest the CIA consciously played on the Cuban legend of "las Niñas" for the sake of demonizing Cuban and Soviet communism: "In 1960, under the Eisenhower administration, the CIA totally invented and propagated in Cuba the false rumor of a law according to which children were to be snatched from their parents by the revolutionary government and sent for early indoctrination in the Soviet Union. Even crueler lies affirmed that the most appetizing children would be sent to Siberian slaughterhouses to be returned as canned meat."

17. I am indebted to Stephan Palmié of the University of Maryland (College Park) for this anecdote.

18. The Miami relatives established this connection between "family" and consumer capitalism early in the public drama by taking Elián to a long list of amusement parks and family entertainments. Buzachero, in "Elián González in Hyper-Space," 2, contends that Elián was rendered hyper-real from the moment he entered the media. Márquez, in "Shipwreck on Dry Land," 4, claims that the Miami relatives were responsible for endangering Elián's "mental health" by employing "methods of cultural dislocation" that included his sudden immersion in a consumer capitalism virtually unknown in Cuba: "At his sixth birthday party in the Miami stronghold, on December 6, his self-seeking hosts took photos of him in a combat helmet, surrounded by lethal weapons and draped in a U.S. flag, shortly before a child of his own age shot dead a schoolmate with a revolver in the state of Michigan."

19. Márquez, in "Shipwreck on Dry Land," 1, characterizes Juan Miguel González as "a quiet man of good character who also worked in Varadero as a cashier in Josone Park."

20. Ibid., 4.

21. Ibid., 1: "After the divorce [González] had maintained cordial and stable, albeit rather unusual, relations with Elizabeth, as they continued living under the same roof and sharing their dreams in the same bed, with the hope of achieving as lovers the child they had been unable to have as a married couple. . . . After seven miscarriages, and with special medical care, the long-awaited son was born, and for him they had planned just one name when they married: Elián."

22. The otherwise thoroughly cynical postmodern critic Buzachero admits as much in his conclusion to "Elián González in Hyper-Space": "Rest in peace, Elián González, for the embargo will soon fall and you will be reunited with Disneyland once again."

23. "Year after Elian's [sic] Rescue, Florida Feels Effects of Case," *Los Angeles Times*, November 25, 2000, A12.

24. Ibid.

25. Ibid.

26. Ibid.

27. Interestingly, Márquez stresses that the "drugs" some of the passengers, including Elizabeth and Munero, took to ward off seasickness on the ill-fated trip across the straits of Florida may have prevented them from dealing with the crisis. The aura of the usual U.S. antidrug rhetoric seems to be directed by Márquez against the "irresponsible" mother: "One factor operating against the majority of the passengers would have been the Gravinol which does indeed avert seasickness but also provokes drowsiness and slows down reflexes" (3).

28. As early as January 26, 2000, Terry Jackson reported in the *Miami Herald*: "CBS . . . has signed a deal with a production company to turn Elián's saga into a two-part, four-hour miniseries." Of course, there are other ways Elián persists as a character shaped by the mass media. In keeping with what Barbie Zelizer, in *Covering the Body: The Kennedy Assassination, the Media, and the Shaping of Collective Memory* (Chicago: University of Chicago Press, 1992), pp. 151–52, terms television's "anniversary journalism," the U.S. network news stations all reported Elián's seventh-birthday celebration in Cuba, showing Elián cutting an enormous birthday cake (decorated with three children linking hands—two boys and one girl—and dressed in Cuban white shirts and red bandanas) for a large party of children, with Fidel Castro presiding in a deliberately paternal manner. NBC reported that in Cuba Elián was treated as "a national hero," while South Florida political pundits were interviewed to answer the question "Did Elián González cost Vice-President Gore the presidency?" (*NBC Evening News*, December 6, 2000).

29. Indeed, the anomalies in U.S. law posed by the contest over Elián required precedent-setting decisions and revisions of INS policies. For example, the U.S. 11th Circuit Court of Appeals in Atlanta, in upholding the "March decision by a District Court judge in Miami," argued that "the INS had to devise a policy since no federal

law addresses the issue of whether such a young child can seek asylum against the wishes of his parents" (*Los Angeles Times* [June 2, 2000], A24).

30. Victoria E. Johnson, in "Fertility among the Ruins: The 'Heartland', Maternity, and the Oklahoma City Bombing," *Journal of Media and Cultural Studies* 13:1 (1999), 73, reaches this sort of conclusion regarding the news coverage of the Oklahoma City bombing and suggests it is typical of how the mass media (and thus U.S. ideology) responds to crises. I think the Elián González story demonstrates a more complex and flexible ideology at work.

Permissions

Different versions of parts of these chapters were published previously in the following articles and chapters. I am grateful to the publishers for granting permission to reprint them here.

An earlier version of chapter 1 appeared in *American Studies in Germany: European Contexts and Intercultural Relations,* edited by Günter Lenz and Klaus Milich (New York: St. Martin's Press, 1995), 262–78. Reprinted with permission from St. Martin's Press.

An earlier version of chapter 2 appeared as "Postmodernist Studies" in *Redrawing the Boundaries: The Transformation of English and American Literary Studies,* edited by Stephen Greenblatt and Giles Gunn (New York: Modern Language Association of America, 1992), 179–208. Copyright 1992 Modern Language Association of America; reprinted with permission from the Modern Language Association.

An earlier version of chapter 3 appeared in *Cultural Critique* 40 (Fall 1998): 11–28.

An earlier version of chapter 5 appeared in *Henry James Review* 20:2 (Spring 1999): 107–34. Reprinted with permission from The Johns Hopkins University Press.

An earlier version of chapter 6 appeared in *American Quarterly* 39 (Spring 1987): 155–73. Copyright 1987 American Studies Association; reprinted with permission from the American Studies Association.

An earlier version of chapter 8 appeared in *White on White: Essays on Intertextuality and Contemporary American Fiction*, edited by Robert Con Davis and Patrick O'Donnell (Baltimore: The Johns Hopkins University Press, 1989), 214–35. Copyright 1989 The Johns Hopkins University Press; reprinted with permission from The Johns Hopkins University Press.

An earlier version of chapter 9 appeared in *The Violence of Representation: Literature and the History of Violence*, edited by Nancy Armstrong and Leonard Tennenhouse (London: Routledge, 1989), 197–218. Reprinted with permission from Routledge.

Index

John Carlos Rowe is professor of English at the University of California–Irvine, where he teaches U.S. cultures and critical theory. He is the editor of *Post-Nationalist American Studies* and the author of many books, including *At Emerson's Tomb: The Politics of Classic American Literature*, *The Other Henry James*, and *Literary Culture and U.S. Imperialism: From the Revolution to World War II*.